ACCUSED OF TREASON

ACCUSED
— OF —
TREASON

THE US ARMY'S WITCH HUNT
FOR A JEWISH SPY

DR. DAVID A. TENENBAUM

PosT Hill
PRESS

A POST HILL PRESS BOOK

Accused of Treason:
The US Army's Witch Hunt for a Jewish Spy
© 2020 by Dr. David A. Tenenbaum
All Rights Reserved

ISBN: 978-1-64293-451-9
ISBN (eBook): 978-1-64293-452-6

Cover art by Cody Corcoran
Interior design and composition by Greg Johnson, Textbook Perfect

This is a work of nonfiction. All people, locations, events, and situations are portrayed to the best of the author's memory.

Post Hill Press
New York • Nashville
posthillpress.com

Published in the United States of America

DEDICATION

To the memory of my Mother who put up with me all these years,
who taught me the meaning of never giving up,
who encouraged me to do my best.

To the memory of my Father who taught me the meaning of life
and whose wisdom, love, and advice is constantly on my mind.

To my wife and best friend, Madeline,
whose love and encouragement keeps me going.

To my children: Nechama Eta, Yehuda Leib, Nosson and Shaina,
and Yisroel Zev, whose devotion to their Abba keeps a smile on my face
and carries me throughout the day.

To my mother-in-law, Barbara Segal, and my late father-in-law, Leslie Segal,
who have always treated me like a son
and have always been there for myself and family

To my sister Brenda and my brother Jeffrey who always watched over
their "baby" brother as we grew together as siblings and friends.

CONTENTS

FOREWORD

I have been practicing law for sixty-five years. During that time I have represented numerous high-profile clients like John Delorean (for forty-three cases), Mayor Coleman Young (for twenty years), Edward Holland (composer of Motown), Dr. Jack Kevorkian (for ten years and thereafter as executor of his estate), Dan Gilbert, Quicken Loans, Rolland McMasters (Teamsters), US Representative John Conyers, and Michigan Film Coalition among them.

Throughout my practice, I have represented numerous persons who were discriminated against and victims of religious, racial, sexual and disability wrongful behavior, and misconduct.

Many of said matters and suits were handled without remuneration and even with moneys being paid by myself in order to remedy the terrible injustice, pain, and suffering experienced by the victims.

One of those cases and representation was for David Tenenbaum and his family. I have seen and in the past, my family has endured horrible and outrageous discrimination. My wife's father was the only survivor out of his entire family and until the day he passed away, he never would talk about anyone in his family or even give us their names. My mother was brought into the United States at age of nine when her mother died in Poland and was raised by her aunt and uncle in Detroit. I can go on forever, but this book is about Mr. Tenenbaum and not me; however, my background is helpful for the reader to understand that my foreword is not based on rumors or hearsay, but on experience and knowledge.

David first came to me to ask about representing him when he and his family had been invaded on a Saturday at their home during lunch by the FBI. David and his family were being followed everywhere and stalked thereafter.

He also lost his security clearance and job at TACOM (Tank Automotive Command) where he was working on his program called the Light Armored System Survivability (LASS) program which was designed to save soldiers' lives with protection on the vehicles.

The program was terminated and cost lives. As a result of the false accusations, David was suspended and he and his family were totally damaged for the rest of their lives.

I appealed his wrongful decisions and the government's conduct in secret hearings and prevailed in the hearings all the way to Washington. His job was restored and he was granted top secret security—one step up from what he had when wrongfully accused.

The people involved in the wrongful attacks and permanent damage of him and his family were never punished for it and justice was never fully granted. In fact, David suffered and still suffers from discrimination at work simply for being an Orthodox Jew.

He has not been compensated for the horrible injury and damage he and his family have endured and continue to endure and the story must be told so it doesn't keep happening without the punishment of the culprits.

Anti-Semitism did not end with the downfall of Hitler and the Nazis in the war when they persecuted everyone under their domain and killed more than four million innocent adults and children.

Last year in the United States alone, there were more than 8,700 acts of violence and threats against people of the Jewish faith. Nazi groups still exist and march the streets.

Racial discrimination still continues as well and people are harmed, destroyed, and starved based on their race. As mentioned before, people of the Jewish faith are still persecuted. It has to be stopped.

The United States and local governments have to investigate and stop such action and behavior and pursue such misconduct relentlessly. Schools have to educate their students regarding the same issues.

Legislative branches of government have to enact legislation that concentrates on stopping and preventing said conduct by passing strong preventative and punishment for said misconduct and organizations have to speak out and educate the public.

FOREWORD

Slavery ended, women got the right to vote (ridiculous that it happened some sixty years ago), and concentration camps ended fifty-four years ago, but outrageous discrimination continues. It's time to stop anti-Semitism.

—*Mayer Morganroth*, Morganroth & Morganroth, PLLC

"Yet, nearly six decades after the Holocaust concluded, anti-Semitism still exists as the scourge of the world."

—ELIOT ENGEL, US Representative
for New York's 16th congressional district

INTRODUCTION

This book has been an ongoing project for close to eight years. It really became more than a thought when I spoke before the Zionist Organization of America (Michigan Chapter) in 2012. Five hundred people listened to me for more than an hour. After I spoke, I was approached by a journalist who said to me, "Don't speak again until you write a book." I had been considering writing a book for a few years but did not feel I had the expertise. I wrote it anyway and I was right…I did not have the expertise. I wrote it like my dissertation. It was boring when it should have been jaw-droppingly interesting. At that point I considered various ideas and then, Dr. Michael Engelberg, the executive director of the New York Center for Civil Justice, Tolerance & Values offered to fund the book's writing. He as well as many others—both Jews and non-Jews—felt that the story of a government gone wild with no accountability and how anti-Semitism was responsible for US soldier deaths in Iraq and Afghanistan was a story that needed to be told. I was not and am still not looking for revenge. I am looking for justice. We teach our children that there are consequences for their actions and that they need to be held accountable for those actions. The US government and the US Army need to be held accountable as well.

As a US government employee, I was required to submit my manuscript to the Defense Office of Prepublication and Security Review. I submitted it in March 2019. According to its website:

> Some active and former DoD affiliates become or are authors that employ their knowledge and experiences gained during their DoD tenure in crafting literary works that warrant submittal to DOPSR for security and policy review and approval for public release. What do we look for? Inadvertent classified DoD information,

unclassified export controlled technical data on defense articles if needed, and an accurate portrayal of DoD policy if cited (critiquing DoD policy is fine).

The Office of Prepublication and Security Review sends the manuscript to the "entities" involved, which in my case, probably means (no one would tell me) the FBI, CIA, IG-DOD, TACOM, and others. As of the date of the publishing of this book, not all of the entities to which the manuscript was sent have given their stamp of approval. Nevertheless, we have decided to publish this book. My book does not contain any classified material or unclassified export controlled technical data. It contains material and information which is embarrassing to the US Army and government. Embarrassing does not equal classified. Although, from my view, according to the US government and Army, anti-Semitism is a state secret.

A WAR STORY

The first thing a deployed soldier notices about the Middle East is the heat. And the sand. Though soldiers train in the United States, intentionally wearing their Kevlar while marching to get used to the weight of their gear and the temperature, nothing fully prepares them for landing in summer in Iraq, Afghanistan, Iran, Saudi Arabia, or any of their neighboring countries.[1]

From above, the landscape is a seemingly endless sea of sand; on the ground, it's rubble and remnants of urban warfare. Command tries to give new soldiers a couple of days to acclimate. But the reality is that at the height of summer in the desert, soldiers may get used to the misery the way a cancer patient may get used to the pain, but they never get over the heat. The soldiers' equipment and body armor, together weighing forty pounds and up, ensure that the soldiers are drenched with sweat.[2] When the wind blows, sand sticks to the moisture. The sand mixes with the body's salts, creating patterns of swirled white dust on exposed skin. Some feel the effects of heat exhaustion after only a short time in the swelter.

It's a glimpse of hell.

For the soldier manning the crew-served weapon atop a HMMWV, hell couples with guilt. Though the most vulnerable position, it is also the one that allows a bird's-eye view of death.[3] This soldier has a front-row seat. Even though this post is among the most stressful—and most dangerous—the "brotherhood" of soldiering means that no one willingly gives it up. Because giving it up means one of your friends, one of your buddies, the men or women you would die for, they're going to be the ones to die, maybe. And so those manning the weapon prefer to stay put. To risk their lives. Better them than their brothers in arms.

1

Soldiers in the Middle East wars, in those urban warfare theatres, have endured and continue to endure a constant barrage on the senses: heat, thirst, brilliant sun bearing down, and chills at night as the desert devilishly plays with extremes. Then there is the endless tat-tat-tat against a soldier's nerves. It is hard to liken the steady hammering to anything familiar stateside. At home, stress can feel relentless—an overdue mortgage payment, a special needs child, caregiving for an elderly parent, or a marriage tattered beyond repair—but wartime stress is more akin to bursts of terror. It frays at the edges of nerves, gnawing away like rats chewing at a house's wires until the whole damn thing is in darkness because they finally chewed the main electrical line, frying the rats and the house in the process.

CHAPTER 1

THAT THING IS A TARGET

"We can't wait for problems to occur. We must be prepared."

—PRESIDENT BILL CLINTON,
State of the Union Address, January 24, 1995

When the Persian Gulf War began in 1991, David Tenenbaum felt so far away in his suburb of Detroit. An international coalition was on the ground and in the skies over Saudi Arabia. Sixty-two-metric-ton M1 Abrams tanks pressed their parallel tracks into the desert sands, and American soldiers were discovering what it was like to step outside into the intense heat of the Middle East, where the high temperatures felt like they seared a person's lungs with every breath.

On the US Army Tank-automotive and Armaments Command (TACOM) base in Warren, Michigan, Tenenbaum's days as an engineer were full of fresh-air walks between buildings 200, 229, and 230. In the fall, his feet crunched over fallen leaves on the sidewalk. In the spring, the smell of fresh-cut grass revived his winter-weary mind. He preferred face-to-face discussions with the engineers and scientists who were working with him on the ballistic testing of new armor designs of combat vehicles—like the Bradley Fighting Vehicle—and other army vehicles, such as troop carriers and High Mobility Multipurpose Wheeled Vehicles (HMMWVs). Discovering the weaknesses of these vehicles known as Humvees firsthand, rather than in a later report, enabled Tenenbaum to gain the best possible understanding of how to increase the survivability of these vehicles. He worked hard and he knew he was making a difference in the lives of soldiers, who themselves were risking injury and death in the Middle East and around the globe.

Dr. Tenenbaum had been working at the Tank Automotive Research, Development and Engineering Center (TARDEC) since December of 1984. TARDEC is the United States Armed Forces' research and development facility for advanced technology in ground systems and shares its facilities with TACOM. At the time of the first Gulf War in 1991, the army—specifically TARDEC—was looking for engineers to go to Kuwait and Iraq. They needed real-time assessments and remedies for the daily damage to army combat vehicles. Without a doubt in his mind, Tenenbaum knew what he had to do. He contacted one of his supervisors, Dr. James Thompson, and volunteered for duty. He was not a soldier, but he was an accomplished engineer. Over his seven years with TACOM, within TARDEC, and working within the Armor Group, he had seen how the metal of a tank could be deformed by various types of anti-tank weapons and how the armored bodies of Bradley Fighting Vehicles and M113 troop carriers could be turned into shrapnel directed at those riding inside. He knew where his engineering and survivability expertise were needed most in that moment.

The Persian Gulf War was the first war exposed to a twenty-four-hour news cycle, replete with dramatic theme music and images of camels and tanks set against desert sunsets. Unlike with the Vietnam War's violent photography, the Gulf War's carnage was somewhat shrouded from the media.[1] However, working on an army base, Tenenbaum knew precisely what was going on. Bombs exploded. Missiles wreaked havoc. Engineers were in short supply.

Jim Thompson brought Tenenbaum to the chief of the division at that time. Don Rees, Tenenbaum's second-line supervisor, was the one who had the final decision-making ability. Standing in Rees's office, Tenenbaum waited for the official reply. He felt that he had so much to give. If going into the war zone was the best use of him, he would do it.

After a deep breath, Rees looked him straight in the eye.

"We are taking engineer volunteers—but not you," he said. "That thing is a target."

The presence of the yarmulke on Tenenbaum's head had never before been as directly discussed as in that moment.

"We aren't sending you to the Gulf to get killed," Rees continued. "You are a good engineer—and we need you here…alive."

David Tenenbaum's father had been a Holocaust survivor. David understood the depths of anti-Semitism that could capture a culture and endanger anyone outside a society's norms. Tenenbaum knew the dangers of a Jewish man, especially one wearing a yarmulke, in the Middle East.

"I understand what you're saying, but I'd like to go."

Yet Don Rees shook his head. Tenenbaum was denied. It was the first but not the last time that reactions to his Judaism changed the trajectory of his career.

Unable to work alongside the soldiers in the Middle East, Tenenbaum decided he had to do the next best thing: protect them as best he could. A drive inside of him was born, and it was this drive that eventually led him to cocreate the Light-Armored System Survivability (LASS) program.

The concept for LASS was simple: vehicles were going to be hit—either with bombs or with bullets—but how could these hits remain external impacts rather than explosions that broke into the interior, where the vulnerable soldiers were hidden (supposedly protected)? The lost limbs, the burn injuries, the maimings from flying shrapnel, and endless other damages and deaths could be drastically reduced, if not stopped altogether. These pieces of metal or shrapnel, called "Behind Armor Debris," could travel at thousands of miles an hour and cut through the vehicles and the soldiers within them like a knife through butter.

Tenenbaum was working on a method to increase the safety and survivability of deployed forces from weapons like the new threat of improvised explosive devices (IEDs), which produced devastating metal debris. The LASS program was conceived as a joint effort among the United States, the Federal Republic of Germany, and the State of Israel. It involved experts from each country. The HMMWV, which was designed as a type of replacement for the old-model jeeps used in WWII, Korea, and Vietnam, was chosen to be the test-subject vehicle for the LASS program.

Working in the government could be slow, but Tenenbaum was a man who did not like standing still. Whether it was zero or ninety degrees outside, he would still go jogging, and in his professional life, he wasn't one to sit at his desk and wait for new projects and ideas to come to his door. If he had an idea, he was going to pursue it.

Tenenbaum had previously worked with Southwest Research Institute (SwRI), the research and development nonprofit that had been tasked with the analysis of the *Challenger* shuttle disaster only five years before. Having collaborated with them on many projects that dealt with soldier and vehicle survivability, he had strong relationships with the people there, as well as with foreign engineers who had extensive experience with the challenging type of warfare being posed at the end of the twentieth century. His last major project with SwRI, the Computer-Aided Armor Design Engineering Model (CAAD), was still ongoing, and it was the prelude to LASS. It modeled what happened when bullets of various sizes went through a vehicle and examined the damage to the vehicle and the injuries to the soldiers inside. This effort also involved engineers and scientists from countries around the world, including Israel, Germany, and the Netherlands.

When he traveled to SwRI in San Antonio, Texas, Tenenbaum approached colleagues who could partner with him in the creation of this new initiative, which would eventually be known as the LASS program. Besides having some of the brightest ballistic engineers and computer modelers in the United States, SwRI was also well connected in the international defense community. Following efforts by Tenenbaum and SwRI, some of the best and brightest were sought out to work on and develop LASS. Back in Michigan, Tenenbaum walked the familiar quarter or half mile between buildings to finalize the team.

Using the Humvee as the model and utilizing the talents of ballistic engineers from Germany and real-world urban combat data from Israel, the LASS program began to take shape. Tenenbaum lobbied for congressional funding and was making great headway toward obtaining it. The team was assembled, and they were getting to work on a project that promised to lessen the threat on soldiers' lives as they traveled across war fields on mine-riddled desert sands and as they navigated densely-populated city landscapes.

David married his wife, Madeline, in August of 1991, but only two weeks after the wedding, he told her that he needed to go to the Netherlands for an engineering conference dealing with CAAD, which would be the program that eventually grew into LASS. The best and brightest in his field would be gathered. He was the army representative and had been asked to give a presentation.

Madeline smiled as she said, "You're not going without me."

"Of course," he said. "I'll arrange it."

"You really enjoy meetings like this?"

"I'm working with experts in the field from around the world. It's always great to learn from some of the best."

So, the couple went together. Tenenbaum was always learning, trying to determine how to best utilize the talents of those he met and worked with, as well as considering how to apply new ideas to the technology he was trying to develop. The CAAD and LASS project team was an international collection of computer modelers, engineers, and individuals experienced in modern warfare.

In the midst of his work, Tenenbaum didn't allow his mind to linger on moments, such as when a female TACOM employee, who he had never met before, approached him in the hallway and tapped his yarmulke on his head—whether in spite of or ignorant to the Orthodox Jewish tenet that does not allow touching between genders (except family members and spouses), he didn't know.

"Why do you wear that thing?"

Tenenbaum had given a short answer regarding his faith, but after she walked away, the team member he had been standing with asked, "Do you know why she patted your skullcap?" When Tenenbaum offered him a confused look, his coworker continued, "She believes the legend that you wear it to cover devil horns." (See Appendix 1.)

He remembered once returning to his office and finding a bag of pork rinds on his desk, despite the tenet that Jews refrain from consuming pork products. He had an idea of who put it there, someone who had made disparaging remarks about his religion previously, but he never considered it more than an ignorant prank. He wasn't going to be roped into a debate with someone who only wanted to proselytize "the Jew" and other "non-believers" on the base, including non-practicing Christians.

He remembered the early words of a colleague who helped get him the job at TACOM and who also knew that Tenenbaum worked closely with Israel: "Make sure you know who you are working for." As if there was any question. Any doubt. As if his connections with Israel and the fact that he spoke Hebrew gave him a tendency toward loyalties other than to the United States.

The signs were there. How had he not seen the ignorance and the bigotry within his own base, within his colleagues, the people he considered his "friends"?

It wasn't only in the Middle East that Tenenbaum needed to be wary of how others perceived him. This was modern-day America, a country that extolled religious freedom and promised fairness and equality of treatment for every man and woman. Yet Tenenbaum would soon find out that this wasn't always the case, and not only he but countless American soldiers would suffer from it.

CHAPTER 2

WHAT HE DIDN'T KNOW

"But then eject them forever from this country.
For, as we have heard, God's anger with them is so intense that
gentle mercy will only tend to make them worse and worse,
while sharp mercy will reform them but little.
Therefore, in any case, away with them!

Let the government deal with them in this respect, as I have
suggested. But whether the government acts or not, let everyone
at least be guided by his own conscience and form for himself
a definition or image of a Jew."

—MARTIN LUTHER

On July 22, 1992, TACOM nominated Tenenbaum for the Scientist and Engineer Exchange Program (SEEP), which would send a US Army engineer to Israel for a period of time to learn and to share unclassified fighting vehicle technology and other information with the Israelis. In exchange, an Israeli engineer would be sent to the United States to work with US engineers and scientists.

With Tenenbaum's skill set and interests, this program had been on his mind for a while. He had almost applied for it in prior years but had learned that an engineer had to have a certain amount of time working for TACOM before they could even be considered. They had to prove themselves trustworthy, a go-getter, skilled in interpersonal relationships and research abilities. But in the ten years he had worked at TACOM, he'd earned exactly this reputation.

He had flushed with pride when he received word about the nomination. His career was on an upward trajectory. His confidence with where he was and where he was going was at an all-time high.

Yet on the very same day that Tenenbaum was nominated for the SEEP program, a colleague of his, Jaunutis Gilvydis, who heard about the nomination, decided to file a Subversion and Espionage Directed Against the US Army (SAEDA) against him. Tenenbaum only found out about this SAEDA, as well as others, years later. A SAEDA is filed when an army employee suspects that someone they know is plotting to commit treason against the United States of America. *Treason.* It's no small suspicion.

The SAEDA immediately alerts army officials to activities that may threaten army security interests. This report can be filed by army employees, both military and civilian, if an employee gains information showing that another is engaged in treasonous actions. The inherent loophole, however, is that employees can file a SAEDA against other employees without proof.

According to Gilvydis and his filed report, whenever Tenenbaum left the building at the end of the day, he was carrying a shoulder knapsack—and even more suspicious, it looked like it had "heavy things" inside. Gilvydis found this very unusual, even though other engineers and stationed personnel carried backpacks and briefcases to work. Yet somehow, Gilvydis chose to file a SAEDA on the day of Tenenbaum's SEEP nomination based upon Tenenbaum's backpack. He didn't know what was inside but suspected it was something that shouldn't be there. As this charade played out behind the scenes, as the train left the station and gathered steam and momentum, it does not appear as if anyone, from the filer all the way up to the head of TACOM's Counterintelligence Division, ever stopped for a moment to consider that Tenenbaum's personal backpack contained his lunch, a change of clothes for a lunchtime run, and a religious book. Tenenbaum *still* carries a backpack.

It still doesn't contain classified documents and never did.

Instead, since there are no kosher restaurants near the base, Tenenbaum's packed lunch was a simple and economical solution for keeping kosher. He'd never considered how it might come across. It was simply his lunch.

A change of clothes for a jog allowed his blood to flow for a midday recharge amidst days of data and reports. His runs were great for problem-solving and clearing his head, and he loved the exercise.

As for the religious book, in a country where freedom of religion is at the core of its founding, Tenenbaum had never given his choice of reading material a second thought. His religion was a big part of who he was. It didn't define him as an engineer, nor did it drive his professional ambitions. It was no different from carrying a book for a Bible study group for a Christian; it was simply a part of who he was and what he chose to pursue in his personal life.

A SAEDA report, according to regulation, must be filed immediately if the filer suspects someone of being a traitor or planning some type of terrorist activity. So mandatory and critical is this reporting mandate that the *failure* to report a suspected or known SAEDA incident is cause for disciplinary action under the Uniform Code of Military Justice and United States Code.[1] (See Appendix 2.)

Unfortunately, there is nothing that prevents filing for the pettiest of reasons. As long as the filing is not exposed as an outright intentional lie, the filer is protected. The initial interview of Jaunutis Gilvydis and the subsequent report prepared by the 902nd Military Intelligence (MI) Division of the US Army show that Gilvydis filed his SAEDA because he suspected that Tenenbaum was committing espionage on behalf of the State of Israel.

Gilvydis stated that in addition to the suspicious backpack, a prior conversation with Tenenbaum seemed questionable to him. When Gilvydis had been preparing to travel to Israel for TACOM, he stated that he approached Tenenbaum for advice on traveling there. He knew Tenenbaum had knowledge of the location and the culture, and he had hoped that his colleague could be of some help to him. This would be a completely logical direction to turn. Why wouldn't a colleague going to a foreign country ask another colleague who spent time there about the restaurants, the hotels, and the sights to see if there was any downtime?

But according to Gilvydis, Tenenbaum gave him more than just travel brochures and trip tips. Tenenbaum—according to Gilvydis, and *only* Gilvydis—recommended that he "shake loose" from the strict supervision of the personnel from the US Embassy in Israel so there would be no one present to monitor his activities. This way, he could be able to speak "freely" with the Israelis. Tenenbaum even, according to Gilvydis, made his *own* travel arrangements—another sign he wasn't a "team player." In addition, Gilvydis also relayed to the FBI that Tenenbaum told an "unrecalled TACOM employee" that the US president was not Tenenbaum's president.

Anyone who knew Tenenbaum would know that "shaking loose" wasn't in his vocabulary or his personality. A simple phone call, a basic search into his background, or a direct question to him would have put a halt to the ramblings of a distrusting colleague. All of Tenenbaum's travel orders and vouchers upon his return had been signed off on and approved by Tenenbaum's superiors. In all his years at TACOM, he'd never been known to do anything with his travels that raised any flags.

Gilvydis's suspicions only came out on the day his colleague was beginning to get some recognition and elevated status, yet the FBI launched a Preliminary Inquiry (PI) into Tenenbaum without Tenenbaum's knowledge. The 902nd MI Division was tasked with conducting proactive counterintelligence activities and support to protect army and designated Department of Defense (DOD) forces, information, and technology.[2] Had the members of the 902nd checked when they were brought into this matter, they would have found that Jaunutis Gilvydis's accusations and suspicions were completely untrue and unwarranted. They would have found out that Tenenbaum never spent time on an Israeli *kibbutz*, another of Gilvydis's accusations, and they would have determined that there was never an "unrecalled TACOM employee" to whom Tenenbaum remarked that the US president was not his own. Tenenbaum never told Jaunutis Gilvydis how to avoid US security. It simply wasn't how he worked.

The FBI's PI into Tenenbaum found no evidence to pursue any further investigation. However, even the PI was fraught with technical problems. Because Gilvydis had filed a SAEDA against Tenenbaum in July 1992, for events which dated as far back as 1991, the allegations were well over a year old, which in and of themselves were violations of army regulations. At this point, the FBI should have recognized that there was something not quite right—and that this something might have to do with the filer, not the subject of the investigation. But instead of conducting a more in-depth interview of Gilvydis and instead of looking into a few simple-to-disprove allegations, the FBI opened up the PI. Tenenbaum, waiting for the results of his SEEP nomination, had no idea.

The Preliminary Inquiry is a short three-to-six-month investigation to determine if there is any substance to the concerns raised. But, unbeknownst to Tenenbaum at that time, while Gilvydis was filing his report, other allegations surfaced against Tenenbaum from a different front.

Aside from the allegations of the man who suspected Tenenbaum's backpack, Tenenbaum had another "black mark" on his record that was rediscovered at this time. These allegations were based on a 1988 polygraph of one of Tenenbaum's coworkers, named Glen—old news to those in the know by the time of Tenenbaum's SEEP nomination.

During a routine polygraph examination in 1988, this coworker had noted his understanding that Tenenbaum was spying for Israel. When his results displayed skewed, he was asked to explain why his polygraph showed that he tested deceptive. Glen's answer had been that he had a *dream* about Tenenbaum.

A dream.

Glen had claimed that he, around the time of the polygraph exam, had a dream about his coworker. While undergoing his polygraph exam, Glen had explained—as if this was perfectly rational—that his thoughts must have drifted to the dream, which vaguely had something to do with spying. According to this coworker, Tenenbaum had traveled to Israel for TACOM, spoke Hebrew, and had acquaintances at the Israel Ministry of Defense—and so he had naturally dreamed about Tenenbaum and had been *thinking* of Tenenbaum during his polygraph exam. Glen was not accusing Tenenbaum of spying—just that he thought of Tenenbaum when a question arose about Israel. But Glen's "polygraph failure" was connected to Tenenbaum. Tenenbaum was a "dream" spy, whether there was any logic behind this idea or not.

In corporate America, if an executive walked into human resources demanding someone be fired because the executive had a dream the person was untrustworthy, he or she would likely be fired himself or herself or sent for a psychological examination.

In the government, this was enough to open a PI by the FBI—and enough to justify all the wasteful spending of hard-earned taxpayer money that entailed.

Nonetheless, based on Gilvydis's allegations about the backpack and this prior polygraph record stemming from Glen's dream thought process, the FBI opened their PI on Tenenbaum. Thankfully, the FBI closed this PI rather quickly, recognizing that the allegations were baseless. According to legal documents, the FBI refused to open up a full-fledged investigation because the allegations were not specific enough, and opening an investigation would have posed legal barriers. In other words, how would the FBI ever explain that the allegations were based on a deceptive polygraph examination of someone who was dreaming about Tenenbaum, and because a coworker felt Tenenbaum was "being too Jewish"—and had a backpack?

Tenenbaum didn't know anything about Gilvydis's accusations. He didn't know about Glen's. All he knew was that he couldn't go to the Middle East when he wanted to volunteer, and now his SEEP nomination had fizzled away before his eyes. There might not have been a public investigation against him, but the opportunity for career advancement through the exchange program was gone. No one mentioned it to him again, and Tenenbaum himself had to pursue the reasons why. No one would give him a clear-cut answer. All he knew was that the nomination had come to nothing.

MOGADISHU

In winding alleys, ill-designed for the box-like Humvees, the Somalis moved fluidly in the First Battle of Mogadishu in 1993. Delta Force members were on a mission to capture warlord Mohamed Farrah Aidid and other leaders of his militia. Two of Aidid's top lieutenants were detained smoothly. But the street-savvy and well-armed Somalis had the advantage in the urban fighting theatre. A rocket-propelled grenade launcher met its target to shoot down one of the US force's Black Hawk helicopters.[1]

Bulletproof glass on the Humvees shattered in the close-in battle. A second convoy was deployed to aid a first that found itself trapped. Humvees made wrong turns in a city of narrow streets that seemed to hug the buildings that lined them. By the end of the situation, two costly UH-60 Black Hawks were downed. UN personnel were stranded. Wounded were left to fend for themselves, lying desperate in the street to the horror of the world.

The US suffered seventy-three wounded, eighteen dead, and a Black Hawk pilot was taken captive. Over five hundred Somalis were dead. A thousand wounded. Including significant numbers of women, children, and civilians.[2]

In many ways, this is modern warfare, but it doesn't have to be.

CHAPTER 3

SETTING THE TRAP

"Like many physical diseases, anti-Semitism is highly infectious and can become endemic in certain localities and societies. Though a disease of the mind, it is by no means confined to weak, feeble, or commonplace intellects; as history sadly records, its carriers have included men and women of otherwise power-ful and subtle thoughts."

—PAUL JOHNSON

When Tenenbaum was hired at TACOM in 1984, his ability to speak Hebrew and his comfort around liaisons from Israel—an ally the United States collaborated with on defense projects—were considered an asset. All assignments and trips abroad were with the full knowledge and support of his supervisors. He could not travel internationally without such approval as a government employee.

Tenenbaum was never formally told that the SEEP assignment was canceled. He did not even know until years later about Glen's dream or Gilvydis's accusation. He also did not know that one of his former supervisors, Doug Templeton, considered him a security risk. Templeton advised that he couldn't come up with anything concrete, but that he would feel more comfortable recommending Tenenbaum for a position of trust if he had not received approval for a long-term assignment to Israel.[1] Still, after all of these ridiculous, bigoted allegations, the FBI concluded during the 1992 and 1993 time frame that Tenenbaum had done nothing wrong. But the army was not done with Tenenbaum.

17

ACCUSED OF TREASON

On January 13, 1994, members of the army still suspected Tenenbaum of spying for Israel. These army members expressed their concerns about Tenenbaum participating in the SEEP program, even though Tenenbaum had done nothing wrong and even though he was nominated for the SEEP program based on his job assignments and qualifications at TACOM, as well as his Jewish background. In all of this time of suspecting and investigating Tenenbaum, no one ever spoke with his supervisors or looked at his job statement to see what, exactly, his responsibilities were. As a matter of fact, no one even bothered to speak with Tenenbaum.

When Tenenbaum was again proposed for a SEEP assignment to Israel in 1994, certain army individuals became very nervous. The army continued to press the FBI to take a greater interest in the Tenenbaum saga. Eventually, as a result of the army's repeated concerns, the FBI agreed to reinterview the source of the 1992 SAEDA report against Tenenbaum—namely, Gilvydis. The FBI was very firm with the army officials who were pressing for a full-fledged Tenenbaum criminal investigation. The FBI needed a firm allegation from Gilvydis against Tenenbaum. Otherwise, they would not open a criminal investigation.

In response to the FBI's move, TACOM's Chief of Counterintelligence said that if the FBI could not or would not open an investigation into Tenenbaum, then a "Request for Security Determination form could be strategically filed to transfer investigative jurisdiction to the DIS from the FBI."[2] In other words, a document stating that the FBI gave up their right to investigate Tenenbaum and handed that right over to the DIS—without the FBI even knowing about it—would be surreptitiously placed in the Tenenbaum files. The problem with this idea was that the chief of counterintelligence completely ignored the fact that a DIS criminal investigation, which was being proposed, could not be used as a substitute for an FBI counterintelligence investigation. The DIS has no jurisdiction to investigate US civilians in counterintelligence matters. Only the FBI has jurisdiction.

The FBI did reinterview Gilvydis, and at that time, he retracted his allegations concerning Tenenbaum. But still, the army and the DOD would not give up, continuing to press for an investigation to block Tenenbaum's SEEP assignment to Israel. Nevertheless, his supervisors

18

kept assigning him to international programs, specifically Israel, for which he continued to receive highly successful ratings. Tenenbaum was a hard worker and he did his job well. In all of this time, none of the investigators bothered to check his job statements or speak with his supervisors concerning his job assignments. And still, none of them bothered to speak with David Tenenbaum.

In late spring of 1995, Tenenbaum traveled to Israel on US government orders to attend an international ballistics conference and to further the LASS program—every moment of his trip fully coordinated with his supervisor's approval, evidenced by the fact that his supervisors signed off on every aspect of his travels upon his return. LASS was Tenenbaum's brainchild, an idea born out of concern for warfighters in Humvees—vehicles ill-designed for urban conflict. The Battle of Mogadishu and countless other military encounters had shown it to be true. According to Dan Meyer, the former director for whistleblowing and transparency (DW&T) to the Inspector General (IG) of the Defense Department, Tenenbaum was one of "four or five guys" in the entire country who were thinking about survivability and Humvees in guerilla-type warfare at this point in time.[3] Tenenbaum's LASS project, by years, preceded anything the army has done since.

Following any governmental trips to foreign countries, employees at Tenenbaum's level were supposed to be debriefed within a few weeks of their return to the United States. But no one ever debriefed Tenenbaum after his Israel trip. However, in early 1996, when frigid winter weather clung to Michigan like frostbite, it was allegedly Lieutenant Colonel (LTC) John Simonini, head of TACOM's Counterintelligence Division, who decided Tenenbaum should be debriefed—over nine months after his return. The debriefing would be carried out by the 902nd MI Division based at the Selfridge Air Force Base in Michigan.

Had the agents actually been interested in the truth, they could have looked at Tenenbaum's travel vouchers to see that his superiors had signed off on every piece of his trip. Instead, the agents acted as if they had captured an enemy combatant.

"You are being uncooperative, Mr. Tenenbaum," said Special Agent Roy Cochran of the 902nd MI.

"How I am being uncooperative?"

"You refuse to tell us the name of the hotel you stayed in while in Israel, and you refuse to tell us who you met with. Stop being evasive and give us names."

"It was over nine months ago," Tenenbaum answered, disbelief showing on his face. "I've traveled numerous places since then, and for most of those, I couldn't tell you the name of any of the hotels I stayed in. Now, out of the blue, you expect me to remember the name of a hotel I stayed in almost a year ago?"

"And how about the people you met with? Are you telling us you don't remember who you met with and what the subject of conversation was?"

Tenenbaum, with his black, curly hair tucked beneath his yarmulke, appearing not much older than a grad school student, took a deep breath before answering.

"I was at a conference of over three hundred people from around the world. I spoke with at least seventy people throughout three days of the conference about everything under the sun, including armor, baseball, and the weather. I saw conference people at the conference and in restaurants after hours, and you want me to tell you who I spoke with, when I spoke to them, where I spoke to them, and the subject I spoke of with each one of them? Even if you had debriefed me right after I returned, I still would never have remembered all of that information."

This was not the first time Tenenbaum was debriefed or questioned after one of his trips overseas. He had been debriefed previously by the CIA many years before after a government trip overseas and understood that debriefings needed to take place very soon after overseas travel while information was still fresh.

Tenenbaum was frankly puzzled by the line of questioning. All the details and information that they requested was contained in his travel vouchers, as well as the post-trip evaluations submitted by his supervisors. Instead of being on the "same team"—Team USA—these guys were overtly hostile. His trip to Israel had been approved by his superiors and was a trip for the US government.

"You are being evasive, Mr. Tenenbaum."

These guys have no clue what they are doing, thought Tenenbaum without actually verbalizing his thoughts to these agents. *Are they actually protecting our nation's security?*

The 902nd agents, referred to by many on base derisively as the "Keystone Cops," made no effort to verify any suspicions—even by simply seeking a copy of the reports that illustrated the details of Tenenbaum's trip, and the fact that the "minute details" were approved by his supervisor. That low-level effort could have cleared up any problems and may have satisfied the agents. But these agents did not seem interested in clearing Tenenbaum of any alleged wrongdoing. This was not the standard debriefing that federal employees normally receive when returning from an overseas assignment.

These 902nd agents might not have had any intention of filing a SAEDA against Tenenbaum—despite their "misgivings" that Tenenbaum could not remember the name of his hotel and other minutiae[4]—but shortly after their conversation with Tenenbaum came their "eye-opening" experience at a conference in Washington, D.C.

Cochran, one of the 902nd agents who spoke with Tenenbaum, attended a conference where he met Michael Shropshire, who worked in the headquarters of the Department of the Army, in the Foreign Disclosure Office within the intelligence community. At this conference, Tenenbaum's name was mentioned, as was the SAEDA that had been filed against him years earlier. Shortly thereafter, the 902nd agents filed a new SAEDA with this "newfound" information, beginning their own investigation.[5] The facts and evidence behind these men's concerns remained vague, but Tenenbaum found himself on the wrong end of "follow the leader."

Neither Tenenbaum nor the public at large was yet aware of the US government's 1995 secret memo warning that "ethnic ties" to Israel meant Jews working within the US government would be "aggressively" recruited as spies by Israel.[6] The Anti-Defamation League (ADL) later strongly objected to the contents of the now-repudiated memo.[7] However, despite that repudiation, Jewish patriots within the government continued to be falsely profiled.

Back in 1992, the *Washington Post* had exposed the codenamed "Scope" project, a list that the FBI kept of Jewish employees—and the level of their security clearances.[8] In addition, about a decade prior to the questioning of Tenenbaum, Jonathan Pollard, a Jewish civilian analyst working for the federal government, pleaded guilty to providing secrets to Israel. There was a growing tenor of paranoia about Jews within the government.

Unbeknownst to Tenenbaum, Simonini—the head of TACOM security and counterintelligence—and the 902nd were working together to investigate him as a spy for Israel. They wanted to open a criminal investigation, but without any concrete evidence, it would never happen. They had to create a situation that they could then use to approach the FBI. They were going to catch their Jewish spy by any means necessary. Tenenbaum was "dirty," according to Simonini, and Simonini would be damned if he didn't prove it.[9]

The minor details that Tenenbaum admitted nothing out of the ordinary and that the 902nd agents were acting as if the conversation was a hopelessly delayed debriefing didn't seem to lessen any of the intensity of the questioning. Rather than addressing the trip in a calm and rational manner, admitting that too much time had passed for any realistic recall of the events in question, Simonini followed Tenenbaum's interview by proceeding directly to Special Agent James Gugino of the FBI.[10]

Simonini swore to Gugino that at a July meeting the previous year among Tenenbaum, Simonini, and Paul Barnard, who was Simonini's second-in-command, Tenenbaum admitted he had passed unauthorized classified information to Israel. Simonini declared that Tenenbaum was committing ongoing espionage and that he had confessed to both Simonini and Barnard that he was an Israeli spy.[11]

Simonini also swore that Tenenbaum was working too closely with the Israelis on the program Tenenbaum had developed and was heading the LASS program, despite the fact that it was unclassified and part of his job to work with the international team. It was not utilizing secret materials or information, but instead using public information from the three countries with the most experience and sophistication in light-armor vehicle design.

What Tenenbaum was keenly aware of was that if the United States was to prevent future horrors, the free exchange of unclassified information, fully following army rules and regulations, was a necessity.

Israel represented the United States' best source of data because of its unique situation as a landlocked nation, a nation with a high population density (ranked thirty-fifth in the world in population density as of 2016),[12] a nation surrounded by enemies, and a nation with specific and real urban combat experience. Tenenbaum also sought Germany's expertise—another nation with Cold War, urban, real-life experience— and its top-tier ballistic engineers.

Later, when Barnard was asked under oath about the supposed admission by Tenenbaum, Barnard swore it never happened.[13] Tenenbaum's lawyer later asked about the very logic of it. If Tenenbaum had admitted that he had, even inadvertently, provided classified information to Israel—the verbiage Simonini used was that Tenenbaum stated he "probably passed classified information to the Israelites"[14]— the response would have been immediate, swift, and powerful. And what Jew, what person since the Old Testament, would use the term "Israelites"?

Army regulations demand immediate action if a security leak occurs, and those same regulations threaten punishment upon any personnel who fail to report a security leak. Therefore, again, how could Tenenbaum have made any such admission in 1995, let alone to TACOM's director of intelligence and counterintelligence, Simonini, and his second-in-command, Barnard, with no further response?

Even more preposterous, why would Simonini—often called "paranoid" about the State of Israel[15]—sit on his hands and do nothing, allowing Tenenbaum to continue working on projects with Israel and other foreign governments, while counterintelligence cooled its heels? As Barnard would later state under oath, Lieutenant Colonel Simonini had already been instructing him to "sit in on" LASS meetings.[16] If Simonini was suspicious of Tenenbaum's activities—and sniffing around LASS as if it was somehow dangerous to have Tenenbaum working so closely with Israel—why would he then blithely ignore not only Tenenbaum's "confession," but also the rules and regulations of the army? Why didn't he file a SAEDA?

Simonini was known for obsessiveness and overly focusing his attention on minutiae, going above and beyond army requirements. According to Ron Duquette, who worked under Simonini, it was his obsessiveness about minor rules and regulations that led to unnecessary stress and the overworking of his small team.[17] Martin Terry, another team member, said Simonini was known to be a good "staff sergeant."[18] In military parlance, he was effectually a "paper pusher," but the fact that he never moved to his own command would reveal to anyone in the military that his career had remained firmly in the morass of the mediocre.

Would someone like Simonini ignore a confession of passing classified materials? The answer, of course, is that Tenenbaum never said any of it. Not so much as a single word.

CHAPTER 4

THE SECURITY RUSE

"I have long been convinced that Jewry constitutes the cancer in all of our life; as Jews, they are strangers in any European state and as such they are nothing but spreaders of decay."

—PAUL DE LAGARDE, German author and philosopher

Nearly a full year after the initial interview with the 902nd MI Division—a year spent developing the LASS program, holding meetings with its international team on the TACOM base, speaking to soldiers, analyzing vehicles, and doing ballistic tests with armor materials and different types of threats—Tenenbaum was told he needed to undergo another interview, this time by two agents from the Defense Investigative Services (DIS) for his security-clearance upgrade. This was an upgrade that Tenenbaum had already gone on record as saying he did not want, an upgrade request that came from over his head, which was in direct contrast to the actions that should have been taken if there was an existent security concern.

The interview took place on January 8, 1997 at TACOM and was a partial repeat of the debriefing Tenenbaum underwent with the two agents from the 902nd MI Division.

Two DIS special agents, Mark Yourchock and Robert Riley, conducted the interview in a windowless conference room—three chairs, a desk, and a snug proximity Tenenbaum didn't flinch at when he walked in, being used to conversations in similar-sized spaces across the base. The questioning began in the early morning, focusing on his trip to Israel in May 1995 and then on the type of work he had been involved with over the course of his career at TACOM. The questions were initially rather banal, but as the interview continued, he was asked about the types of people he worked with and more about his background.

Tenenbaum wasn't initially wary. Yourchock, who seemed to be playing Good Cop, asked the questions. He was relaxed, professional, and courteous in his demeanor. But then Yourchock angled back toward the trip to Israel.

Tenenbaum's posture began to tighten, the windowless room feeling more like a cage than it had only moments before.

The agent asked what hotel he had patronized. Who had he talked to? What had they discussed? The same questions he had already been asked, the same questions that had already been answered in Tenenbaum's travel vouchers showing every detail of his trip and signed by his superiors.

Didn't any of these people speak to each other? thought Tenenbaum.

Tenenbaum had a head for figures and problem-solving. He wasn't a man who focused on meals eaten, sights seen, or the social chatter of colleagues. He was the classic engineer—an excellent mind for facts and figures, design and detail—but taking in only what he thought important and necessary information. In the calm, respectful voice Tenenbaum was known for, he gave the same answers he gave to the 902nd agents: he traveled so much, and with so little concern over his hotel accommodations, that he regularly had only bare memories of where he'd stayed only a week after he arrived home. His Israel trip was filled with a conference and dozens of meetings; he likely had been passed the business cards of a hundred professionals. While he could not recall which hotel he had stayed at months before, he did know that his hotel had been little more than a place to shower, shave, and sleep off jetlag.

Had this not started giving Tenenbaum an uneasy feeling that something was afoot, he would have laughed at the military being so concerned as to where he put his head—on what pillow and in what hotel. He wondered if they would next ask him what kind of shampoo the hotel provided in their little bottles, about the lighting fixtures, the bedspread, or the pattern on the carpet.

A year later, Tenenbaum would not be able to recount the art on the wall in this small conference room either, not for any lack of observational skills but due to a simple prioritization of importance in his mind. Analytical problem-solvers look for information that has relevance to the challenge at hand; the number of the room and the detritus on the desk were not among these remembered details, but hardly is this a condemning personality trait.

That nagging sense that this seemed more invasive than a typical debriefing and security-clearance interview kept gnawing at Tenenbaum as the questioning dragged on. It brought back memories of the CIA debriefing he had undergone after a previous overseas trip, but the contrast between debriefings was, to say the least, mind-boggling. The CIA debriefing was conducted professionally, with pertinent questions geared toward obtaining real facts. This debriefing seemed piloted by incompetency.

Tenenbaum wove his fingers together and tried to answer everything he could as patiently as possible. After hours, they broke for lunch. Tenenbaum wasn't hungry and went back to his desk to catch up on work he was missing with this exercise that felt so useless.

Yourchock and Riley, on the other hand, met with Lieutenant Colonel Simonini during the lunch break and were apparently instructed to get Tenenbaum to agree to the next step of their "investigation."[1] Simonini said Tenenbaum violated numerous federal laws. The agents didn't ask for the details or the proof that didn't exist. They followed their orders.

After lunch, Riley, consistently acting as the Bad Cop of this interview, leaned forward in his seat, hands in front of him on the conference room table. "I am disturbed you can't remember details, Mr. Tenenbaum."

Suddenly, after their break, they started using the phrase that Tenenbaum had "committed numerous violations of federal law and had violated army and DoD regulations."

Riley had been specifically chosen to speak with Tenenbaum because he had experience in espionage cases. Tenenbaum thought Riley's eyes literally seemed to dance with delight at seeing the engineer squirm.

"I talked to a hundred people on a dozen topics," Tenenbaum repeated. "I told the 902nd guys, and I'm telling you, you should have debriefed me *last year*. This is ridiculous."

Tenenbaum wanted this whole thing over with already. His hands balled into fists he held as graciously as he could in his lap. How many different ways could he tell them the same thing—that *nothing happened* on this last trip to Israel? That nothing had happened *ever*? He did not want to be here. He did not want to upgrade his security clearance. It was not his idea. He wanted to be working on LASS. He wanted to be saving lives. They were wasting his time.

"We have a different take on it." Riley leaned forward on the table. He exhaled, a jagged breath that had an edge to it, as if Tenenbaum was personally annoying him. He narrowed his eyes at Tenenbaum's face and held the stare.

The other guy—Good Cop—was looking away, as if he wasn't going to watch this. Then, Bad Cop pushed away from the desk and stood to his full height. He paced back and forth a minute or two, apparently unconcerned that the anticipation of what he was going to say next was driving Tenenbaum crazy.

Tenenbaum felt his heartbeat thumping in his chest. He'd been sitting still for too long. He hated sitting still. He itched for a walk between buildings, a quick visit to his team in the lab, or a long, fresh-air run. It took a lot to get to Tenenbaum, but now he was angry—angry and doing his best not to show it.

Riley finally approached him, leaned down, and said, in a terse voice, close to Tenenbaum's ear, "We think you are lying."

Tenenbaum's fists unclenched themselves. *Lying?* He just wasn't wired that way—not for career advancement, not in his personal life. He felt like shouting, "Ask my wife. Ask my friends. Ask anyone from my community. Ask *anyone* who knows me." He could forget things, perhaps. But lying? Not a chance. And who cared what hotel he stayed in the previous year? And then Bad Cop said it aloud:

"I find it difficult to believe you *haven't* been passing classified information on to the Israelis."

The rip current was pulling Tenenbaum under. He was a happily-married, quiet engineer with two young children, and his career was taking off. He created and was now the head of the LASS program and was its driving force. He was known as a face-to-face leader, one who would walk across the TACOM base to forge alliances to propel his life-and limb-saving program forward. He was one of the good guys.

"What about the phone calls you make from the office in Hebrew, Mr. Tenenbaum? What about those?" Special Agent Riley sat back down, pushed his index fingers together, then moved his fingers to his lips, pursing them, seeming to consider something.

Tenenbaum's breathing turned shallow, and he pressed his palms against his slacks, sweating and worried. His mouth was dry, and he struggled to form his response. When he had been hired, years before, his fluency in Hebrew had been considered an asset. He traveled to the Israeli embassy and Israel—but he also worked side by side with colleagues from Germany, Great Britain, the Netherlands, South Africa, Canada, and others. The LASS program itself involved cooperation between the United States, Israel, and Germany. Was his own country tapping the phone lines in his office? Listening in? He tried to swallow. His throat was too constricted. Were they listening in on him? His own country, his own government, his own *office*—had they bugged him? He later learned that his colleagues had heard his conversations in Hebrew and suspected he was passing classified information to Israel. They had been the ones who passed on their suspicions to security. But it seemed that the people who knew him and should have known how loyal he was to the soldiers and his job were playing spy games with him.

And what about the other languages spoken in the office? Russian, Farsi, German, Taiwanese—were these people suspected of passing on classified information as well?

Tenenbaum swallowed again. His emotions were jumbled. "I speak to my children in Hebrew. I want them to be bilingual."

"We don't believe you."

Tenenbaum felt like another wave struck him down. If they had gone to the trouble of listening in on his calls in Hebrew, couldn't they have discerned he was speaking to his own kids? Was his preschool-aged little girl now a spy too because she could recite the Hebrew alphabet?

At the time, he didn't realize that his own colleagues suspected him of being a spy. Unbeknownst to him, his own "colleagues" used to call him the "little Jewish spy" behind his back.[2]

Riley shook his head. "You understand that your career is over, right?"

Tenenbaum felt like screaming, *Over what? Because I can't remember the name of my hotel over a year ago, and I speak in Hebrew to my little girl when I call home to check in with my wife?*

Yourchock folded his hands on the conference room table and spoke matter-of-factly. "David, I think you know how our government treats people who betray their country. Think of what this will do to your family." He put on a compassionate face, pretending to wince in solidarity with Tenenbaum's newfound predicament.

Betray their country? Where had *that* idea come from? They were, essentially, branding him a spy, and worse—a traitor.

Tenenbaum considered asking for a lawyer. If he asked for a five-minute break, he could hurriedly phone a family friend who was an attorney and ask him what he should do. But that wasn't even the kind of law his family attorney—and friend from the Orthodox community—practiced. He drew up wills.

What the heck kind of lawyer even handled this? Were there lawyers who handled espionage cases? He remembered from history in his elementary school days reading about Benedict Arnold, a traitor to the US colonies. Wasn't he hanged? *Don't they give the death penalty to traitors?* But Tenenbaum struggled to understand what on Earth they were basing their suspicions on. In his work with LASS, he was *using* Israel's data. If anything, Israel had more to lose in this situation than the United States did.

Tenenbaum refused to believe that "they"—his own government—thought that he was a spy. This was a misunderstanding. He pushed it out of his mind. He assumed if he had nothing to hide, this would all be cleared up with a few phone calls. Asking for a lawyer—as he believed from any Hollywood movie—meant the suspect was guilty. The innocent do not need lawyers.

"You know, at worst, you're going to jail. At best—at the very best—you're going to receive the Gordie Howe mushroom treatment." Tenenbaum heard the words and immediately imagined himself as the late Gordie Howe, Mr. Hockey, the twenty-six season NHL pro who had been relegated to a dark office to twiddle his thumbs after retirement.

Tenenbaum wasn't a man who liked to twiddle his thumbs. "You will sit in a corner and do nothing—absolutely nothing—for the rest of your career. You will be a pariah. Your colleagues will avoid you. They will look at you in disgust. You'll be a living dead man on this base. If I were you, I'd be looking over my shoulder every day I came to work. Word gets out, you know…about guys that don't belong…about engineers who can't be trusted."

A living dead man? Tenenbaum's mind scrambled to try to fathom the veiled threat. *A dead man?*

Tenenbaum's skin felt cold. He was clueless that the FBI had noted in their correspondence from FBI Detroit to the director of the FBI in Washington, D.C., Mr. Louis Freeh, on September 24, 1996, language that helped to fuel the fire for the Yourchock and Riley inquisition of Tenenbaum:

> Detroit's investigation has relied on reporting from Roy Thomas Cochran, Special Agent US Army Intelligence and Security Command (INSCOM), 902nd Military Intelligence Group, Detroit Military Intelligence Attachment, Selfridge Air National Guard Base, Michigan. According to Cochran, Tenenbaum should have no official reason to be in contact with Lieutenant/Colonel Eli DavidPur, an officer of the Israeli Defense Forces (IDF) who is a certified foreign national liaison officer (INLO) assigned to TARDEC. Despite no official reason for Tenenbaum and DavidPur to have contact, Cochran has received reporting from his source at TARDEC that Tenenbaum is frequently in DavidPur's office. [REDACTED PORTION.] During FBI interview, Laurain [code name] stated that she is suspicious of Tenenbaum because he made an application under the US Army Scientist Engineer Exchange Program (SEEP) to visit Israel as an exchange scientist. However, Laurain could provide no articulable facts or evidence to support her suspicion, other that the fact that she has seen Tenenbaum in DavidPur's office and she knows that Tenenbaum has been friendly with every Israeli Liaison officer assigned to TARDEC.[3]

Both Cochran and "Laurain" failed to relate that not only was Tenenbaum authorized to have contact with the Israeli liaison officers at TARDEC—in fact, he was allowed to have contact with the Israeli liaison officers as well as the other liaison officers on base—but Tenenbaum's contacts and frequent discussions were indeed necessary based on the US-Israel programs to which he was assigned, as well as the programs he was developing with the State of Israel. Laurain's suspicions of Tenenbaum because he applied for the SEEP program, a program for which any engineer and scientist could apply if they so wished, further muddled this investigation. There were other engineers within TARDEC and other army organizations who applied and were accepted to other countries such as France, England, and Australia, but they were never suspected of espionage because they applied for the SEEP for those countries. Only Tenenbaum who applied for the SEEP program with Israel was suspected. The Jew was suspected of being a spy—treason, because he applied to be an exchange engineer with a "Jewish" country.

Other engineers would speak with the Israeli liaison officer in his office, but they were never suspected of treason. Cochran stated that Tenenbaum had "no official reason to have contact with DavidPur," yet as an intelligence officer, he should have been aware that there was no regulation to back his claim. As an intelligence officer, he should have spoken to Tenenbaum's supervisors, checked Tenenbaum's job statement, or even spoken with Tenenbaum about his work. Both he and "Laurain" seemed to have done none of these. They also did not seem interested in logic and truth. Tenenbaum supporters believe Laurain and Cochran were looking to catch a spy in little old Detroit.

The final paragraph of this Summary of Interview (SOI) to FBI Headquarters summed everything up in a way Tenenbaum would have approved of if he had seen it:

> Although INSCOM officials continue to be suspicious of Tenenbaum, FBI investigation has developed no evidence to support the contention that Tenenbaum is involved in espionage or treason against the United States Government. Detroit (FBI) believes that there is insufficient fact to predicate further investigation regarding Tenenbaum. As a matter of fact, the allegations against Tenenbaum remain so sketchy that there is little information upon which to base an intelligent and logical interview of Tenenbaum.[4]

"Insufficient fact." "Sketchy." "Little information."

Yet despite the FBI's misgivings and direct written report that Tenenbaum had done nothing wrong, Lieutenant Colonel Simonini had convened a highly classified briefing at TACOM on October 21, 1996, two months prior to Yourchock and Riley's interrogation of him, where he labeled Tenenbaum an Israeli spy and where he concocted the idea of using a security-clearance upgrade as a ruse to investigate Tenenbaum without him being aware that he was considered an Israeli spy by high-level US government officials.

Attending the October briefing were high-level senior officials from TACOM and from Washington, D.C., including Jerry Chapin, the director of TARDEC; the deputy to the TACOM commander; Dr. Jack Parks, Tenenbaum's first-line supervisor; representatives of the Program Managers' Office (PEO) Ground Combat Systems; LTC John Simonini, a TACOM DIC for Special Access Programs (SAP)/Black Programs; 902nd MI special agents; a representative from the Department of the Army Office of the Chief of Staff for Intelligence; as well as the Chief of Administrative Law at TACOM; and a representative from the FBI. And they all went along with Simonini's scheme. They had all bought into it. Innocent until proven guilty be dammed. Simonini was the conductor and running the show, labeling Tenenbaum a spy without providing the sworn statement that the FBI requested.

According to Gugino of the FBI, "In the eyes of the counterintelligence and security personnel, people are assumed guilty until they can be proven not guilty."[5] But the catch with the "Tenenbaum affair" was that the counterintelligence and security personnel in this case seemed only interested in proving guilt. They had their spy. They just had to manufacture the "proof."

In the words of Gugino, who was the lead investigating agent at this high-level meeting, Simonini spelled out his plan to catch what he thought could be one of "the biggest spy cases ever," and Simonini specifically informed the briefing participants that they should keep Tenenbaum oblivious to this DIS counterintelligence investigation.[6]

Prior to this secret meeting, Simonini was informed by the 902nd that Tenenbaum may have compromised three Black programs (highly classified military or defense projects publicly unacknowledged by the

33

government) by handing over extremely classified information to the Israelis. These allegations were going to be briefed to the Program Executive Office (PEO) Combat Systems that is responsible for providing ground combat equipment to Joint Warfighters, as well as to the vice chief of staff of the army. Simonini wanted more information from the 902nd, and he received a secret draft memo that was unsigned and was dated October 11, 1996, ten days prior to the secret October meeting. It summarized the previous SAEDAs and noted that the FBI had recently closed a PI on Tenenbaum stating that the previous SAEDAs were exaggerated.

The 902nd MI Group said, "There is no substantive evidence to indicate any unauthorized disclosure on the part of Tenenbaum; moreover, he is not currently the subject of any Army Counterintelligence Investigation."[7]

Simonini, on the other hand, informed the meeting participants that Tenenbaum fit a "classic profile" and had natural religious tendencies that the Israelis could try to exploit. He pointed out to the meeting participants that Tenenbaum traveled to Israel for both official and personal reasons, and he noted that the, "host nation [Israel] is known to try to exploit nationalistic and *religious* tendencies."[8]

Simonini neglected to inform the meeting participants, some of whom were hearing these allegations for the first time, that the first two SAEDA reports generated by Tenenbaum's "colleagues" were either completely recanted or greatly "softened" when reexamined by the authorities. He also did not tell them that the FBI and the 902nd MI Group considered the reporting way back in 1994 to be "exaggerated," and that the LASS meeting, which was held at TACOM, was coordinated with Simonini himself and Army Material Command (AMC), who both sent representatives. (See Appendix 3.)

They were on a mission. His idea was to make sure that the paperwork for Tenenbaum's security-clearance upgrade went through the system and to use this bogus upgrade request as a means to criminally investigate Tenenbaum for treason against the United States of America. The army and the investigative agencies felt they could keep the upper hand as long as Tenenbaum was kept in the dark regarding the truth: that there was never any intention to upgrade his security clearance. In actuality, it was all a sham, and Tenenbaum was being investigated for espionage.

On November 4, 1996, one of Tenenbaum's higher-level supervisors, Jack Parks, under the auspices of Simonini and the DIS, submitted a formal request to have the DIS open its rueful "security clearance" investigation. The form that Parks submitted is called the "DoD Request for Personnel Security Investigation." There is a place on this form for supervisors and security personnel to mark and explain if there was ever any derogatory information on the person for whom the form is being submitted—in other words, David Tenenbaum. Similar to the 1992 request form, the form submitted by Jack Parks indicated that there was no derogatory information that existed on Tenenbaum. Those who filled out this form never mentioned at least three—and possibly up to seven—separate SAEDAs that previously had been filed against Tenenbaum, nor did they mention at least three PIs that the FBI conducted on Tenenbaum. They lied. It would be considered a federal violation and false statement if one were to lie on this form, which both Jack Parks and Simonini did by saying that no derogatory information existed. Simonini appeared to assume that Tenenbaum was a spy, but he never mentioned this information on the form.

Simonini later categorized the damage Tenenbaum had done: "This is a serious thing. There are literally hundreds of thousands of army lives at stake, and there's hundreds of millions of dollars at stake."[9]

If this were indeed the case, why would Simonini never file a SAEDA report or derogatory information report against Tenenbaum before the FBI criminal investigation began, despite the enormity of such a purported confession?

Seven months later—seven months after the alleged event—Simonini filed a derogatory information report, but only after the FBI criminal investigation began, and the report had nothing to do with Tenenbaum's supposed confession. (See Appendices 4 and 5.)

But Tenenbaum didn't have any of that background; he was clueless as to what was going on behind the scenes as he sat in the room with Yourchock and Riley. The conference room felt cold. His head ached. His disbelief showed on his face. The words "betrayed your country," "traitor," and "jail" seemed to echo in the small space.

The two agents opposite him remained still. Tenenbaum's heartbeat pounded against his skin, reminding him he was alive. And somehow, he wasn't dreaming.

"You have another choice," Yourchock said hopefully, sounding almost casual.

Tenenbaum's ears perked up, and his heart lifted for a minute. Could they really be tossing him a life vest?

"You can take a polygraph exam," the Good Cop said, almost off-handedly. "That would rule out these charges, and you can move past all this—if you pass it."

To Tenenbaum, this sounded like a sliver of hope. He was honest to a fault. Of course he would pass it. Then this whole incident would be over. He'd pass the test, walk out cleared, and get back to working on LASS. Tenenbaum didn't have an inkling that according to Major Mike Zembrzuski, "This investigation continues to draw attention at the highest levels of the US Army/Army Materials Command (AMC), to include a scheduled 10 Feb 97 briefing to the AMC Chief of Staff."[10]

If Tenenbaum didn't take the polygraph, it sounded like he might as well draft his resignation letter because they had no intention of letting him out of a dark cubicle in the basement somewhere. That would be the kiss of death for his career, but also for LASS. The LASS program was more than an acronym. It was a program meant to prevent devastating permanent injuries and horrific deaths in urban combat. Tenenbaum knew that putting soldiers in Humvees as they presently existed was like putting young men and women into powder kegs on wheels. These vehicles needed to be redesigned and/or retrofitted in a way that protected the soldiers. He *had* to get past this thing.

Of course, it crossed his mind that in Pollard's case, the result was a plea deal that meant *decades* in prison. That if this didn't go the right way, Tenenbaum might be executed. But he had an ace up his sleeve: he knew he was innocent.

Tenenbaum pictured three straws. The first straw represented agreeing to the polygraph and clearing himself. The next was not agreeing to the polygraph and watching his career end in disgrace. His reputation would be mud. The short straw, the one he didn't want to draw, was agreeing to the polygraph and a ridiculous outcome occurring—failing.

Which, of course, meant a trial for espionage, the potential outcome of which he didn't even want to think about. The idea was so ludicrous he didn't even give it much credence. Instead, what he was weighing was one thing and one thing only: he was *innocent*. He'd take the polygraph. He felt that he had no choice, which was exactly what these agents in partnership with Simonini seemed determined to convey to Tenenbaum. But as soon as he agreed to it, a new thought tugged at the corners of his mind. As an innocent, would he be *believed*?

Furious that his dedication to the country and the US government had been reduced to a debriefing about a forgotten trip to Israel, Tenenbaum, with no clue of his rights, agreed.

On February 4, 1997, Gugino was briefed of the results of the Tenenbaum "interview" at the Detroit Field Office. Gugino stated that he would request FBI Headquarters to authorize a full field investigation based upon Yourchock and Riley's DIS findings. Gugino told FBI Headquarters that the DIS should conduct the Personal Security Interview (PSI)-related polygraph examination. Gugino further stated that a second interview should be conducted with Tenenbaum, and that he should sign a sworn statement should he change his mind about the polygraph. Gugino wanted to know when and where the polygraph was going to take place. The FBI remained very interested in the Tenenbaum affair.[11]

THE OLYMPIC PARK BOMBING

In Atlanta, Georgia, rhythm and blues wailed late into the night for the 100th anniversary of the revived Olympic Games. Even close to midnight on Friday, July 26, 1996, nearly fifteen thousand people crowded Centennial Olympic Park. Many athletes might have been resting, but masses of tourists and fans traded pins and basked in their surroundings of endless foreign tongues. International unity was at its height in this extravagant celebration of varied nations, peoples, and sports. Then, a security guard discovered the abandoned olive-green backpack, casually laid under a bench near the sound and light tower that faced the AT&T stage. A bomb squad was called and police began to clear the area; however, it was no simple task amid revelers.[1]

When the explosion burst into the night, some of the crowd cheered, believing it to be part of the festivities. But the line of officers that had formed to clear the area took the worst of the explosion. Smoke tinged with gunpowder filled the air. The vacuum from the heat shoved them forward as the shrapnel flew into the masses. The pipe bomb was filled with nails and screws that ripped skin and muscle and punctured bone.

A woman who had simply wanted to bring her baby to the Olympics lay dead. Over one hundred people were injured, including a stagehand who suffered a collapsed disc in his neck that nearly paralyzed him.[2]

Bombs like this weren't yet called improvised explosive devices or IEDs, a term coined in 2003, but that's precisely what this bomb was.[3] And incidents of extreme violence just like this were on dramatic rise across the globe, in war zones and civilian terrorist attacks alike.

An IED can be almost anything with any type of material coupled with an initiator. It is a homemade device with the sole purpose—what it was born to do—of causing deaths or injuries by using explosives alone or in combination with toxic chemicals, biological toxins, radiological material, nails, screws, or anything that can penetrate the body and do maximum damage. Unlike conventional weapons of destruction, IED builders improvise with the materials at hand, whether military ordnance components or materials purchased at their local hardware store.

Atlanta cringed. Investigators jumped on the case. Tenenbaum watched it on the nightly news. This was exactly the type of blast his working life was dedicated to fighting, but this wasn't a war zone. Explosions weren't supposed to rock the lives of civilians so close to home. But he was finding out they could and they would, and, for him, improvised explosives of a different nature had been set into motion, ticking away, ready to blow everything he loved about his life to shreds.

CHAPTER 5

WIRED

"Injustice anywhere is a threat to justice everywhere."
—MARTIN LUTHER KING JR.

David Tenenbaum drove home in a daze. He hadn't eaten lunch—not with thoughts of Good Cop/Bad Cop dancing through his head. He hadn't eaten all day—and he *still* was not hungry. Just numb. He'd spent hours with the two agents, and they had pressed him to tell his entire life story. It was obvious that they were on a fishing expedition. They were looking for clues or hints that he was passing on classified information to Israel, some sort of quid pro quo arrangement, perhaps. But there was simply not the slightest shred of truth to their accusations. They could fish all they wanted. There was nothing for them to find.

They scheduled the polygraph for two weeks' time. It seemed to Tenenbaum that his colleagues were avoiding him more in the office, casting suspicious and furtive glances his way. Was he being paranoid? He was starting to look over his shoulder more and more. Tenenbaum increasingly felt that the polygraph was his best chance to put this blip on his (until now) unblemished, stellar career behind him.

Tenenbaum had been chosen for the highly competitive Weapon System Sustainment Management (WSSM) program as well as another competitive congressional program, the AMC Civilian Leadership Development Program, which meant that he was being "fast-tracked" for upper management. Tenenbaum had been nominated to go to Israel on the Exchange program. Yet now, it seemed that the more he succeeded in his job, the more it was assumed by his coworkers that he was doing something wrong.

He didn't want to scare his wife, Madeline, and referred to this new "security clearance upgrade" in the vaguest terms at home. He had been given different clearance levels in the past, such as NATO clearance or clearance for various Black programs, but these were always pursued in response to supervisor requests for work being conducted. This was different, and Tenenbaum knew it.

A desired security-clearance upgrade—the words were a spectacular lie—but believable to anyone working within the US government at the levels at which Tenenbaum was employed. Polygraph examinations were not commonly used for security-clearance upgrades, nor were they required. As a matter of fact, Barnard once mentioned to Simonini that he only knew of one other person, in all his years at TACOM, who went through a polygraph connected with his security clearance.[1]

Tenenbaum wandered through his own life like a zombie, distracted and going through the motions. What-ifs played like a perpetual drumbeat in his brain. He worried about LASS and whether this whole exercise would doom his program. The soldiers needed him. He could not bear the thought of the next explosion severing some soldier's legs when his work could help.

Certain the polygraph would prove his innocence, he still felt personally stung by the inquisition. He knew he hadn't acted in any way that would arouse suspicion, but after the Pollard incident, he worried that people around him were looking to target Jews on base. He assumed some basic fact-checking by the government would be occurring. By now, surely, they had located his travel itinerary from Israel, made a few calls, looked at his stellar reviews from his supervisors and others higher up the chain of command—and even the fact that he had volunteered to serve as an engineer in the first Gulf War. They were now realizing how mistaken they were. They had to be.

He still could not wrap his mind around his faith now being a target of suspicion. Tenenbaum's faith had always been a part of his life. As a child of a Holocaust survivor, he had been raised to *never forget* the specter of the fog of ash and war that had come close to destroying humanity in World War II. His father, the only survivor of his immediate family, had immigrated to America. He had survived the horrors of Auschwitz for almost a year, Dachau for a month, and horrors in other concentration camps—as well as the poverty, hunger, and abuse of a ghetto for two years. America had represented hope. The Tenenbaums, as a family, fully believed in the American dream, in the land of freedom, and in the Statue of Liberty. Freedom of religion and separation of church and state were ideas that were a part of his country's identity. He'd never doubted this. The US Constitution would protect him. He had rights. Though Israel represented the Biblical promised land and was an ally, Tenenbaum knew that the United States was his home. He took his governmental oaths and responsibilities with utmost seriousness. Serving his country was his honor, and he preferred that calling of a higher purpose, a career path within the government doing work for the greater good.

On February 6, 1997, Special Agent Gugino notified Special Agent Riley that he had just transmitted a formal request to FBI Headquarters requesting the authority to expand the current preliminary investigation to a full field investigation, meaning a criminal espionage investigation, based upon the investigative developments furnished by the Yourchock/Riley interview and investigative developments. However, Gugino wanted to remain in the background. Gugino did not want to assume full jurisdiction in this matter until the polygraph had been completed on February 13. Riley faxed Gugino the draft, unclassified version of the Tenenbaum interview the DIS (Yourchock and Riley) conducted on Tenenbaum as requested by the FBI.[2]

Two days before the Tenenbaum polygraph, the DIS and FBI were putting everything in place. On February 11, 1997, Gugino advised that he had reviewed the draft Report of Investigation (ROI) furnished by the DIS and found numerous investigative leads of interest to the FBI. Gugino said that the DIS should plan on closing and referring the Tenenbaum case to the FBI upon completion of the polygraph on February 13, 1997.[3]

When the day of the polygraph arrived, Tenenbaum was not yet aware that Simonini and the 902nd and the DIS were feeding the FBI false information. Tenenbaum was distracted and anxious, but confident in the outcome. He set off for the Livonia, Michigan, office of the DIS. All he wanted to do was clear himself of all of these ridiculous accusations and get on with his life.

Special Agents Yourchock and Riley arrived with Albert Snyder, the DOD's senior polygraph examiner. They presented Tenenbaum with a consent form and rights advisement, which to his horrified surprise indicated that he was being polygraphed for the crimes of espionage and false statement.

"I thought this was to clear up confusion about my trip and my security clearance. There is no way I am going to sign this form." Tenenbaum had been wracking his brain these past two weeks, trying to remember everything he could about his trip to Israel. He didn't even pick up the pen lying on the table. His head swam, and the words on the paper were fuzzy, as if his body was shutting down. His vision grew hazy, and the sheet in front of him faded in and out of clarity. He felt like he was hyperventilating. He wanted to throw up. There was no way he was even cut out to be a spy. Give him some materials problem to solve or a tank to redesign. That he could do.

"Don't worry, Mr. Tenenbaum, the words 'espionage' and 'false statement' were merely put down on the consent form for administrative purposes and nothing more," Snyder assured him.

Tenenbaum didn't have any choice—or so he thought. He wanted to get up and leave right then and there, but like the rule follower he was, he thought that he would not be allowed to. No one ever told him that he was free to leave if he wanted. He didn't know if they would arrest him if he refused to sign the forms or if he decided to leave. They never told him that he was free to secure an attorney. He didn't realize that his cluelessness was the point, an elaborate ruse to make sure that he would not secure an attorney.

The remainder of the consent form was standard DIS polygraph paperwork. Tenenbaum continued reading it with newly elevated precision.

He took a deep breath.

"Will you be taping it?"

Snyder informed him that the DIS did not, in fact, record their polygraph examinations.

"I brought my own tape recorder and would like to tape the session," Tenenbaum said. He wanted it as a safety net—just in case there was a discrepancy between what he said and what they heard. After all, men were executed for espionage. Better safe than sorry. Or dead.

"We don't allow that," Snyder told him. "You need to leave your tape recorder outside the room where the polygraph examination will be taking place."

Feeling powerless, Tenenbaum signed the form and was escorted by Riley and Snyder toward the room for the polygraph. Good Cop was being left behind. Yourchock wasn't an ally, but he was the best that Tenenbaum had that morning. Special Agent Yourchock didn't even look in his direction.

After walking down a long, narrow hallway, they stopped at a door that looked like every other door that they'd passed. When they entered, the small windowless room they stepped into felt cold. Tenenbaum's skin tingled. The two-way mirror he was expecting wasn't there. Neither was a video camera that he could see. Why weren't they recording this? Tenenbaum *wanted* to be recorded. He felt it would be a recording of his innocence—evidence that others would see. He wanted the proof to be taped.

According to information Tenenbaum found out later, it was standard procedure to surprise those being polygraphed with startling language of accusations right before they were to take the examination. At that point, almost universally, those being polygraphed feel they have to stay. Leaving—to the innocent—implies guilt.

Bad Cop excused himself too.

The out-of-shape and heavyset Snyder wheezed slightly as he pored over his equipment. He was slovenly, his skin greasy. With just Tenenbaum and Snyder in the room, Snyder's face was coldly impassive. In silence, he wired up Tenenbaum. The wires of a polygraph are enough to make anyone feel unnerved—even the innocent. Snyder attached wires to Tenenbaum's fingers, and wrapped a belt-like measuring device around his chest. Tenenbaum knew the device would monitor and record his blood pressure, body temperature, pulse, respiration rate, and skin conductivity. He believed that he could end this nightmare by telling the truth. He took a deep breath, confirming to himself that it would soon be over. It soon had to be over.

Snyder, author of seminal works on polygraph tests and considered the top defense expert on the polygraph exam, would, Tenenbaum was certain, see immediately in the movement of the needle that Tenenbaum was innocent. So Tenenbaum tried to make the polite and awkward small talk of strangers thrust into an intimate situation. But as Snyder finished attaching his equipment to his subject, he was having none of it.

Baseline questions were asked that would establish whether Tenenbaum was telling the truth or not.

What is your name?

Your occupation?

He was also asked to lie—intentionally—to see what that looked like as the needle shifted on the paper.

Tenenbaum did not know that the control questions are not "scored." He also did not know that polygraph examinations, according to some experts, are skewed to hurt the innocent.[4] For example, if asked the question, "Have you ever stolen anything on the job?" someone might answer, "No, of course not." The examiner might press the person, saying, "Come on. *Everyone* steals Post-it Notes."

If someone—for example, a very honest person who scrupulously avoids theft of even a paper clip, or for whom even white lies are not acceptable—continues to maintain that they do not steal and this is the truth, the examiner will likely assume they are, in fact, *lying*. This can skew the baseline. The assumption is that *of course* everyone tells lies to benefit themselves. Those who are exceptionally honest are, in essence, punished for being so.

In addition, polygraph examinations often—especially for the innocent—lead to "over-sharing," with the examined man or woman trying to be so helpful that he or she offers information above and beyond what is necessary. The innocent say more than they need to. They fill in the silences. The honest are inherently unnerved by the polygraph examination. They wonder if they've said the wrong thing. So, they volunteer still more and more, aiming to help the examiner.

Tenenbaum looked around. He had no idea if he was being watched from outside the room somehow. He was sure he had to be. He knew what the middle-aged Snyder had *said*, but was that even the truth?

Was he alone with Snyder—really alone, the most alone he had ever felt in his life? It made him nervous just sitting there, aware the needles were recording his breath, his blood pressure, and his heart rate. His impassive examiner didn't look him in the eye.

Tenenbaum did know that a final report would be delivered to his superiors. This was comforting at least—once they saw that he was telling the truth, the government would have a little egg on its face, but this whole charade would be over. He did not know that his superiors were part of this ruse; they were fully aware of what was happening and were completely complicit in this illegal criminal investigation. The entire security upgrade pretext was a lie. None of the events in that room were being watched, taped, or recorded. Snyder, he would learn later, would ultimately *destroy* all evidence of the exam and all the notes that went into his final report.[5]

Tenenbaum tried to sit up straighter, forgetting the strap fastened around his chest. He took a deep breath and tried to sit still. He was as ready as he ever would be.

CHAPTER 6

THE FLUCTUATING NEEDLE

*"The piles of propaganda produced by the polygraph profession
rival Hitler's propaganda machine."*

—DOUG WILLIAMS, noted polygraph expert

"I've gotten big names in the spy business to confess," Albert Snyder bragged. "Now stop tensing up," he admonished. "You'll negate the polygraph results."

Stop tensing, Tenenbaum thought. As the reality sharpened that he was now wired and being asked questions that might ultimately land him in Leavenworth for the rest of his life, he felt like his own body was betraying him, panic coursing through his veins, causing him to want to jump out of his own skin, a crawling sensation up his spine as if a cockroach were skittering up into his hair and scalp. *Tense,* he thought, *I haven't even begun to be tense.*

"I said stop it!" Snyder barked, looking down at his own equipment in apparent frustration.

Tenenbaum, knowing his innocence, felt a new emotion as the exam continued on and on. Anger was taking root—and growing. The longer Snyder hounded him, homing in again and again on his faith and the "ethnic ties" he had with Israel, the more Tenenbaum realized he was being railroaded. But Tenenbaum, again despite what he'd been told, assumed every inch of this building was wired for sound and visual. There had to be a hidden camera and microphone in the air vent, a bug under the table. Someone, somehow, had to be listening on the other side of the wall. Wasn't that how it was in every spy movie?

Snyder intimated that he had been the examiner who "broke" Pollard. And then he stated that he would get "this Jew"—Tenenbaum—to confess too.

This was blatant bigotry, overt and hostile. Tenenbaum straightened his posture, the strap around his chest tight and uncomfortable.

Someone in the building had to be hearing this rant about Jews and how Snyder knew how to extract a confession out of them. Tenenbaum imagined a hunt for Nazi war criminals. Nazis extracted confessions. But a US polygrapher going after another US citizen? Any minute, the US government Tenenbaum had pledged his life's work to, the government whose soldiers' lives he was desperately trying to save, was going to burst through that door and end this charade. But this was no charade—this was a nightmare.

Snyder berated Tenenbaum, peppering him with questions and accusations and questioning his loyalty to the United States government. Tenenbaum tried to come up with answers for why anyone would mistrust him or even worse suspect him of treason, but he kept drawing a blank. He was naïve. He couldn't believe, and perhaps did not want to believe, that anyone could think he was giving classified information to the Israelis or anyone for that matter. One of the main reasons he was hired was to specifically work with the Israelis, and now, of all things, he was being accused of spying for them. It made no sense.

Snyder claimed that Tenenbaum was obtaining different clearances to have access to more and more classified information—NATO clearance and various Black programs—except the engineer did not run after those clearances. His supervisors had directed him toward those clearances for the specific work he was conducting during different projects at various times over the years.

Why had his orders to go to Israel the previous year been cancelled? Why was he pushed to increase his security clearance by his supervisor, Dr. Jack Parks? Why had a number of his colleagues been so standoffish, if not downright rude, toward him? He couldn't put it together because he was missing key parts of the puzzle. It would not be until years later that Tenenbaum would realize just how close he came to being locked up for the rest of his life.

He wanted a drink of water. His throat was parched. Anger was fighting with fear, and from minute to minute—second to second—he and Snyder were jockeying for dominance. What was Snyder planning on doing next? Assaulting him? Snyder seemed less in control of his own emotions and demeanor with each blip of the needle. Sickening drops of spittle gathered in the corners of his mouth. Tenenbaum expected him to, without warning, tip the table over, grab Tenenbaum by the throat, and throw him against the wall to begin beating him.

Please be listening. Someone, anyone, please be listening. Please be listening.

Tenenbaum had never been in trouble with the law in his entire life. He couldn't even recall being stopped for speeding. He assumed polygraph experts needed to remain neutral and unreadable. Even without any experiences to compare it to, Tenenbaum fundamentally intuited that something was very wrong here.

Later Tenenbaum learned that once the suspect—or victim in this case—starts to become angry, the polygraph results go down the tubes, rendering the examination and its results worthless.[1] But whatever the results, this was still amounting to an anti-Semitic rant full of slurs that, if leaked to the media, would result in a firestorm of protest.

Snyder's voice's decibel never softened. He repeatedly referred to a number of DIS documents—all allegedly given to him by Simonini[2]—related to Tenenbaum since 1988. Snyder would ask Tenenbaum a question, refer back to the documents, which he made sure that Tenenbaum saw were carried in their folder with the "SECRET" tag on the outside—which, of course, Tenenbaum was not allowed to see—shake his head, and say, "You're lying."

Tenenbaum felt his rapid heartbeat and the sweat on his hands.

The polygraph examiner shifted in his seat and turned to a new subject, "Black" programs or SAPs. These are the programs that "don't exist." At least not on paper. While Americans love a good conspiracy about Area 51 and "aliens" at Edwards Air Force base, in truth, Black programs are the *real* secrets the government doesn't want anyone—its citizens, allies, or enemies—knowing about. Black programs are so sensitive that, even if a government employee has a clearance level high enough to learn about a SAP, the employee is still restricted from such information absent a specific and direct need to know and authorization for such knowledge. Even the names of the programs themselves are considered classified. Snyder had apparently been fed information on one or more Black programs by someone in TARDEC, Simonini perhaps—without the need to know. This was highly illegal and ethically faulty; Snyder was not allowed to even *know* about the programs. They were far, *far* above his pay grade.

Tenenbaum sat up in his chair and grew even warier.

"Do you have access to those programs?"

Snyder shrugged dismissively. "Yeah."

But that was a lie. Yet another in his and Simonini's long list. Snyder didn't have the clearance level. In fact, he had no formal education in human physiology—not even a degree in psychology.[3]

Still, as the needle fluctuated, Tenenbaum assumed it was securing his future. It was telling Snyder—and the unseen (and at the moment for Tenenbaum, unknown) puppet master pulling his strings behind him—that there was nothing but a bright and dedicated army tank engineer in front of them. But the reality was that Simonini and Snyder were so determined to break this "Jew," so certain they had the next Pollard, that this case would make their careers, that the results of the examination were immaterial.

Tenenbaum just didn't know that yet.

"Stop fidgeting. You'll skew the polygraph results!" Snyder screamed again, his voice so loud it echoed off the walls in the confines of the room.

"I'm stiff," Tenenbaum answered. "I've been sitting here for hours. I need to—"

"Stop it! Just stop it. I can't get accurate results if you keep moving," Snyder muttered half under his breath and half out loud, irritation in his voice. The needles of his polygraph equipment were moving, but Snyder wasn't liking what he was seeing.

Tenenbaum, wired and uncomfortable, sat ramrod straight opposite his examiner in the small, cold room in the Defense Security Services office. The shifting needle reminded him of the jagged ups and downs of an EKG. He tried to fathom what was happening to his career—and his life—and how he came to be in this windowless room.

51

But as the hours dragged on, all the while the needle moving and Tenenbaum sweating as the questions focused over and over again on Israel and the Jewish religion, he kept thinking of the Pollard case. And then even of Ethel and Julius Rosenberg—strapped to electric chairs for conspiracy to pass secrets to the Soviet Union during the Cold War. The Rosenbergs were given the death penalty, and Pollard a life sentence.

A single bead of sweat trickled from his collar and down his spine. He wanted to shift in his seat, but he was second-guessing himself. If he fidgeted, he might appear guilty. But guilty of what? Being a Jew? He was finding his mind twisting and turning into itself. Was this what they wanted? For him to drive himself crazy with conflicting thoughts, fighting himself?

Tenenbaum tried to focus on his answers. Snyder kept on hooking and re-hooking Tenenbaum to the polygraph. The invasion of personal space only exacerbated the bespectacled engineer's nerves.

Roughly *seven hours later*, the test wound down, and Tenenbaum was relieved his ordeal was over. He had confessed to nothing. And he knew he hadn't lied.

Exhausted but pleased, Tenenbaum stretched slightly as Snyder stopped the machine. It was time to go home.

Instead, a legal pad was placed on the table in front of him. And a pen.

"I need you to write out your confession," said Snyder matter-of-factly. "That you have given over *every* piece of classified intelligence you've ever possessed to every Israeli you've ever had dealings with from the first day you set foot on this base. That you have *always* been working for Israel. That you have been and still are committing espionage. That you are an Israeli spy."

Tenenbaum felt the world slip away, as if a hole had opened in that room, and he was falling, falling, falling into nothingness. He struggled to wrap his mind around Snyder's request. He struggled to understand what this demand *meant*. That after all Tenenbaum had said in this room, hours upon hours of questions answered, after all his cooperation, after a career spent dedicated to the soldiers out in the field, after LASS, after all of this, they were framing him.

He looked over at the machinery. He could not have failed because he *knew* he was telling the truth. He wondered if this was how someone who had literally lost their mind felt, this funhouse mirror where nothing was as it seemed. This was so unreal, so beyond his own understanding, and now the results of the so-called debriefing and the polygraph examination were more accusations—sweeping accusations. This was not going to be about preserving his career.

Tenenbaum now, first and foremost, needed to preserve his own *life*.

He shook his head, incredulously. In fact, during the whole exam, he'd been unconsciously shaking his head. He looked at the legal pad.

"What? Do you want me to confess to being a Jew?"

Snyder sneered. "No. I want you to confess to giving classified material to Israel." His voice had a derisive edge, as if speaking to Tenenbaum disgusted him.

Tenenbaum knew they had nothing on him because there was nothing *to* have on him. He knew he had done nothing wrong. He had violated no letter of the law—or spirit of the law. But he also knew that it was likely he was leaving this office in handcuffs.

"I can tell by the look in your eyes: You're lying. I've gotten other Jews to confess. I once dealt with, polygraphed, a Jew married to an Israeli and got him to confess. I'll get you to confess too."

The flush of anger traveled up Snyder's neck into his face until he looked like a lumpy beet. He needed a confession to open up a full-fledged criminal investigation. Simonini and the FBI were waiting. But Tenenbaum was not cooperating or giving him anything to work with. This was not good for Snyder's impeccable record as one of the DOD's top polygraph experts.

"I am not confessing to something I haven't done."

"We're going to take a short break. When you come back in here, be prepared to write your confession."

WAR ZONE TRAINING

Detecting IEDs is not as simple as combing beach sand with a metal detector in search of lost treasure. Battlefield signals and frequencies can interfere with detection equipment; soil around the world has various traces of metal within its natural mineral compositions; IED builders have begun to construct their explosives with materials that aren't picked up by traditional sensors and indicators.[1] Training soldiers at home before they are on the ground in a war zone is essential.

What was once a textbook discussion and slides on a projector has recently developed into training environments built on army bases worldwide. Soldiers can "walk the streets" of a war zone and be surrounded by charred cars, abandoned Humvees, and mounds of dirt. They can practice with detection devices but also hone their own sense of their surroundings. Packages might hide inside the holes of a cinder block. Wires that resemble coat hangers might poke out of a rubble pile. Graffiti or a neatly stacked pile of rocks could act as a timing mark for an insurgent one hundred yards away with a line of sight and a modified garage-door-opener triggering device.

The IEDs can be single bombs or a series daisy-chained together. Through this training, soldiers become aware of possible threats and to be conscious of what may be hidden in everyday objects like coffee cans, or even in unexpected packages, like animal carcasses. [2]

Mine detectors seek explosives using a combination of metal detectors and ground penetrating radars that let out chirps and warbles as clues to what is under the soil or sand. But differentiating between explosives and the buried rubble of war is not easy. Basalt mined from a quarry in Massachusetts combined with black iron oxide is mixed into the dirt of training areas across the United States to mimic the natural soil of various war environments.[3]

Yet because no detector device is perfect, the best tool for spotting IEDs is often a well-prepared eye.

When the training is over, soldiers sometimes fear they won't be able to remember it all when faced with the real thing. But when they're on the ground in the intense heat of the desert, surrounded by flying sand and the smell of gunpowder, they often find this training has become so ingrained in them that they can react without thinking. A soldier can shout out "Take cover!" and enable his or her team the few seconds to find a barrier of protection from the fire or gas or shrapnel blasting into the air.[4] These reactions can save lives. But not every IED allows a hint of its hiding place. Tenenbaum had his role to help at least some of these soldiers, if only he was allowed to continue his job.

CHAPTER 7

CAT AND MOUSE

*"Anti-Semitism is a noxious weed that should be cut out.
It has no place in America."*

—WILLIAM HOWARD TAFT

The moment Snyder uttered the word "Jew," spat out as an epithet, David Tenenbaum had known his questioning was not about passing a security clearance, and it wasn't about just his trip to Israel in 1995. This was not an "unbiased" polygraph examination but an inquisition. This was a Jew hunt: he was the mouse and Snyder was the cat. There were more cats too, more than Tenenbaum even imagined. Simonini and his minions had their claws out and were circling for the kill.

During the administration of the polygraph, Albert Snyder advised that deception was indicated regarding unauthorized disclosure of classified information and that Tenenbaum was admitting to the inadvertent disclosure of classified information. Gugino instructed that Tenenbaum be allowed to leave at will.[1] But there was a very significant problem with Snyder's accusation. It wasn't true. However, at this point in time, Gugino did not know that Snyder was making things up.

Tenenbaum was unhooked from all of the wires. He wanted to take a deep breath to enjoy the new space around his chest, but the blank legal pad and the pen sitting on the desk in front of him stared back at him. He stood, chair legs screeching on the floor. His heartbeat reverberated across his skin. Without even looking at Snyder, Tenenbaum walked to the door and pulled it open.

He left the room and raced down a couple of flights of stairs to look for a pay phone. There had to be a pay phone. There was always a nearby pay phone. When he found it, his fingers punched in the number of a close friend, and the ringing began against his ear like miniature alarms sounding again, and again, and again.

After his friend picked up, Tenenbaum spit out the entire story. The wires. The questions. The slurs.

"Get out of there! They're playing with you."

"Can I leave? Won't that upset them more?" Again, Tenenbaum's honest nature was working against him. He still remained focused on not breaking the rules.

"Just leave. I mean it. *Now*."

Tenenbaum hung up the phone. He was in a daze, palms sweating and headache emerging. This was supposed to be about an upgrade in his security clearance—one he never even wanted. Then this was supposed to be about clarifying some overseas travel. Somehow, disturbingly, despite nearly seven hours of answering every single question Snyder had asked, Tenenbaum was now accused of committing espionage—treason! The events were so strange, so far from reality, that he thought he was dreaming. There had to be some rational voice in all this. He weighed what his friend advised him to do as he climbed the stairs again, step after step matching his breath that he fought to keep steady. When he returned to the interrogation room, Snyder confronted him immediately before Tenenbaum even sat down.

"Who did you talk to on the phone?"

The irony of being spied on while being accused of spying was not lost on Tenenbaum.

"I called a friend of mine."

"Who?"

"Why do you care?"

"Did he tell you not to talk to me?"

"Look, I—"

Later, Tenenbaum discovered that the government traced his phone call and knew *precisely* who he called. But in that moment, Snyder cut him off, slicing the air with his hand, before slamming it—*bam!*—on the legal pad, sending the pen sailing across the table and causing Tenenbaum to jump.

"Today is Thursday. You have until Monday to write out your confession. In full detail. And don't forget to sign it. Here's my card with my private number," he said as he handed it to Tenenbaum, and stared at him maliciously, menacingly.

Tenenbaum remained standing. He didn't know what to do, but he wasn't going to stay another minute longer with Snyder. Not knowing if the agent would tackle him and arrest him on the spot, Tenenbaum said, "You can wait until Monday, but nothing's going to change."

He exited the interrogation room drained. He hadn't just run. He'd concluded the interview. He'd given his answer. Tenenbaum walked slowly down the stairs in a daze. His feet carried him down hallways and out the front door, where the sunshine didn't warm him. The parking lot felt like a maze and, for a moment, he forgot where he'd parked. He just wanted to get out of there as soon as he could. His keys jangled in his hands. He still wasn't sure if he would be arrested, and he tried to avoid constantly looking over his shoulder to see if anyone was following him.

Unaware that Snyder immediately went to the FBI and told them he *had* a confession from Tenenbaum—that he had confessed to espionage, to being an Israeli spy—Tenenbaum reached his car and got inside.

All hell broke loose between the FBI and the Department of Defense. They caught a spy. Here in little old Detroit. Snyder didn't record the exam and ultimately destroyed his notes,[2] but he had just made Simonini's day, and perhaps his career. A real-life spy on his base. Albeit a manufactured one at best, but still....

The "additional evidence" of this espionage claim included the same unverified information that had led to Tenenbaum being investigated by the FBI in 1992, 1994, and 1996. In addition, Simonini also provided the FBI with a facsimile that he was given by one of Tenenbaum's colleagues. This fax was sent to Tenenbaum by Tenenbaum's Israeli contact for the LASS program, regarding a trip that Tenenbaum had been approved to take to Israel in furtherance of the LASS project. The fax was taken from the communal fax machine in Tenenbaum's work area where all of the engineers sent and received faxes in concert with the work they were conducting in the office. One of Tenenbaum's colleagues felt that it was highly suspicious of Tenenbaum to be Jewish and receive a fax from Israel—from another Jew! This colleague took this fax and handed it to Simonini. The obvious question of why a supposed Israeli spy would utilize an open, public, communal fax machine to aid in his spying activities was never considered. Baseless suspicions drove the investigation further, as they had from the start.

Some government players later admitted that Tenenbaum should not have undergone a polygraph. (See Appendix 6.) It wasn't procedure. But in this moment, all Tenenbaum wanted to do was get to his car. Tenenbaum tried hard to focus on his driving. He tried hard to focus on the rest of his day, to breathe, to respond when spoken to, and to act like things had any degree of normalcy.

He did not sleep that night except in bursts of a few minutes here and there. Every time he dozed off, he'd replay the dialogue exchanges of that day, and of the Good Cop/Bad Cop events of weeks prior. He listened to his sleeping wife's breathing. The house creaked with the sounds that only seemed audible in the still of night.

As morning dawned, his body ached from exhaustion. His heart ached from the betrayal of his own country toward him, and his head pounded from lack of sleep and lack of food. His stomach remained knotted, and he again could not bring himself to eat.

A practical man, he decided to do what he often did when he needed to clear his own mind—either run or work. On this day, Tenenbaum decided to head into work early and immerse himself in his programs, especially LASS. As he drove the familiar streets in the early-morning quiet, he tried to focus on lab results and assessments he still needed to do, but his heart wasn't in it. His thoughts returned again and again to what Albert Snyder warned him about before he left the DIS office the evening before: "You have until Monday to write out a confession. I'll be waiting."

Tenenbaum kept asking himself what he was supposed to confess to. Working with the Israelis on programs he was supposed to be partnering with them on? Speaking Hebrew with his daughter and baby son, who had just mastered "Abba" (father) on the phone? Tenenbaum allowed himself a rare smile since this whole thing started. Maybe he should confess that he thought Special Agent Snyder was a dweeb.

Sleep-deprived and stressed beyond anything he'd ever known, that thought made Tenenbaum actually laugh out loud. His faith and character had made him a man who didn't even curse. But if he were to take up cursing, this would probably be the occasion to do so.

After showing his ID and seeing the guard eye the parking sticker on his windshield, he passed through the TACOM gates and into the parking lot. Tenenbaum felt the now-familiar gnawing sensation in his gut. The sun was just peeking over the horizon as he walked toward the facility. Even it seemed to be watching him. He ducked his head self-consciously as he entered the building and moved through the sterile hallways toward his office.

His desk, at least, was a haven. Tenenbaum put down his bag and pulled up his chair, but his desk was oddly bare. Only a couple of personal items, pens, and paper stared back at him. His computer was missing. Tenenbaum shut his eyes. He hadn't really slept. Maybe this was really a dream or an exhaustion-based hallucination. He opened them again. There was a blank, dusty space, where his computer used to be. He looked under his desk. He stood and walked around it to the other side, just to make sure the IT department staff hadn't come for maintenance and somehow placed it on the floor.

But it was gone. Vanished into thin air.

Obviously, Dr. Tenenbaum's computer was not stolen. Still he needed to report the "theft" to base police. He picked up the phone and listened as they told him they would send someone over to his office within twenty minutes. They were following procedure—even if this was anything but procedure.

Trying again to quell the panic—and anger—Tenenbaum approached a colleague, a man he considered a friend, and asked if he could borrow his computer.

"I just need to log in to the system for a minute."

When his colleague agreed, he sat down beside him and typed in his name and password.

Nothing.

People walked by them in this shared open area. Tenenbaum ran a hand over his face. Not trusting his own senses, he said, "Would you search and try to find me in the system? Send me an email or something."

Was he imagining this whole thing?

His colleague looked up after clicking on the keyboard for a minute or two. "That's strange. You're not here. Not in the directory. Not here."

"What do you mean I'm not there?"

"I mean, I type your name in, and nothing comes up. It's like you've been erased. It's as if you never existed as a government employee. Your name just doesn't show up anywhere in the system."

Tenenbaum nodded and whispered, "OK. Thanks. I'm going to go to my office and see if I can straighten this out." What else was there to say?

The base police would give him some sort of answer. They had to say something.

He was still ignorant of the fact that after he left the Livonia DIS office the day before, after Snyder lied and said he confessed to being an Israeli spy, Snyder immediately contacted Special Agent James Gugino at the FBI. He told him that Tenenbaum confessed, and like toppling dominoes, Gugino called DIS officials, who then called Simonini as well as representatives of the 902nd MI detachment. Simonini then advised that a command decision had been reached by the US Army to disable Tenenbaum's access to all network information at TACOM. The understanding was to make sure Tenenbaum got onto the base the next morning like a rat in a trap. The criminal investigation was steamrolling ahead.

The walk to his office was agonizing. He focused on staring straight ahead, but every eye was on him. He felt laser gazes boring into his back. When he did glance at faces, their eyes were filled with disdain. Word was traveling quickly.

By now the base police had arrived, taken Tenenbaum's statement, and left. Tenenbaum sat at an empty, computer-free desk, trying to digest what was happening and what to do next. He couldn't work without a computer, so he stared blankly at the place on his desk where his computer *should* have been for maybe fifteen minutes when his phone rang. It was the base police who wanted him to come to their building and provide some additional information on his missing computer claim. He was grateful for *something* to do and took the short five-minute walk to the building where the base military police were housed. The policeman in charge seemed irate that something like this could happen on his base, took some additional information from Tenenbaum, and drove him back. But this was part of the ever-expanding trap. The base police had been instructed to come up with a reason to get and keep Tenenbaum out of his office for fifteen or twenty minutes, to give the FBI and other investigative agencies time to get to TACOM to interrogate the engineer.[3]

Little did Tenenbaum know, but at approximately 0925 hours on February 14, 1997, Robert Riley of the DIS arrived at TACOM. Gugino was already present along with a second FBI agent and Paul Barnard from TACOM security. TACOM had already secured Tenenbaum's work computer. Barnard said that upon arrival for work, Tenenbaum notified TACOM public safety that his hard drive was missing. Barnard said that this event had allowed TACOM to keep Tenenbaum busy pending the arrival of the FBI and the DIS.[4] They were swooping in for the kill.

It had been the day before, just after Tenenbaum's polygraph and Snyder's immediate report to the FBI, that Special Agent in charge Jon McCann authorized a command notification to TACOM, essentially letting them know they had a spy in their midst. Simonini advised that at 1731 hours, TACOM disabled Tenenbaum's access to TACOM computer networks and instructed the DOD police at the gates to deny Tenenbaum access until the morning of February 14, 1997.[5] When Tenenbaum arrived back at his building after visiting the police, he was immediately met by agents from the FBI, the DIS, the 902nd MI Division, the counterintelligence/security division from TACOM, and other assorted intelligence personnel who did not identify themselves or their agency. They were assembled and ready, and Tenenbaum was soon surrounded by their pack.

To Tenenbaum, it was a blur. The lead investigative agent, Gugino, introduced himself and did most of the talking. All of this was happening in a public setting, in front of all of Tenenbaum's coworkers. People averted their eyes from the crowd of suits and freshly shaved, stern faces. Colleagues stepped around the group or chose to turn and try another direction. The pile-on was designed for maximum embarrassment, degradation, and humiliation. No one spoke quietly or discreetly.

At full volume, Gugino said that he had some questions for Tenenbaum. He said he needed a place where they could sit down and speak. What he really wanted was a place where he could interrogate Tenenbaum—uninterrupted. The group ended up in a conference room where anyone within fifty feet of the room could hear every word of the conversation without straining. The door wasn't even closed. Tenenbaum realized depressingly that his entire life was about to be laid bare for all on base to know. He was certain what was said in that room was going to be broadcasted base-wide in gossip. What was happening was bad enough. Once the rumor mill took hold of this, he thought he might as well prepare for the firing squad because distortions of the already grotesque lies would fly, increasing in strength until all believed this insanity was fact.

The group settled into their chairs, Gugino sitting opposite Tenenbaum.

"Mr. Tenenbaum, we know there is spying going on here at TACOM with Israel, so why don't you just tell us what's going on?"

At one point, Tenenbaum may have been naïve, but now his emotions had changed. Anger, fear, and disgust vied for dominance inside. His hands balled into fists in his lap.

"So, there is spying going on with Israel, and I am the Jew who deals with and works with Israel, so that makes me the spy?"

"Why don't you just tell us what is going on? Let's just end this charade."

"Why don't you just tell me what is going on?" Tenenbaum replied. He felt the tension from his clenched hands climbing up his arms and into the rest of his body. He was no longer going to passively take this.

Gugino reiterated that there was spying going on at TACOM. He consulted notes—Tenenbaum assumed these were from his exhaustive polygraph examination and his interrogation by Good Cop/Bad Cop. If Gugino was expecting a repeat of the confession he was told Tenenbaum had already given, he wasn't going to get it.

"Mr. Tenenbaum, tell me about this close friend of your father, an Israeli engineer who was introduced to him by one of the previous Israeli liaison officers on the base," Gugino said calmly. "How did your father introduce him to you?"

Tenenbaum frowned. Some of this had to have come from Snyder—but the information was not accurate. Gugino's facts were incorrect, and Tenenbaum told him so. Tenenbaum—not his father—first met the Israeli liaison officer at TACOM. The Israeli liaison officer introduced the Israeli engineer to Tenenbaum, and Tenenbaum was the one who introduced the Israeli engineer to his father.

"How could my father have met someone on *my* base and then introduced him to me? It was the opposite. I introduced him to my father."

Gugino's forehead wrinkled, but the agent pressed on, looking at his notepad. He revealed he had additional information about programs Tenenbaum had worked on and other Israelis he had met in the course of his working at TACOM.

Tenenbaum was incredulous. Obviously, most if not all of the information—or misinformation—had to have come from Snyder and probably from Simonini and the other agents who had interrogated him in the past year. This "information," of course, had been adapted to fit their agenda. Visions of supermax facilities danced in his head. Bars on a cell. Chains on his ankles. Seclusion from his family and friends. The least these guys could do was get basic facts straight. Was anyone doing their homework? They couldn't find the name of the hotel where he stayed in Israel, which could have been verified by a simple phone call regarding his travel vouchers? In the lab and in Tenenbaum's own research, meticulous notes weren't just happenstance; they were expected. They were necessary to get the job done. Why weren't these people doing the basics of their jobs? It seemed to Tenenbaum that being a part of the intelligence community did not necessitate possessing intelligence.

He continued to demonstrate point by point to Gugino that the information he received from Snyder and other sources was not only skewed but was outrightly deceitful or deliberately misinformed. He felt a small bubble of hope. Gugino's eyebrows lifted. There was a glimmer of something there. Doubt? Confusion? Tenenbaum pushed on, pointing out discrepancies and offering details as a way of demonstrating his honesty and integrity, clarifying to the special agent how much of his information was wrong. Perhaps finally someone sane had entered into this whole fiasco.

Special Agent Gugino paused his questions and squinted at his papers, as if analyzing the notes. By the look on his face, the agent was beginning to have some kind of epiphany. That's what it looked like to Tenenbaum—he hoped he wasn't becoming delusional with panic. Gugino had entered TACOM thinking that he was going to catch a traitor, and all of a sudden, things were not moving along as smoothly as he expected. Tenenbaum was cooperating—and giving him conflicting information from that of the polygraph examiner, information the examiner had not filmed, had not taped, and of which he had no witnesses.[6] Tenenbaum was giving actual information that could be verified. (See Appendices 7 and 8.)

But despite Gugino's apparent reservations about Snyder, he continued to ask Tenenbaum a number of other questions regarding his work. Tenenbaum, from time to time, glanced around the table at the assortment of faces, most of whom he did not recognize. Expressions were steeled. Emotions were hidden.

Yet one face he *should* have recognized was not there—Simonini, the director of the counterintelligence group at TACOM. Where was Simonini? This was supposed to be, as Gugino swore to in his later deposition, possibly one of the greatest spy cases of modern history right there in Michigan at TACOMUS. Wouldn't Simonini want to cement his reputation as the guy who took down an Israeli spy? Why was Simonini not at this interrogation to "reap" his rewards?

Tenenbaum took a deep breath between his answers.

Then, Gugino asked Tenenbaum if the FBI could search his house.

"Search my house?" he repeated into the stale conference room air.

By now, Tenenbaum knew, from the outright lies and misinformation being planted about him, that telling the truth was simply not enough to satisfy them. And if they could not even get their facts straight and were weaving a spy case around him, what was to stop them from planting evidence in his house? His home. Around his family.

"I'd like to speak with an attorney."

Gugino nodded.

"In that case, I guess we cannot search your house."

"I guess you can't." Tenenbaum was tired, antsy, and angry. He rose from his chair. "If you want to arrest me, go ahead and arrest me, but if not, I'm leaving."

He stood still, almost wobbly. He felt the ears of his colleagues leaning toward the room.

"We have nothing to arrest you on. We have no basis for an arrest," Gugino said.

The word "arrest" was like having a bucket of cold water dumped on his head. Tenenbaum straightened, and his eyes narrowed. Around the table, the men seemed to also straighten, and they looked at him more closely, perhaps having noticed the change in his demeanor. Tenenbaum no longer seemed apprehensive. He had changed. However, it wasn't some sudden recall of a past crime. Instead Tenenbaum realized that he had never been read his Miranda rights. In fact, he had never been told this was a criminal investigation. The "interrogation" itself was a blatant violation of the government's own laws.

Tenenbaum asked himself if it really made any difference to the FBI if they had any evidence or basis to arrest him. Maybe they would arrest him anyway. They were making things up as they went along—breaking the law as they went along, too. Since Snyder and Good Cop/Bad Cop had fabricated untruths, clearly the various agents and intelligence agencies had no morals or scruples. They would do anything to charge and arrest him—with or without any real evidence. And Tenenbaum alone knew the truth. There was no evidence. In a sense, that was worse; it meant that in order for this investigation to seem to all of these agents' higher-ups that it was worth the time and resources, they would have to manufacture the evidence. And clearly, Snyder had no problem doing so. And neither did Simonini. A government full of people out to change the world for the better, and a few bad seeds could destroy any shred of integrity and honesty of the whole. Tenenbaum still believed the best of his country. This was not his government. This was something desperately wrong.

If David Tenenbaum's father was alive, would he have flashbacks to his youth? Would he remember government officials that rearranged the truth and people's lives for their own purposes? In his father's time, they were called Nazis, stormtroopers, Gestapo, but what were they called now?

In the pit of his gut, Tenenbaum felt that they could very well arrest him at any moment, and his focus was to at least return home and see his wife and children before that happened. Surrounded by agents as he was, he really believed that the only way he would leave the base was in handcuffs.

Tenenbaum slowly made his way to the door of the conference room. He never turned around, sidling around chairs and people. He didn't know when the door had been closed. He grabbed its handle with utter trepidation, waiting for what he thought would be that inevitable hand on his shoulder and Gugino telling him he was under arrest for espionage.

But it didn't happen.

He continued to walk toward his office, which was no more than fifty feet from the conference room. His colleagues, out in the open, were all just staring at him. Tenenbaum kept his eyes focused straight ahead, never looking back and never looking to the side. He picked up his knapsack at his desk—the desk with no computer—and walked toward the exit.

His mind started taking him places he did not want to go. He hadn't said goodbye to his wife Madeline that morning. He hadn't kissed his son and daughter goodbye. They had been sleeping. He hadn't wanted to disturb them. Would he see them that night? Or any night in the near future?

He hurriedly left the building, forcing himself to walk not run. A jog wouldn't relieve any stress right now. It would only make him look guiltier. But it would feel so good to start pumping his arms up and down, lifting his feet into a run, becoming a part of the wind that cut between the buildings on base. A glance backward caused him to feel like someone had punched him in the sternum. He felt that wherever possible, faces peered out, watching his departure and walk of presumed shame across the parking lot. The base, a series of low-lying buildings, Quonset huts, and displays of tanks and other military vehicles, sat mostly squat amid the blacktop, sidewalks, and parking lots surrounding it. Fences enclosed the space, only ending at guard booths that controlled the entrance and exit gates that rose and fell.

As David Tenenbaum made his way toward his car, he felt the eyes of his colleagues bearing down on him. The walk to his parking spot felt like an eternity. It reminded him of a dream in which someone is being chased and the person is trying to run away, but can only run in slow motion. He felt like he was barely moving. Any minute, he waited for someone to stop him, to arrest him.

Just as he reached his car, a glimmer of relief started to wash over him. He'd made it. He could go home now. Nothing was solved or answerable, but at least he could go home. Home, where his wife and kids were waiting. Where they would smile when they saw him. But as he opened his car door, he felt a hand on his shoulder.

This is it, he thought. A military base police officer stood behind him. *It's finally happening.* He was not going to make it home after all. He was going to be arrested.

The police officer stopped him from entering his car.

"Mr. Tenenbaum, I need your badge." He put out his hand and waited.

This was the badge that enabled Tenenbaum to enter and leave the base. Tenenbaum remembered how proud he was when he started his position. How proud he was of the LASS program. He stared down at the badge, then he handed it over.

Slowly and tauntingly deliberate, the police officer used Tenenbaum's own badge to scrape the parking decal off his window. Then he kept the badge and said, "You can go now."

Tenenbaum again looked up and could see others staring. Everything about the day seemed designed to be as demeaning as possible. It felt like the whole base was watching him. All he wanted to do was get home and see his wife and kids. That was his focus. It was a mantra he kept repeating to himself: *just get home, just get home.*

Despite being allowed to drive off base, Tenenbaum still felt that he was not going to make it to his house. He watched the cars driving behind him, examining closely if they followed him from turn to turn. Any moment now, a police officer would pull out with sirens blaring. He eyed the shoulder of the road for the spot where it would all end. Where he would have to park his car, step out, and not be able to step back in. Tenenbaum kept glancing in his mirrors and down every side street looking for the surely inevitable blue and red lights. He spent more time looking backward than forward. Any moment now, he was going to be pulled over and placed in handcuffs, never knowing when or if he would see his family again. The trip took fifteen minutes—the longest fifteen minutes of his life.

His career and life shattered, exhaustion pulling hard on every muscle in his body, Tenenbaum pulled into his driveway. His home had never looked so beautiful to him—the big picture window, the hedges that made their comfortable brick home look so welcoming, even if they might need to be trimmed. He sat there for a moment and considered if the government might come in the night to take him away. His hands began to tremble uncontrollably. Like every Jew, he had been raised to know—deeply—the horrors of the Holocaust; in his case, his father was a survivor of the atrocities, and Tenenbaum felt the pain of those thoughts even more keenly. Now he was waiting for his own government—the government of the country he had dedicated his career to, that he pledged allegiance to—to rouse him in the night and take him from his family, friends, and community for no reason other than being Jewish. Then he remembered what his father used to tell him: "Don't think it can't happen again." He felt the fear, anger, and embarrassment welling up inside him, behind his eyes and behind every muscle.

He was incredibly grateful his father, the oldest of three children and the only survivor of his siblings from the Holocaust, had recently passed, that he was not here to see the United States of America lie and now try to destroy a man—let alone his own son—for the crime of being a Jew.

CHAPTER 8

FINDING A SUPPORT SYSTEM

*"Experience hath shewn, that even under the best forms
of government, those entrusted with power have, in time,
and by slow operations, perverted it into tyranny."*

—THOMAS JEFFERSON

At approximately 1125 hours on February 14, 1997, a short while after Tenenbaum left the base, Riley arranged for Gugino to speak with Al Snyder by telephone. Gugino had expressed reservations regarding the accuracy of Snyder's account of the Tenenbaum polygraph interview the previous day.[1] Things were getting a little confusing for Gugino, but this moment of pause wasn't able to help David Tenenbaum.

At home, Tenenbaum now realized there was no shielding his wife—and in turn his children, friends, in-laws, and others from his nightmare. But Madeline had to be told first. Madeline, the love of his life.

In many Orthodox Jewish communities, young men and women generally do not "date"—not in the way most people consider dating. There are no exchanges of numbers with strangers or conversations struck up with someone who happens to catch your eye. There are no nightclubs or wild parties—no Tinder or Match.com. There isn't even JDate, the Jewish online dating site. Instead, as Tenenbaum phrases it, Orthodox Jews are "set up." Dating for dating's sake does not exist. Instead, young Orthodox Jews seek to meet and marry a spouse. But amid this structure, he and Madeline were a true love match.

As Tenenbaum sat in his driveway after the nightmare he'd just been subjected to, he was hoping to avoid his wife until he at least contacted Stuart Snider, a close friend and a family attorney. Stuart, he knew, could help him find a good criminal attorney because that is what he was going to need now more than ever. Stuart's expertise was estate handling and planning and that, obviously, would not work for Tenenbaum at this point in time. He was still trying to somehow put the pieces in order in some way that made sense. But like a jigsaw puzzle tossed in the air and then put together again, there were missing pieces. He was sure of it. Because this could not be happening.

He also wasn't a stupid man. He had not had his Miranda rights read to him and had not been advised he could have an attorney present. The way they had entrapped him in that polygraph room was with a lie about security clearance. He now wondered in what other ways they would twist his words—and leave him twisted and hanging in the wind.

His face tightened and distorted into a grimace. He shook off the shadow of family history, of uncles and aunts and grandparents. His body felt cold, but it wasn't the Michigan temperatures.

He wanted to speak with Stuart and fill him in on the last few hours of happenings. Stuart was a confidant. Tenenbaum had let him know a little of what was happening, but this was beyond anything he could just keep to himself. He needed legal advice, and he knew that Stuart would be helpful in providing some input; any input from someone other than himself was welcome. He was tired of spinning things around in his head over and over, and he needed to hash this out with Stuart before he even began to broach the subject with his family.

Tenenbaum stepped out of his car and walked the short walkway to his front door. His mind was on nothing else but getting to the phone. But his wife caught him first.

"Why are you home so early?" Like any young wife and mother, she assumed he was sick—and with what? Would the kids catch it?

Why am I home? Tenenbaum thought. Perhaps that was the most loaded question in their time together up to this point.

How could he possibly tell her? Their eighteen-month-old son was toddling about. A picture of innocence, his dark-haired young daughter was belly-down on the floor, coloring. Tenenbaum inhaled and exhaled. Once he told Madeline what was going on, there was no going back. She would have to tell her parents; he would have to tell his mother. Their friends in the community would eventually know he wasn't working—his badge had been taken. At this point, he didn't even know if they were going to continue paying his *salary*. Any hopes that this "little misunderstanding" would be cleared up by the polygraph were shattered. His life was unraveling.

"I am having a few problems at work." He massaged his temples, wishing he knew what to say.

"What kind of problems?"

Tenenbaum lowered his hands and looked straight into the eyes of his wife.

"They think I'm a spy."

Saying it aloud was preposterous. Anyone who knew him, really *knew* him, would be aware this was the most ridiculous accusation in the history of false accusations.

"A spy for whom?" Tenenbaum could tell that to Madeline, it sounded farcical. This was the man who fathered her two children. The man she pledged her life to. She knew from their years together that he was fundamentally incapable of lying. For some, it just wasn't in their DNA, their makeup—Tenenbaum was one of those. He knew it. She did too.

"Israel."

"Are you?"

Their children giggled on the carpet at their feet. Crayons lent every color of the rainbow to the masterpiece of the young artist at work.

Madeline Tenenbaum didn't think her husband was a spy, but she had faith in the US government. She knew her husband was meticulous, a fervent notetaker. He was an engineer, and that piece of him ran like veins through all aspects of his personality. She assumed he had taken notes on a project he should not have. As he began to explain, she became more and more sure that once he straightened it all out, they would be OK.

Tenenbaum didn't have the same confidence, but he reassured his wife. He wasn't a spy. He wasn't even an "accidental spy." He told her not to worry and then left his young family so he could make a call.

When Tenenbaum contacted his friend Stuart, he gave him a quick rundown on what happened over the past few hours.

"Stuart, what am I supposed to do?"

"Stay by the phone. I'll call you right back."

Tenenbaum nodded, knowing his friend couldn't see him. He hung up the phone and waited. He wanted to sit, but he couldn't be still. He couldn't deal with still. His body was hot, then cold. His pulse was rapid in his chest. The children talked to their mother in the next room, but he couldn't face them.

Thankfully, it wasn't more than ten minutes before Stuart called back.

"I just got off the phone with a guy, an attorney, Marty Crandall."

Within that short time, Stuart had lined up a meeting with a man highly respected in the criminal defense game in Michigan, the kind of attorney you call when a wayward child faces drug charges, you get pulled over for a DUI, or you are the subject of much more serious allegations. He had agreed to meet with them immediately.

Stuart picked Tenenbaum up and they drove downtown together. The highway and surrounding suburbs barely processed in Tenenbaum's mind. The bare winter trees swayed in the wind. Blooms of frost trimmed stop signs and streetlights, but Tenenbaum didn't see any of it. He was a man who had never accumulated a single unpaid parking ticket. What need did he have for a criminal attorney? Still, he reasoned, people hired lawyers to fight their battles. Maybe a tough lawyer would scare this whole thing away.

Twenty minutes later, they were in downtown Detroit, though Tenenbaum's sense of timing was all off. Minutes had seemed like hours lately, especially at night, when he'd stared at the ceiling in his darkened bedroom and tried to fall asleep.

They were ushered into Marty's sleek offices, and introductions were made in a room with tall glass windows and plush chairs. Tenenbaum reviewed what had transpired up until that point. Repeating it was almost painful; it was as if through repetition, the story went from a crazy flight of fancy to reality. It didn't sound real—more James Bond than David Tenenbaum.

Stuart Snider had thought of Crandall because he knew he had been part of the US attorney's office, having worked there as a US prosecutor from 1979 to 1985, so he knew all the players there. Marty

Crandall, at the time in his fifties, was the kind of defense attorney an innocent man wants. He genuinely believed in the system of American justice. He had an unshakable belief that everyone deserves a fair trial—and that someone being "different"—whether an Orthodox Jew, a Muslim wearing a hijab, a black youth wearing a hoodie, or someone who speaks no English—deserves the same blind justice as everyone else. But he also was a realist. He knew Lady Justice was not always actually blind. Her scales were not always balanced.

Crandall nodded as he listened to Tenenbaum's recounting, a longer version of what Snider had told him on the phone. Tenenbaum detailed his trips to Israel, his work at US TACOM in Warren, Michigan, the LASS Program, and the technology he was working on to protect the Humvees. The wonderment about whether he was giving, selling, and trading intelligence and technology because of the coincidences of his visits to Israel came out as bafflement and disbelief. Tenenbaum's hands shook as his finished his recounting.

"Part of your job, Mr. Tenenbaum, is working with Israel, Germany, and other allied countries, correct?"

Besides Stuart Snider, Crandall was the first person who seemed to not only believe him but to understand the weight of the issue.

"There's no cause for a search warrant, but…" Crandall reviewed his notes. He had learned Martin "Mike" Liebson was on the case. Liebson was a talented ranking investigator and prosecutor who had become a friend of Crandall's when they worked together at the US attorney's office. "I can make some phone calls."

The sum to retain Crandall was five thousand dollars. To a modest engineer with two young children and a wife at home, it was an astronomical number—which realistically wasn't going to go very far unless Crandall could make this all go away. Still, Crandall was a calming presence, clearly smart—and he knew Liebson.

After Tenenbaum agreed to retain Crandall formally, Crandall made the initial call to the US Prosecutor's Office in Detroit. Marty explained to them that he was now acting as Tenenbaum's attorney. Crandall sounded authoritative and strong, his natural height and easy gait giving him a commanding presence that somehow translated to his confident, intelligent manner on the phone, and Tenenbaum felt some small bit of stress lift. A good lawyer could make this go away.

The attorney spoke into the phone while Tenenbaum and Snider sat across from him at his desk. Crandall's admiration of Liebson was clear—and there was a level of trust there. The connection could only help Tenenbaum's predicament. He tried not to listen to the phone call and instead stared out the wide windows to the city, the skyscrapers and the far-off Detroit River that connected Lake St. Clair to Lake Erie. The water looked brown, contrasting with the snow collected on the banks.

Crandall hung up the phone and laid his hands flat on his desk, looking at them only a moment before meeting Tenenbaum's eyes. Through Liebson, in an unprecedented show of trust, Crandall learned the government's plan.

"Mike was candid," Crandall said. "They've got the necessary information. They're considering executing a search warrant—for Saturday."

Tenenbaum put his face in his hands, incredulous. It only added to his feeling that his inquisitors wanted to get him no matter what. He had only just been questioned—had only just *told* them that he had nothing to hide and was innocent.

"Saturday?" Tenenbaum pulled his hands away from his face.

"I told Mike he couldn't do that," Crandall said. "I know it's your Sabbath."

Tenenbaum, still recoiling from his treatment on base, now would put nothing past the government. He almost wondered if they would *intentionally* come on the Sabbath, just to further intimidate him.

But Crandall was hopeful. He took great pains to explain how unusual it was for Liebson to let him know about the warrant before the fact. "This is usually not how search warrants are executed. Usually you want absolute surprise. You knock on the door, and if they don't open, you batter it down. These are usually drug houses, not family houses in the area you are from."

Crandall was familiar with Oak Pak and Southfield, another piece that made Tenenbaum feel a degree more of trust.

"You see an Orthodox Jewish population," Crandall said later. "You see the hats and the hair and traditional dress. This is not a hotbed area of crime."[2]

He assured Tenenbaum that Liebson's courtesy in letting Crandall know about the warrant was highly unusual. Knowing Liebson, Crandall felt it meant his new client would get a fair shake.

He explained the basics of a search warrant. "The form says 'You are *commanded* to search these premises,' and 'You must execute the search between 6:00 a.m. and 10:00 p.m.' Traditionally, at 6:01 a.m., you bang on the door. If people don't answer, you batter the door down, and you're in." Liebson wouldn't give a warning on a warrant, Crandall assured Tenenbaum, except in highly unusual circumstances.

The heads-up was good. It was something in their favor. But battering down his front door on a Saturday afternoon in a predominately Jewish neighborhood would be like alarm bells for the situation in the quiet, Orthodox community.

"How much experience do you have handling a case like this?" Tenenbaum asked. "You know, espionage cases?"

There was a momentary beat before Crandall answered.

"Well actually, you're my first one…I've never handled an espionage case or anything even remotely similar to an espionage case before."

A wave of nausea hit Tenenbaum. It just kept getting better and better, he thought. He forced himself to look at it logically. How many spy cases were there—ever—in the United States? Forget Michigan—what attorney *anywhere* would have experience on espionage cases? Now he was going to write a check to an attorney who had never even defended an accused spy. And worse, it gnawed at him that the reason he was going to have to decimate his small life savings had to do with the yarmulke he wore rather than something that he had done.

Tenenbaum wore the yarmulke, also known as a *kippa*, on his head at all times—a sign of *Yirat Shamayim*, or reverence to God. Everyone he worked with knew he was Jewish, and it never seemed to be an issue before, at least not one of which he was seriously aware—until now. How had his faith become a liability? When he had first interviewed with TACOM, his fluency in Hebrew was an asset for projects working with Israeli allies in the engineering universe. In one of the portions of his initial interview with TACOM, his interviewers became animated when he said he had spent about a half a year in Israel furthering his

Talmudic studies and was fluent in Hebrew. Now it had spun around and was part of the reason he was in this mess.

After Crandall assured Tenenbaum that he would be in contact with him, Tenenbaum and Stuart Snider left the sleek, sophisticated office. As Stuart drove, Tenenbaum just sat back in the passenger seat and shut his eyes. He wondered if his situation could get any worse. He'd just agreed to decimate his savings account. Now he'd have to tell Madeline how dire this situation was.

The drive was nearly silent, and Tenenbaum arrived home approximately twenty-five minutes after leaving the office of Marty Crandall, who was now Tenenbaum's criminal attorney. At home, he pulled aside his wife and finally poured out the bigger story of what had happened and what he had been shielding her from, though he still left out the worst of it, hoping she would never have to know. He told her about the polygraph, leaving out the Jewish slurs, knowing it would upset her. He also told her about the interrogation by Yourchock and Riley and how he felt that it was all a setup. He knew how much pain the anti-Semitism would cause her. Unlike himself, Madeline had not been raised in an Orthodox household. She came to a deeper embracing of her faith later, after high school. Being singled out because of his—their—faith would be hard for her to reconcile. She valued the Orthodox way of life so much—it had become her world.

He reassured her that he felt that there was absolutely no way that he would be arrested given that he had never done anything wrong. At least, he was trying to convince himself of that, but he was not always doing a good job. He also knew that the people he had dealt with so far did not seem to be interested in his version. They had an agenda, seemed to have already made up their minds that he was a spy. It was not until years later that Tenenbaum found out the behind the scenes "goings-on," including the anti-Semitic words and actions of the various players who wanted Tenenbaum put away for life. That drive coupled with Tenenbaum's "colleagues," who gladly came out of the woodwork to say that they knew the whole time that he was a spy for Israel and that his fluency in Hebrew was one more reason it was so clear. The common sentiment seemed to be: "And that is what Jews do: they spy and can't be trusted."

78

This whole mess was all about this myth of dual loyalties. What was so frustrating to Tenenbaum was that this "dual loyalty" concept only seemed to apply to a Jew working for the army. No other religions, nationalities, or ethnicities of people who worked for TACOM were being treated the same way with accusations of dual loyalties. Only Jews. In this case, an American Jew, born and raised in the United States who had dedicated his career to helping America's fighting warriors.

The Tenenbaums tried to be calm for each other, and especially for the children. It was Friday, and tomorrow, on Saturday, they were having some friends over for Sabbath lunch. They prepared as best they could for the Sabbath, which begins about an hour before sundown on Friday and ends about an hour after sunset on Saturday evening.

Tenenbaum wasn't much help as his mind rehashed the events of the past few days. This rehashing and reviewing just served to agitate him more and more, so he went for a run to calm his nerves. The rhythm of running, his breath in and out, the sound of his athletic shoes hitting the pavement, his heartbeat and a whoosh of blood in his ears, all of it usually helped him focus and relieve stress. But on this day, it didn't help at all. He passed by familiar trees, naked without their summertime leaves. The sidewalks were so familiar he could almost run this route blind. But he kept his eyes open. He watched out for patches of ice. He was possibly facing life imprisonment or even the death sentence, and he had no clue how this all started. Who had gotten this crazy idea that he was a *spy*?

A few hours later, in the midst of the Friday evening Sabbath meal, the phone rang. But as Orthodox Jews, the Tenenbaums don't use the telephone on the Sabbath, and they always let the answering machine pick up the call. This time, they didn't realize they had left it on a setting that allowed them to hear the message being left.

"David, this is Marty." The now-familiar voice spoke through the machine, filling the silenced room with trepidation. "I was just informed by the prosecutor's office that the FBI is coming to your house tomorrow around noon to conduct a search of your house."

David and Madeline Tenenbaum exchanged glances. He tried to smile feebly at her and she at him. Then they both looked at the kids and smiled and tried to pretend that all was right in their world.

But nothing was right.

Tenenbaum needed to speak to his rabbi and get some much-needed spiritual and emotional advice. He did not want to go alone, so he told his wife that he would walk over to the Sniders, who lived down the block from the Tenenbaums, and ask Stuart to accompany him. Rabbi Asher Eisenberger, a trusted advisor and old friend for years, lived only a few houses away from the Sniders in their largely Jewish neighborhood.

"Go," Madeline urged him. "Just go."

Tenenbaum stood from the table and nodded to his wife before wordlessly slipping away.

He quickly left his house and strode down the empty sidewalks toward the Sniders. He felt like he was keeping secrets from the houses he passed by. No one would guess what was happening to him. No one would believe it. He knocked on the Sniders' door and gave Stuart the latest update of the impending search before asking his friend to accompany him to Rabbi Eisenberger's home. Stuart, of course, agreed, and they both made their way down the block. On the walk there, the two men discussed the idea that, if those in charge of this investigation were so intent on "getting" Tenenbaum, would that also include planting evidence?

Tenenbaum's cheeks were cold. He clenched his fists to keep them from shaking. He was tired of the trembling that wouldn't go away.

The knock on the rabbi's door felt heavy. He tried to keep from pounding in desperation. One of Rabbi Eisenberger's children answered. They were still in the middle of their Friday evening meal, but Rabbi Eisenberger was a rabbi in every sense of the word and always available for questions or advice. He ushered Tenenbaum and Stuart into his study and asked what the problem was.

"We need to discuss an issue which you have never been asked about before," Tenenbaum began. He rubbed his hands together, not even knowing where to start.

"I have heard it all." Rabbi Eisenberger, a humble man, was not stating thisout of ego but more in the reassuring way that priests, rabbis, psychologists, and other advisors have of letting others know they won't judge, that they really *have* heard it all—marriages broken, embarrassing secrets, wayward children, warring in-laws, too much to drink.

"OK," said Tenenbaum. "I am being accused of being an Israeli spy. My attorney just called and left a message on my answering machine saying that the FBI is coming to my house tomorrow to conduct a search. We are worried that they might plant evidence and arrest me."

For a moment, there was complete silence, and then Rabbi Eisenberger spoke.

"You're right. I haven't heard it all. This is a new one."

The rabbi, Stuart Snider, and Tenenbaum proceeded to discuss everything. There was nothing the Tenenbaums could do about the search. Stuart assured his friend that he could see his house from his dining room and would be available when the FBI came. Still, after Tenenbaum left Stuart at his house and continued to walk the short distance home, he had this feeling of foreboding that would not go away. It was going to be a long Sabbath—a very long Sabbath.

"GOING BOOM"

Hitting an IED has been described as being hit by a wave. Not an ocean wave, familiar to many because of summers at the seaside. This is more like one of those monster waves, tsunamis three stories high. It's over in moments—a hit with a force unlike anything any soldier has ever encountered. Followed by silence and dust—unspeakable amounts of dust in their lungs, up their nose, in their eyes and ears. And then pain. Their ears may bleed for weeks. Like seamen who have not yet acquired their "sea legs," those hit by IEDs—the ones who survive with their limbs and lives intact—may fall over for weeks, their inner-ear-controlled sense of equilibrium destroyed. Soldiers call it "going boom."[1]

Those are the ones who survive.

Harry Stokes, a medic in an army infantry unit, didn't see the IED when he set down his bag and took a step outside the cement school in Afghanistan. But then came the boom. His eye protection and helmet were both blown off in the blast, and so was his right leg. His left leg was shredded.

With dirt in his mouth and the smell of the explosives still hanging in the air, he breathed the best he could. Then Stokes started to tourniquet his own legs. He administered his own morphine while enemy fire broke out all around him. There was the terrible boom, and then it just kept getting worse.

Eventually, his team stopped the enemy assault, and they all got to safety. Together, they survived. He survived. A double amputation awaited him, as well as more pain and fear and hurdles to overcome, yet his family and friends were there. [2]

No matter when and where the improvised explosive strikes, if a soldier survives the initial blast, having that core unit of support changes everything.

CHAPTER 9

SEARCH AND INTIMIDATION

"The right of the people to be secure in their persons, houses,
papers, and effects, against unreasonable searches and seizures,
shall not be violated, and no Warrants shall issue,
but upon probable cause, supported by Oath or affirmation,
and particularly describing the place to be searched,
and the persons or things to be seized."

—US CONSTITUTION, Article IV

Tenenbaum's house is seemingly as far from a war zone as one can imagine, but these explosions in his life improvised by those working against him rocked his balance, his body, and his core.

Within his suburban neighborhood, there is normally a silence, a serenity, that is missing from most modern residences. In the Tenenbaum home, there is not even any television. Without waiting up to see the latest late-night talk show monologue like much of America, the family (to this day) seems to follow a more natural biorhythm: early to bed and early to rise. He and his sons go to *shul* most mornings.

Yet on this eve of the search, Tenenbaum's nerves were stressed at every shadow of a neighbor taking a walk down the street and at every caught breath of Madeline, who was processing the coming day in her own steady way as she prepared for bed. He wasn't in a war zone, but nonetheless, he waited for the boom.

"If David Tenenbaum did not have his faith, he would not have survived the intense psychological warfare inflicted upon him through his ordeal," said New York Center for Civil Justice's Dr. Michael Engelberg.

Engelberg, one of Tenenbaum's oldest friends, had retired as a very successful pediatrician on Long Island and had established the Center as a way to secure justice for victims of civil injustice, such as going after Libya's bank accounts after their involvement in terrorism. He knew how much Tenenbaum's faith meant to him. He had also seen firsthand how cases of injustice destroyed lives.

It was his deep faith that Tenenbaum turned to now.

Tenenbaum went to bed late and did not sleep well, if at all, that Friday evening. After tossing and turning for a good three hours, he finally just got out of bed at about 3:00 a.m. Sleep was a hopeless cause. His heart beat inside his chest. Madeline's deep-sleep breaths weren't enough to calm him.

He pulled a *Tehillim* off his shelf and recited the complete Book of Psalms for the next few hours. Tenenbaum was and remains a deeply religious man, but he had never recited the full Book of Psalms before in one sitting. However, there was reassurance in the Hebrew words and sad comfort in the knowledge that countless Jews before him through time and persecution, back to Biblical times, had also sought solace in these words written by King David and in the rhythm of prayer lifted to God.

By nearly 7:30 a.m., bleary-eyed and heavy-footed, Tenenbaum knew it was time to go to the synagogue for morning Sabbath prayers. He walked rather than drove, as was the way on the Sabbath. It was less than a mile, and the solitary walk did him good; Tenenbaum liked being out in the fresh morning air, which also always seemed to make him feel closer to his God. It was mild and not very cold for a Michigan February. A very private individual, Tenenbaum was thankful that none of his friends or anyone within the small Jewish community in Southfield, other than Stuart Snider and Rabbi Eisenberger, were yet aware of the events of the past few weeks in the Tenenbaum household.

Within the synagogue, Tenenbaum sat down near the back. Exhausted from lack of sleep and worry, he found it difficult to focus, as hard as he tried, on the morning prayers. Yarmulke-covered heads surrounded him, something that had always made him feel the ultimate kinship in his journey of faith, yet today they only inspired sadness. He didn't know how many Jews before him had feared for their futures, their families, their lives, because of senseless government actions. But he never thought it would happen in his United States.

Tenenbaum was thankful when the service ended so that he could return home. He knew that no one in the synagogue knew what was going on, but he still felt like he had a sign plastered on his forehead that said "spy." He was becoming paranoid. The call had said noon, but he was certain they had chosen this day, the Sabbath, the holiest day of the week for Jews, for maximum effect. The game of psychological warfare had gone to the next level. If they surprised him by arriving early, he did not want his wife to have to face the FBI alone.

Dr. Mark Meissner, a very close family friend, joined Tenenbaum on the sidewalk as they walked toward their respective homes. Conversations among neighbors and friends were common after services, and Dr. Meissner was a frequent companion. This day, the two walked shoulder to shoulder, an awkward silence hanging in the air between them.

Tenenbaum felt like a stone had lodged in his chest. He did not like surprises, and he was nervous that when he arrived at the corner of his street, there would be FBI cars pulled up in front of his house with revolving red and blue lights in his driveway. He envisioned yellow tape surrounding his house with the words "crime scene" printed across it, and everyone from the neighborhood would be looking out of their windows, if they were not in the street getting a closer look. With his friend, he was distracted and distant. They engaged in a conversation, but Dr. Meissner understood that Tenenbaum was lost away in thought and what he perceived as worry. Tenenbaum was right next to him, responding politely, as was his way when spoken to, but his eyes didn't settle. They searched the streets, the sidewalks, and the faces of passersby.

Tenenbaum almost didn't notice when he parted ways with Dr. Meissner. He just saw his house was undisturbed. Like a drowning man given a life vest, Tenenbaum clung to the idea that maybe they weren't coming after all. Maybe they were going to call off this whole insane idea, and life could go on as before. Maybe someone higher up had read the search warrant, looked at the case objectively, and laughed and dismissed it all as absurd.

His kids were smiling when he walked in the door. He sat down with them while Madeline moved from the living room to the kitchen and back, making sure everything was in place before their neighbors arrived—their neighbors, the Phalens, who had to be given a short version of the story so they knew what was happening and might happen when the FBI arrived at the door.

"We may be having more company." Tenenbaum held up his chin and tried to smile, determined to add levity to their gathering. "We just aren't sure what time they will get here and how many there will be."

Madeline invited everyone to the table where she'd set out the cholent, a meat stew that had been slowly cooking in the oven over-night—filling the house with warmth and the scent of beef, onions, and garlic—and allowing her to conform with the Jewish Orthodox law of not even cooking on the Sabbath.

By 11:45 a.m., everyone was seated for the Sabbath lunch meal. Tenenbaum made *kiddush*, reciting the familiar prayer in song over a glass of kosher grape juice in lieu of kosher wine. It was often one of the holiest moments of his week. The familiar words allowed a trace of calm into his heart, but it didn't last. They could not have been eating for more than fifteen minutes when, like clockwork, three cars pulled up into their driveway. At least seven FBI agents with guns stepped out.

The neighborhood in which the Tenenbaums lived was primarily Jewish, and a good portion of those who lived there were Orthodox. The Orthodox do not drive on the Sabbath. One car pulling into the Tenenbaums' driveway was an anomaly; three was a miracle.

Crandall later recalled, "I remember talking to Mike Liebson and saying, 'You can't execute it on a Friday night,' and he said, 'You can come see us execute the warrant on Saturday morning.' And it ended up being at 'high noon.'"

If it was high noon, then the lead cowboy was Gugino, who knocked on the Tenenbaums' door with an authoritative rap. Tenenbaum, who had refused to leave the table, finally stood. When he opened the door, he was presented with a search warrant for his house.

Madeline had stood from the table too. Just as Tenenbaum was answering the door, she had moved to step outside, past the FBI agents, to get Stuart Snider. But Stuart was already one step ahead. As Stuart was raising the traditional *kiddush* cup filled with wine at his house to recite the special blessing before the Sabbath lunch meal, he spotted the FBI cars—nondescript dark sedans—pull into the Tenenbaums' driveway. His family was waiting for him to say the blessing when he paused, the cup midair. He quickly put the cup down before he began the blessing, looked over at his wife and kids, and said, "gotta go," promptly leaving the house without any word of explanation to his family and leaving his wife literally "holding the cup."

At the same time, Tenenbaum's wife was leaving the Tenenbaum house. Special Agent James Gugino stated, authoritatively, "No one is allowed to leave during this search."

Madeline, a calm and spiritual person, told him, "It's OK, don't worry. I'll be right back." She donned a jacket and dashed out the door, leaving Gugino with his mouth hanging open—but surprisingly, he did not do anything.

Madeline met Stuart halfway between the Tenenbaums' and the Sniders' houses, and they returned to the Tenenbaums' together. Madeline felt strengthened with another witness there, another person who could see what was happening to her husband, her home, her family.

Within a few minutes, Marty Crandall arrived too. Tenenbaum was to find out later that it was highly unusual for the US Attorney's Office to notify and allow the attorney of the defendant's house to be present at a search. Marty took over as Tenenbaum's spokesman, and the FBI communicated directly with him. Crandall examined the search warrant to ensure everything was in order—of course it was, at least to someone not familiar with the actual happenings in the case thus far. But in reality, the search warrant was a lie. It was based on false information provided by the polygraph examiner, Albert Snyder. Snyder, with the pitbull Simonini driving the charge, provided the FBI with the sole information to concoct a search warrant in order to trap Tenenbaum even further. But even armed with this so-called search warrant, Special Agent Gugino appeared to be having a very difficult time using it and conducting a search on a personal, moral level.

In later depositions, he said he was concerned at the rapidity with which the government was proceeding based on the flimsiest of innuendo. He had problems believing Albert Snyder, and he had problems with the other players in the Tenenbaum case as well, such as Simonini, Yourchock, and Riley. He would later state in his deposition that he could not fully "trust" what the government's players said.[1] But it didn't matter. Gugino was overruled and was told to "do the search."

Tenenbaum, though, could sense Gugino's moral dilemma. He saw it in the agent's softened face. He was struck by the strange utterance Gugino muttered when he had first entered the house: "I don't know what I'm doing here." They were words he repeated over and over, under his breath over the next hours.

Gugino informed the Tenenbaums—and Crandall, "We're taking your records. Where are your computers, your laptops....?"

Tenenbaum didn't act like a spy. He wasn't fidgety. Or evasive. Or hostile. Tenenbaum contradicted almost everything Snyder had said about him. And Tenenbaum's information was in the process of being verified as factual and true. Someone was lying, and it did not seem to be Tenenbaum. Gugino had experience with polygraph examiners before, and as the sole basis of a spy hunt, something seemed off. He had told FBI Headquarters in Washington they needed to slow things down and not conduct a search of the Tenenbaum house. He had left his Detroit office late Friday with the understanding that there would be no search, only to receive a call at home close to midnight from one of his subordinates, Special Agent Sean Nicol, who said that he was overruled by the higher-ups in Washington's FBI Headquarters and ordered to conduct a search of the Tenenbaum home.[2] Gugino wasn't happy—and it wasn't just the midnight call and lack of sleep. It was this whole scenario, and he let Nicol know that. (See Appendix 9.) However, now, the search was happening, and Gugino was leading it.

Crandall, meanwhile, knew that the agents were intent on finding intelligence on the Tenenbaums' home computer versus Tenenbaum's work computer, things that they thought Tenenbaum was secreting out of the Warren TACOM base—documents and plans that he would take to Haifa or wherever. They would look for discrepancies. Lies. White lies. Anything that showed the engineer was who Simonini said he was: a spy. This is how, Crandall knew, cases were built, bit by bit of evidence. A trail.

Crandall said he thought Simonini and his allies at TACOM believed they had the new Pollard.[3] Emotions ran high.

Like an elaborate game of telephone, if Gugino had a question, he would ask Marty Crandall, who would then repeat the question to Tenenbaum. Tenenbaum would then respond to Marty who would then restate Tenenbaum's response to Gugino. They stood in an off-kilter triangle having conversation after conversation like this, making every moment more absurd.

The children were kept busy with stories, with the adults putting on the false face that everything would be fine, pretending nothing was wrong, exaggerating their voices for maximum soothing effect. But children are perceptive. For years after, the Tenenbaums' oldest child, their daughter Nechama, would flinch at unexpected knocks on the door.

The search team began going through every cabinet, every drawer, every book, and every paper. Cushions were overturned and examined on the underside. When Madeline saw agents entering the sanctity of her bedroom, she followed them. The violation was powerful. They opened the drawers of her dresser, going through her clothes and her personal belongings. Like all married Orthodox women, Madeline covers her hair unless in the privacy of her home, and she wears modest clothes, dresses and skirts well below the knee, stockings, and long sleeves. To have strangers in her marital bedroom, pawing through her things, was deeply upsetting.

The agents in the bedroom asked her seemingly innocuous questions: "Does your husband work from home?" "What does he bring home with him?" "What does he tell you about his projects?"

Crandall later told her it was the same as their seeking discrepancies on the work computer versus the home computer. The agents were hoping to catch the Tenenbaums in a lie—Madeline saying one thing, her husband saying another.

Gugino's demeanor, while authoritative, was somewhat apologetic. The agents were professional toward the Tenenbaums. Madeline even went so far as to offer them some of their Sabbath meal, a reflex based on both her personality and her religious convictions of empathy and compassion. But Gugino continued to be troubled as he walked from room to room. He kept muttering, "I don't know what I'm doing here." Nothing about Tenenbaum screamed "spy." He looked Gugino directly in the eye and was devoid of any evasiveness. He was either a cold-blooded sociopath or innocent. And since little children were tumbling about and Madeline Tenenbaum seemed deeply supportive of her husband, no red flags were raised. Any thinking, sane person would be bound to the latter.

"I told them not to do the search," Gugino muttered under his breath. He did not look happy.

The Tenenbaums, still fearing the planting of evidence, attempted to follow the agents around their house as they conducted the search but couldn't follow all of them—they had sent too many. The Tenenbaums additionally feared that not only might they plant evidence, but that the FBI might possibly be planting "bugs" and listening devices throughout the house. If they had nothing on Tenenbaum—and Madeline and David both knew he was totally innocent—they would have to manufacture evidence.

From that dark day of the search on, when the Tenenbaums needed to discuss anything important, especially relevant to the case, they left the house and spoke outside. Their privacy was shattered. The sanctity of their home had been violated forever forward.

The search took approximately six hours. The FBI looked inside mattresses and went through all the closets, coat pockets, and boxes of memories tucked away onto shelves. They took the neat and tidy Tenenbaum brick rancher apart, room by room, drawer by drawer.

Tenenbaum had known, of course, they were going to search the house. He assumed they would take his computer, but now *boxes* were being assembled. The agents were putting personal effects in them—not just his and Madeline's belongings but the children's too.

"Wait!" said Tenenbaum, who'd had enough of the indignity. Their visiting friends ushered the kids into another room to read stories and keep the children in their routines as much as possible. No one wanted them seeing their things being taken by the government.

Tenenbaum faced Gugino, not even using Crandall as an intermediary. "Why are you taking my music books and my daughter's coloring books and drawings?"

"There could be something covert or codes embedded in the music notes or the drawings," responded Gugino.

Tenenbaum asked himself exactly what secret codes could be embedded in a five-year-old's drawings or in a bluegrass fiddle book. That might be the stuff of movies and spy novels, but in his house, a coloring book was a coloring book.

He closed his eyes; he closed his fists; he forced himself to breathe. Toward the end of the search, Gugino returned to Marty Crandall. "We'd like his passport."

"David, will you give the government your passport?" Marty asked, turning to his client and giving a small nod.

"Yes, I'll go get it." Tenenbaum stepped out of the awkward telephone game's triangle, relieved at the momentary escape, confused why they were asking his permission when everything else was simply being carted away.

"Yes, he'll give up his passport," he heard Crandall answer the agent behind him.

Tenenbaum had no plans on running away. He was innocent, and he would prove it. But still, perhaps more than at any other moment, this was the symbol of what his government was doing to him. They were seizing his identity. As the child of a Holocaust survivor, the idea that he was now restricted in his movements brought forth a rush of panic and rage. The passport represented his freedom, his right to travel anywhere as he pleased, vacation or work-related, if he even had a job to go back to. It represented his American citizenship. Tenenbaum gave his blue-covered passport to Marty, who, in turn, handed it to Gugino.

Tenenbaum whispered to Marty, "Are they going to start following me?"

Marty was incredulous that this could lead anywhere. Taking coloring books reduced this to comical proportions—if it wasn't all so deadly serious. Still, he replied to Tenenbaum, "I can't believe that the FBI would waste their time and resources, at this point, to follow you, to devote man-hours to it." Even Crandall was not aware at this time that the FBI considered Tenenbaum a flight risk and he would be under twenty-four-hour surveillance.

The next obvious question, now that his house was taken apart, was putting it back together—and keeping it. Tenenbaum asked Gugino directly, "What about my job?"

"The Army is placing you on administrative leave while the FBI opens a formal criminal investigation." Gugino met his eyes, but there wasn't fierceness in them. There was almost sympathy.

Tenenbaum's leave was with pay—but every minute that Crandall stood next to him was devouring this retainer. At this rate, he would need to take out a second mortgage.

He knew there was nothing in those coloring books, or the fiddle books, or anything they seized. The drowning man again grabbed for that life preserver. Surely, they would realize this and end this line of inquiry.

Gugino took a deep breath beside them.

"Things are moving too fast," the agent said to Tenenbaum's attorney. He continued to tell Crandall that he was going to tell the powers at be that they needed to slow everything down. "There is something not right here."

Gugino had informed Special Agent Roger Pendenza, a supervisory special agent with the Detroit FBI field office, that from the outset he was concerned that Snyder may have manufactured some of the information he provided to the FBI.[4] In addition, "Gugino informed Special Agent Sean Nicol at one point in time that Simonini, Snyder, and possibly others had met prior to the polygraph and that they had discussed SAPs Tenenbaum had been assigned to. Gugino expressed to Nicol that he felt that they were using that information to put words in Tenenbaum's mouth."[5]

Tenenbaum let out a sigh of relief when the agents left without arresting him. Gugino's statements offered him a little hope, but the FBI agents still carted away seven boxes of his family's belongings, including those children's coloring books and music books. Included in their haul were telephone records, a computer, and other personal business records. Tenenbaum and his wife just stood in the doorway and watched as the agents loaded pieces of their lives shoved into boxes into the government sedans.

Crandall told Tenenbaum that the agents would comb every digital byte of his computer. Every file. Every email. Every bit of everything—search histories, phone records. Everything in those seven boxes—every inch of their lives would be gone over. And hopefully, that would be the end of it.

"I still don't understand what they expect to find in a five-year-old's coloring books and in my music books," Tenenbaum said. "I wonder if FBI special agents have to go through a psych evaluation as a sort of prerequisite to become a special agent. Who thinks that there's something devious in fiddle music?" One by one, the cars pulled away with his family's belongings in their trunks. "I think this is only the beginning, and it is only going to get worse...." His voice trailed away.

Tenenbaum, Crandall said, would have made a good prophet. Things were about to get much, much worse.

CHAPTER 10

THE SMEAR CAMPAIGN

"It's very hard from the Jewish cultural perspective to separate religion from their heritage. It's a big element of their heritage. It's hard to separate Jewish history without their religion. Other societies and cultures are a little bit different."

—JOHN SIMONINI[1]

Gugino would find himself butted up against a stone wall in the face of Lieutenant Colonel John Simonini. The words "slow down" were not in Simonini's vocabulary.

Unbeknownst to Tenenbaum, Simonini, head of TACOM's Counterintelligence Division, had been eyeing Tenenbaum as a spy for Israel for *years*—with no grounds for suspicion other than Tenenbaum's faith and a cesspool culture of paranoia in the Counterintelligence Division that Simonini was breeding. According to Ronald Duquette, a security specialist who worked side by side with Simonini, "John was a known anti-Semite. He did not like Jewish people. In reality, our enemies—US enemies—are countries like China, Russia, and Iran. You could have told John the base was *crawling* with Chinese agents and he wouldn't react. But if you told him *one* Israeli liaison officer was on base, he would explode. Literally explode."[2] Duquette even sent an email to an online site with legal experts who deal with military law questions. He asked:

I am retired Army. I've worked for the Army as a civilian since November 2001. My supervisor, John Simonini is the TACOM G2 (GG-15). In the last few years, he began screaming and using profanity against employees to include threats such as "if you say

96

that again, I'll punch you in the fu**ing face." I reported him. They did an IG sensing session in which they interviewed all employees. Every employee verified the behavior. The command drug [sic] their feet, and over a year later, he is still in his position. I continued to complain to include the commanding general, and I was moved to another organization. G2 employees continue to call and email me and say his behavior remains the same. I don't wish to ever go back there, but I think he should not be a supervisor.[3]

Simonini controlled through fear and rages, even physical threats. The Tenenbaum case would come to haunt him, stoking a simmering fury that threatened to boil over at the slightest provocation. Whether it was Simonini or another of the government players who failed to seal the search warrant, the standard practice in even the most minor of criminal cases, Tenenbaum would never know. Yet on that Monday, two days after the FBI's search, the headlines of their hometown newspaper screamed out that he was an accused spy.

For Tenenbaum, the idea of an accused individual being presumed innocent until proven guilty was becoming a myth. Whoever the mastermind behind the torment of the Tenenbaum family, he or she was conflating the order of the presumption of innocence. The publicity of the search warrant was a beacon for every journalist and media outlet, and they jumped on the story, which made top-of-the-fold headlines in the local paper. The Tenenbaums could only assume the government's players tipped off reporters as a way to turn up the heat and isolate them from their own community—to expose them to more shame and humiliation.

While Tenenbaum was out speaking to close confidants about the recent happenings, Madeline had taken the children for a walk in their stroller. She had bundled the two—her toddler son, Yehuda Leib, and her little girl, Nechama—on the chilly day, certain the fresh air would do them all good and would help ease her nerves. She needed to clear her mind from the events of the Sabbath, and though the children seemed all right, her daughter remained more self-contained and quieter than usual.

As Madeline and the children returned to their own block, she became aware of two men walking slowly from mailbox to mailbox. Still new to the daily disturbance the persecution was having on their lives, she at first did not connect the dots that these men could have anything to do with her, with her husband.

But Madeline's nerves began to fray. Something was not right. Living in a Jewish enclave, one in which people walked to temple and socialized together and worshipped together, most people were familiar by sight, if not by name. Even those neighbors who were not Jewish were a pleasant and friendly part of the community. However, these men weren't wearing yarmulkes. And she had never seen them before.

The two men stopped in front of her home and stayed there. So Madeline walked past her own house, appearing, for all intents and purposes, like any other Orthodox mother in this neighborhood, dressed modestly, head covered, taking her children for a stroll.

After she walked past, she immediately went to a friend's home, panic rising inside her, protective mothering instincts wanting to simultaneously shield her children and do anything she could to retain a semblance of normalcy for them. She felt her cheeks burning. How dare they do this to her family?

From her friend's house, she monitored the situation on the street. More strangers arrived, along with vans. Men and women began setting up equipment on the sidewalk. The block grew congested with vehicles, and all of this was happening without her husband being aware. He was out, and Madeline was trying to figure out how to deal with the journalists and TV cameras camped out on their front yard. *Were they allowed to be in her front yard?*

More news trucks appeared and parked, with their camera crews unpacking still more equipment. Large lights were affixed to the rooftops of vans. Professionally dressed on-camera news talent milled about, along with more casually dressed production personnel, some with journalist credentials in clear plastic holders hanging from lanyards.

The Tenenbaums' brick ranch house sits on a small parcel of land in Southfield, Michigan. The front room has a room-wide set of large—nearly floor-to-ceiling—picture windows. Anyone on their lawn is almost intimately "in" the Tenenbaums' space. The effect was terrorizing.

Looking at the sea of camera crews and reporters, Madeline became aware that her husband was now part of the headlines. Madeline realized that now her parents and her entire world, really, would have to be contacted and told the story from *their* perspective before anyone could be so fooled to think the news as reported was true.

Madeline knew she needed to return to her home. The children were too young to be displaced like this, with none of their toys and clothes. They needed to sleep in their own beds. They needed their routine. There was no telling how long this would go on for. She couldn't stay away forever.

Suddenly, Madeline and her synagogue's group of close-knit women were playing spy games. They cleverly loaded Madeline and the children into a car and had her duck down in the backseat, shielding the children with a coat. Knowing the neighborhood better than any of these invaders, they turned into the Tenenbaum driveway and continued until they reached the back of the house, so she could enter her home through a back door, hidden from prying eyes.

Yet even that didn't go smoothly. She was spotted. She rushed up the concrete steps, carrying her young children, heart beating in her throat. Reporters yelled—male and female voices vying for her attention.

"Mrs. Tenenbaum! Mrs. Tenenbaum!"

"Stop her. Just one question!"

Camera shutters clicked. Lights flashed. Fight-or-flight took hold; even if these people weren't there to *physically* harm her, Madeline's body and mind didn't react that way. These journalists didn't ensure that she was safe. She feared dropping the baby and hurting herself and the kids, so she only clutched them tighter. When she made it in the back door, she locked it and then went straight to the front of the house to see, through her windows, the media circus on her lawn.

Madeline Tenenbaum crawled on her hands and knees in her living room, smiling at her children, trying to pretend it was all a game.

But it wasn't.

On her lawn, news trucks from around the United States, and, for all she knew, around the world, were encamped. She could hear reporters' chatter, even if she could not quite make out their words. It sounded like a buzzing of bees, and her house was the hive. Her lawn was trampled—so much for not trespassing on private property. The dead winter grass now looked like tufts of hay. Bright lights shone into her living room. She was desperate to close the blinds and draw the curtains to keep her children from being frightened. Madeline was furious that the journalists on her lawn cared not one iota that the Tenenbaums had very young children, who were undoubtedly—and rightly so—terrified. Someone in the crowd even went through the Tenenbaum's mailbox, which is a federal offense. But no one seemed to care. They wanted a story—the story—and the Tenenbaums were not cooperating.

She prayed to her God for protection, for strength, for safety. She prayed for her husband. She prayed for her children. Through the ever more and more horrible happenings, she prayed.

Her faith remained unshaken.

Madeline Tenenbaum grew up in a Reform Jewish family in suburban New York, with the benefits of an upper-middle class upbringing and all that entailed. She attended private schools and a private college, the very best of education offered to her. There were family trips and vacations. She memorized parts of the Torah and learned to read and recite Hebrew for the obligatory bat mitzvah.

Yet even in high school, Madeline had been a seeker of faith. She relentlessly sought "something." Something more than this existence. She took offered courses in school on Daoism and Buddhism. She was looking, she later realized, for that deeper connection to something bigger than herself, a connection to the vastness of the universe and eternity. If each human being is a puzzle, she was seeking the God-shaped piece.

She had set off on a trip to Israel in her late teens, a trip that would change her life. There, amongst the cedar and olive trees, in the brilliant sun, amongst Hebrew-speaking Jews and wise men and women, she met experts in Kabbalah, an esoteric discipline, more experiential than her own Reform Jewish background. She was exposed to what she termed "spiritual secrets" and discovered areas of Israel that felt vibrant and more alive than traditional Judaism. There, she discovered a dynamic, breathing Judaism, not a static form of rote prayer. Centuries and centuries were stripped away. A *living* faith emerged. Staying at a women's school, with other women who weren't raised steeped in

Orthodoxy, she connected with a sisterhood that could trace its origins to the ancient world of Rebekah, Rahab, Esther, and Deborah. From that point on, Madeline's soul was fed. She returned to the United States a deeply religious woman whose internal compass, whose soul compass, pointed directly to God as her true north.

She also dedicated herself to a career in social work, which spoke to her compassionate and empathetic side. She felt complete—almost.

After attending Oberlin, she increased her dedication to her faith. But now it was time to consider settling down, to create her own Orthodox family, to raise children in the faith she had come to love and know as intimately as she knew her own face in the mirror. One last piece of the puzzle was missing. Through friends in Rockland County, she was introduced to Tenenbaum. Many aspects of this dark-haired man appealed to her. She loved his sense of humor. He made her laugh. But his inherent goodness and decency, his honesty, and, of course, his faith were what truly drew her to him. This was a man with whom she could have extended conversations about the Torah, about living as a faithful Jew, and about life in general.

In 1995, as a parent to two children, keeping an Orthodox Jewish kosher home, Madeline was content in her community, and she blossomed in a network of Orthodox women with whom she was very close as they shared their journey raising their children in a spiritual environment within a secular world.

But in this moment, she was trapped, literally trapped, in her own home. Vans, newspaper reporters, and dozens of people, if not over a hundred—camera operators, anchors, print and television journalists, and the terminally curious—camped on the Tenenbaums' front lawn.

Everyone now knew. Every neighbor, every person in the synagogue. Everyone.

"Back then I was naïve," she said later. "I assumed if you did the right thing, if you were a good person, if you lived your life in this free country, your own government would not treat you this way. I was wrong."

Throughout history, Jews have been abused in every country they have been part of—from Poland to Germany to the KKK rallies in Skokie, Illinois—but this was their neighborhood, among their own people, their friends and community. And yet, even here, they were not safe.

Toward the evening, Tenenbaum called her on his cell phone, still oblivious to the happenings in his own front yard.

"I'll be home in about thirty minutes."

"No, you cannot come home."

Madeline heard her husband pause, and then in his typical sense of humor, he asked, "Why? Did I forget to take out the garbage?"

She relayed the gathering circus on the lawn. "Just wait, David. Don't come home right now."

And so she found herself alone, in her house with two young children, crawling on the floor, drawing the blinds, trying to smile and be brave so her son and daughter would not think anything was wrong. That it was just a typical day and Daddy was away on an ordinary trip. Like when he traveled overseas for TACOM business. Though, that same TACOM business was now being used against Tenenbaum, and for Madeline Tenenbaum, nothing would be ordinary again.

Not ever.

IMPROVISED ARMORING

Soldiers would put their flak jackets on the floor of their transport vehicles for an extra layer of protection, the Kevlar a patchwork rug underneath them. The "thin-skinned" Humvees were designed for the traditional battlefields of the past wars in Europe, not the explosive environment of the Middle East.

Sandbags were transported empty from the United States, to be filled with desert sand and stacked with the Kevlar. Reports as early as 1993, following the Battle of Mogadishu, called out the security concerns with using Humvees in tight-quartered, guerilla-style battles.

Soldiers welded any available metal they could find to the sides of their low-slung vehicles. They called it "haji" armor, "haji" being the word for a Muslim who has been to Mecca. And in these efforts, they needed their own salvation.

Sometimes, the soldiers would call home, drawing strength from their family or friends. Sometimes, they would admit the fear they felt in their thin-skinned Humvees that were not designed to protect them, that felt like a gamble every time they stepped inside. Sometimes, that whispered fear made up the last words they would ever speak into the telephone line.[1]

Vehicles returned from patrols dented and bloodstained.

Soldiers continued to do what they could, retrofitting the transport vehicles from care packages and what they could order beyond army channels. Spare parts for the plasma-cutting torches and goggles were sometimes paid for via their own credit cards.

LASS had been initiated in 1995 to fix exactly this problem. Vehicle redesigns shouldn't have ever been up to the soldiers. They risked their lives. The risk was far more than it ever should have been.[2]

CHAPTER 11

A MAN WITHOUT A HOME

"There is no crueler tyranny than that which is perpetuated under the shield of law and in the name of justice."

—CHARLES DE MONTESQUIEU

The *New York Times*, the Gray Lady of journalism, the most venerated newspaper in the United States, actually reported that Tenenbaum *admitted* being a spy for Israel. There was no "allegedly," none of those softening adjectives or adverbs. Lies were perpetrated by people like the anonymous source who claimed classified documents were found under the baby's crib—this lie added a dramatic flair. The government's smear campaign was hard, fast, and brutal.

For Tenenbaum, a lifelong Detroit-area resident, Southfield was home. It was more than a tidy brick home on a tree-lined street with sidewalks for children to walk to school. It was *home* in every sense of the word—spiritual, emotional, psychological. But now he wondered how he could engineer some kind of armor around it. What layers of metal could he weld? What sandbags could he stack? Each new explosion that hit him was grueling enough, but his kids were too close now. And no Kevlar vests could offer them any protection.

Driving into the small community where Tenenbaum and his family resided still gives visitors a sense of a different time and place. Signs are in Hebrew, or English and Hebrew. Within a mile or so are two or three *yeshivas*—day schools for Orthodox children—and an apartment complex for Jewish senior citizens. Driving into Southfield, there are kosher pizza parlors and kosher markets. All around the

Tenenbaum home was a true community that nestled the Orthodox families of Southfield within its embrace.

Tenenbaum could walk the street, pointing out that Rabbi So-and-So lives here, Jerry Abraham lives there, Stuart Snider lives there. For Saturday *shul*, the men would walk together in pairs or small groupings.

For Madeline Tenenbaum, the community of women was perhaps even more vital. As the sexes are sometimes separated, the women were especially close. In the basement of the Tenenbaum home, Madeline, part-time, offered therapeutic massages to her female-only clientele, often easing the aches and pains of her friends and neighbors.

Women, immediately recognized as Orthodox by their dress, walked in safety and security on tidy sidewalks. The streets were quiet. On the Sabbath, no one operated a computer or used electricity. A serenity abounded.

And into this serenity, the US government invaded.

"You cannot come home." Madeline's voice was coming through the telephone, but to Tenenbaum, the message was inconceivable. "There are reporters and camera crews all over the lawn."

"How many?" In Tenenbaum's mind, he assumed a couple of newshounds were milling about on the sidewalk.

"A crowd of them. I can't even count them all," Madeline relayed about the cameras, lights, news vans with satellite dishes on top, reporters, photographers, and more than a few curious onlookers.

Tenenbaum soon found out that the *Detroit News* had screamed out that classified documents were found in the Tenenbaum house. Their front-page headline read, "Search Yields Classified Items: FBI Finds Documents Throughout Southfield Tank Engineer's Home." The article went on to state:

> FBI agents found boxes of classified military documents stashed throughout the Southfield home of an engineer suspected of sharing military secrets with the Israelis…The classified documents which were seized Saturday were found in several locations of the home of David A. Tenenbaum including the baby's bedroom, the laundry room and under the basement steps.[1]

Found. Classified documents. This was Monday. There was no possibility that a search warrant executed on a Saturday, concluding Saturday in the early evening, was now affirmed in the positive, especially because he had never had any such documents in his house. In fact, his main program, the LASS program that everyone seemed to be all fired up about, was unclassified, as were all of the programs that he was working on. Tenenbaum knew and continued to reassure himself that as stressful as this all was, the computer—and everything else down to his child's coloring books—was clean. But the press was being fed something else entirely—a falsehood that wasn't even *possible*. No doubt anything they seized still hadn't made it out of an evidence locker yet. They were putting the screws to him.

And now there was no going home.

Worse, the media feeding frenzy was showing no signs of relenting. Every hour that passed, more press arrived according to Madeline.

"What about you and the kids?"

"We'll be fine for now. You just stay put."

Tenenbaum hung up the phone. He closed his eyes and pinched himself. *This can't be real. I must be dreaming...a nightmare...yes, a nightmare.* He opened his eyes very slowly, but he wasn't asleep. He was being accused of spying for Israel, and now the whole world knew. His coworkers, his mother, his neighbors, his wife's parents—and total strangers. His name was plastered as an *admitted* spy across newspapers—and soon the evening news. He needed to slow down and think.

No, first he had to call his mother.

Tenenbaum's father had passed away a little over a year before, and his mother lived alone. He knew she was an avid news-watcher and did not want her to be surprised with the news headline saying her son was accused of espionage. She was elderly, and she didn't need any surprises of that sort. She also didn't need more heartbreak after the death of her husband. But she was also a very strong woman who was very protective of her kids. Tenenbaum had many friends who were into martial arts, but they all knew, you didn't mess with Mrs. Tenenbaum...ever.

"Mom, there's something in the newspapers coming out, but I want you to know I didn't do anything."

He explained it as simply and clinically as he could, with assurances that she should not worry. She was his mother—*of course* she was going to worry. But he wanted to keep that to a minimum. He just wished he believed the words he was telling her.

His head and heart ached as he hung up the phone, but Tenenbaum didn't let it leave his hand. Next, he called his attorney, Marty Crandall. In his mind, he could see dollar signs, eating away at his retainer. *Ka-ching.*

"David, you can't go home. Not right now," his attorney responded to his questions. "I'm in Florida on a case and will fly back to Detroit tomorrow. You need to sit tight, and we'll work all of this out. I'll contact the US Prosecutor's Office and brief you when I get back. But for now, don't speak to any journalists, don't give any interviews—and don't go out in public."

Where would he go? He could stay with friends from the community—for now. But how long could he remain away from his family? And when was this going to let up?

Those billable minutes were going to eat up his retainer pretty darn fast. And then what? He'd already tapped into his life savings for this. Tenenbaum's future was looking bleaker and bleaker. Why had he even gone to work for TACOM? If he hadn't, if he had been working for a private corporation, none of this would ever have happened. He wouldn't now be broke and on suspension. He'd be with his family, in their tidy brick ranch, going on with *life*.

Tenenbaum's original career was in chemical and biomedical engineering at Wayne State University. He even toyed with going to medical school—he was certainly bright enough—but he knew that *one* nonnegotiable element, *time*, was not on his side. He'd spend how many more years in medical school? And wanting the joys and comfort of family—a wife and children—was not conducive to starting medical school. Plus, in the biomedical research field, he felt that his career aspirations would be limited without an M.D.

Post-graduate school, Tenenbaum headed to General Dynamics. He was placed in operations research, but it wasn't a fit. The company was fantastic, his peers easy to work with, his boss a terrific guy; however, it was operations research itself that wasn't quite right for him. Then a fateful meeting occurred.

He represented General Dynamics in a conference room of people who were conducting research in materials engineering. Tenenbaum—always a go-getter—was on fire. This was his field of expertise. He asked all the right questions about materials research. He had all the right answers. It was Tenenbaum's own boss who said, "You're working in the wrong field and in the wrong place. Operations research is not for you. Go work in an area that can use your skills in materials research and bioengineering." His boss didn't mean it as a slight. Tenenbaum, by nature of his personality and ambition, would have done just fine at General Dynamics. But it was a recognition that the real passion in Tenenbaum was in precisely the type of work TACOM did.

A former high-level executive from TACOM had recently retired and recommended Tenenbaum to his former group heads at TARDEC/TACOM. So, after a series of interviews, in December 1984, Tenenbaum was hired by TARDEC/TACOM to work in their armor group, which at that time was part of the survivability division. The group was responsible for looking at ways to increase the survivability of tanks and other combat vehicles by developing new types of armor and seeking out other means to increase the survivability of both the vehicle and the soldiers inside the vehicle. Tenenbaum would be part of a group working to ensure the safety of US soldiers and to make sure they came home safe and sound.

Tenenbaum arrived at TACOM bringing with him certain unique aspects and qualities not necessarily seen in some of his peers. This was brought out in one of his job interviews with his future employers.

When he initially interviewed with Dr. Jim Thompson and Sam Goodman, they asked all the usual questions about his education and background. Tenenbaum wore his yarmulke to the interview, but because of human resources and employment rules and laws, they could not overtly ask about this symbol of his faith. However, the opening to ask about his background was there in his education.

Tenenbaum had studied in Israel for a number of months between earning his bachelor's degree in chemical engineering and entering graduate school. In Israel, he continued his studies in Talmudic law.

He also had friends who served their time in the Israel Defense Forces (IDF) in the tank area.

The information about his time in Israel seemed to interest the two interviewers, and the three of them entered into a discussion on the army's various allied programs with Israel. Both interviewers concurred that Tenenbaum's ability to speak Hebrew and his experiences living in Israel would be an asset for his working on those programs. The discussion flowed—literally more of a conversation than an interview. Culturally, they assured him, he would understand any liaisons sent from Israel. In return, he could represent US interests in those dealings. According to his interviewers, no one with Tenenbaum's specific background worked on the base, and they felt he would be a good fit to work the Israeli programs.

Perhaps, in hindsight, Tenenbaum should have considered that detail of no other Hebrew speakers on base. Was he the only Jew on the base who had connections with Israel? Should that have factored into his decision? But even with hindsight, the interview had been positive. They had spoken of his background as an *asset*. They seemed excited about what he would be bringing to the program. There were no clues he was about to enter a viper's nest of anti-Semitism.

The "assets" his interviewers spoke of became his invisible yellow star as his colleagues mistrusted him and became suspicious of him for those very same qualities. All this time, Tenenbaum realized, as he'd had colleagues for dinner in his home and travelled with them overseas, he had not been "one of them." He had been an outsider.

Later, much later, Special Agent Gugino would acknowledge as much under oath, declaring, "Well, I think there was a lot of jealousy on the part of his coworkers. My recollection is a lot of them were just very jealous that he had success at work because he was able to be personable and relate to and converse with and talk with these foreign nationals where they couldn't have that kind of success because they didn't have a commonality in which to engage in conversations."[2]

Tenenbaum's experience with Israel was but one aspect of the jealousy. The other, it turned out, was his sophistication. Through his travels, he was able to comport himself with foreign visitors as an almost "insider." He had a natural ease with people from other countries. That ease, instead of being seen as an asset at TACOM, apparently stirred resentment.

His dealings with Israel especially gnawed at Simonini. Later, the Office of the Inspector General for the Department of Defense (IG-DOD) investigation would uncover bias within TACOM against Jewish employees, a bias that was attributed to the Jewish experience in the Babylonian captivity, which gave them divided loyalties as a class and triggered guidelines of the Defense Department's Personnel Security Program.[3]

Simonini's anti-Jewish sentiments ran deep, according to those around him. As his former right-hand man said about Simonini, "The Tenenbaum case, for John Simonini, is like an *infected wound*. He can't let it go."[4]

As Tenenbaum embarked on his TACOM career, he was responsible for representing the United States on survivability aspects of combat vehicle systems as the technical project officer/co-chairperson/member of US delegation to discharge Department of the Army obligations for mutual agreements. One of the main reasons he was hired by the army was to work on international survivability programs, specifically with the State of Israel, and ultimately with the cooperation of Germany and additional countries.

In layman's terms, he worked with US allies, sharing information—with the government's full knowledge and cooperation—that would hopefully save the lives of United States Army soldiers in the field. When he created the LASS program, the intent was to use modelling with the data allies provided to get the best real-time, real-life predictions of tank and combat vehicle performance in urban theatres.

As one walks through TACOM, above many doorways, on walls, on plaques, and on displays of tanks and other military gear is the constant reminder to "protect our warfighters." Our servicemen and servicewomen. Our soldiers. It is a reminder Tenenbaum did not need. When working on a computer model, when talking to others on the base, he had—and still has—a clear-minded drive, a relentless drive, to ensure soldiers come back home alive and in one piece.

Tenenbaum was sent by the US government to Israel three times: in 1985, 1986, and 1995. While Snyder had been accusatory and abusive, and the Good Cop and Bad Cop and Gugino had focused on these trips to Israel as suspicious, these trips were not Tenenbaum's idea. However, this did not seem to dampen the fervor with which his adversaries were accusing him. Gugino, as much as he had wanted to slow down the investigation, still referred to Israel as "the Homeland" when applying it to Tenenbaum.

Tenenbaum was sent to Israel by the US government with an itinerary and assignments—this was part of his *job*. Each time, he traveled to Israel to discuss and work on specific programs with the Israeli Army and Ministry of Defense. It was not like he could have strolled into their defense ministry casually or without an appointment. Traveling to Israel as a DOD employee meant having to submit travel orders through a system, which required numerous approval signatures from TACOM all the way up to Washington, D.C., as well as from the country to which the US government employee would be traveling. Orders had to be submitted months in advance, and these orders included a detailed itinerary that articulated with precision who the employee was meeting with, when the meetings were to take place, where they were to occur, and for how long the meetings were to last. Everything had to be approved before the employee could even set foot on a plane headed for foreign soil.

In fact, it was his comfort and ease with foreign nationals that the US Army deliberately developed to build up a relationship with the Israelis. In both the 1985 and 1986 trips to Israel, Tenenbaum was sent for six and two weeks, respectively, to further his development of relationships with the Israeli military. For each of the trips, Tenenbaum wrote lengthy trip reports, which were kept on close hold and commended by high-level management and army personnel. These were uniformly praised by his superiors regarding the reports' level of detail and information. When Tenenbaum later (in 1998) requested to see these trip reports so he could prove to the FBI and other investigators that one of the main focuses of his job was working with Israel at the government's behest, these trip reports had mysteriously vanished. He was later told that the trip reports had been *destroyed*—shredded. To this day, whoever did this is unknown. The reports would have helped clear Tenenbaum's name—and would have certainly been a damning piece of evidence against the witch hunt. A witch hunt Tenenbaum would later call a "Jew hunt."

Ultimately, though, Tenenbaum's main connections were with four foreign liaison officers on the TACOM base in Warren, Michigan; the officers represented Great Britain, Germany, Canada, and Israel. Tenenbaum had been invited, at the beginning of his career, to go on maneuvers with the British Army. Tenenbaum had traveled to Canada and the Netherlands, and he had connections with civilian and army personnel from many other countries, including South Africa, Canada, Germany, Britain, Sweden, Switzerland, and Singapore. In addition, he was assigned the job of Assistant Technical Point of Contact (ATPO) with the Netherlands. Yet only Israel caused suspicions of spying. He wondered aloud to Crandall and others throughout the process: Why wouldn't Germany want to bribe him? Or South Africa? It was that thread of anti-Semitism that saw Israel as the boogeyman. Maybe it was the Pollard case that had the government on edge. But why paint every Jew as a potential spy? Or, more specifically, why paint him as one?

Even more strange to him, the group to which Tenenbaum was assigned was known as "the United Nations" on base because the group was made up of people from various countries of origin, including Iran, Russia, Germany, Taiwan, and others; they spoke different languages, including Russian, German, Farsi, and Taiwanese. The Cold War was only just thawing. Tenenbaum fumed, *why not the Russian guy?* Iran sponsors terrorism, is on the list of travel-restricted countries, and has no US embassy. *Why not the Iranian guy?* Tenenbaum wouldn't wish this on anyone. He didn't *really* want to cast aspersions on his colleagues. But he knew he was being singled out as a Jew. Tenenbaum was the only person on the entire base, as far as he was aware, to ever be accused of treason and certainly the only one to be accused publicly.

How had his star risen so brightly only to fall from the sky?

This is what ran through his mind as he stayed at friends' houses and only dared to enter his neighborhood on the fringes, far away from his home.

Tenenbaum was stranded in limbo, thinking of his wife and children, thinking of the work he desperately wanted to do, of the lives of soldiers he desperately wanted to save—yet he was unable to do anything but sit and wait.

CHAPTER 12

A CULTURE OF PARANOIA

"I'll tell you right now, during that four-month investigation,
I did not interview one person or find anything in David
Tenenbaum's background that led to any evidence whatsoever
that an act of espionage was committed by him."

—SPECIAL AGENT JAMES GUGINO,
lead investigative agent for the FBI[1]

The isolation from his family began to gnaw at Tenenbaum. At some point, whether he liked it or not, he would have to go home and face the news cameras, the articles in various newspapers, and the aftermath of the government's aggression toward him.

After about four days, he phoned Madeline, who had remained painfully apart from her husband but was buoyed by her dear friends. He instructed her to leave the back door unlocked.

"Why? What are you going to do?"

"Just do it, please. I'm coming home."

The Tenenbaum marriage is a definite love match. Tenenbaum readily calls Madeline throughout the day like a touchstone. They check in with one another, and he considers his wife his best friend. Around one another in the house, there is the constant back-and-forth of a close-knit couple and family. Affection and warm chatter fill their home; the Tenenbaums are a family always used to knowing where all its members are, always in touch with one another, always bonded.

Tenenbaum donned his running gear, left the house of a friend with whom he had been staying, and under cover of darkness, literally ran home at around 2:00 a.m., the night air helping to clear his mind and the chronic tension headache he had developed.

For David Tenenbaum, his nightmare had numerous points of entry—from the distrust and anti-Semitism of his coworkers, to the Pollard case, to Simonini's seeming obsession with and hatred of Jews, to the very nature of those on his base and with whom he worked being required—by law—to "rat" on their coworkers at the faintest whiff of suspicious behavior.

His feet hit the pavement. Running felt good. He liked his body in motion. He hadn't shaken the need to escape since he'd been attached to the wires for his polygraph. Snyder's slurs filled his mind. Sweat crawled on his neck. Maybe things had gone wrong before that interrogation, but it was that antagonistic questioning that echoed through his memory again, and again, and again.

David Tenenbaum didn't yet know that the American Psychological Association (APA) stood firmly on the idea that polygraphs were and are unreliable. The issues with the polygraph are numerous and have filled many books. They range from the emotionality of the subject, the results being only as reliable as the polygraph examiner, the nature of *how* questions are asked (how broadly versus specifically) affecting the results, the behavior of the examiner, the deception of skilled liars or sociopaths, and numerous other concerns. "Most psychologists and other scientists agree that there is little basis for the validity of polygraph tests," says the APA. "Courts, including the United States Supreme court (cf. *US v. Scheffer*, 1998…), have repeatedly rejected the use of polygraph evidence because of its inherent unreliability."[2]

The United States government listened to the scientific community—at least as it pertains to the private sector—when the Employee Polygraph Protection Act (EPAA) was passed. This law, for the most part, prevents any private-sector employer from using a polygraph examination either for screening purposes prior to hiring, or within the course of employment. The law, however, does not cover federal, state, or local government agencies.

David Tenenbaum pumped his arms and lifted his knees, trying to pretend it was just a casual jog in case anyone was watching. He had no idea if anyone was watching. He didn't dare to run with a flashlight, headlamp, or anything that would draw attention.

To Tenenbaum, in a country in which someone is supposed to be innocent until proven guilty, he was targeted by hearsay, by jealousy, by a dream. The token Jew was a convenient scapegoat. His Jewish faith was reason enough for some of his colleagues on base to call him, behind his back, "Our Little Jewish Spy."[3]

It would, Tenenbaum mused, be comical—if it wasn't destroying his life.

He entered through the back door and immediately saw Madeline. "I am so sorry."

"There is nothing to be sorry for," she assured him.

Tenenbaum went into his children's bedrooms, first his daughter's, then his son's. Something about their sleeping innocence, no sign of the cares of the world on their faces, soothed him. For now, he was home.

In the morning, some of the press had started to drift away, clearly realizing that Tenenbaum was not about to stand on his front stoop and make a statement to the media. But this did not stop the headlines.

Someone in the government was spoon-feeding journalists information. Unnamed government "sources" in newspaper after newspaper declared that classified information had been found in "every" room in the house, despite the fact that Tenenbaum had not even been working on classified programs for a long time before the whole nightmare circus began.

In fact, the government got downright creative. Not only were the boxes the FBI had carted off "filled" with classified documents that Tenenbaum had taken home from the base; classified documents were found "under the stairs" (a physical impossibility) and even under the "crib in the baby's room." There was a certain dramatic flourish to finding classified documents beneath an innocent child as the baby slept—the very baby he had stared at just the previous night—but none of it, not a single detail, had been true.

He hoped things would quiet down as the government went through his bank statements and computers. They would find no secret codes, no hidden emails, and no unusual deposits.

Later, under oath, Gugino would say, "There were two individuals that said, 'Boy, Mr. INSCOM [US Army Intelligence and Security Command] representative, you better investigate Tenenbaum because he goes to Israel by himself. He's vacationed there, he wants to reside there, and as a matter of fact I think he has lived there.'"[4]

Gugino would testify:

> I had to be very cautious in conducting any investigative activity relating to Mr. Tenenbaum because INSCOM representatives would make statements to me and never support those statements with documents, a report, anything but words, and I was just a little bit skeptical that some of this information was accurate because it was hearsay…I never saw any documentation…it just seemed that as an impartial investigator, that I like to view myself as, I was going to have to not only listen to what they were telling me and take Tenenbaum's notes and look into allegations that they were bringing forth or information that they were bringing forth, but I was going to have to double-check it someplace along the line like I would, just because they were never able to show me supporting documentation. What I ended up with after leaving their offices or them leaving Tenenbaum's office was not too much more than I had gone in with other than information that they got from an unknown source.[5]

Tenenbaum would come to discover that in addition to the SAEDA filed against him from Jaunutis Gilvydis and the "dream accusation" from Glen, still another of Tenenbaum's coworkers, Thomas Furmaniak, had filed an additional SAEDA against Tenenbaum on March 17, 1994. Furmaniak's allegations were centered on his suspicions regarding the amount of time Tenenbaum spent speaking with the Israeli liaison officer at TACOM, as well as other Israeli officials who traveled to TACOM. But while Furmaniak filed his SAEDA in 1994, his suspicions and allegations took place in 1985. He filed his SAEDA nine years after the events occurred. Given that SAEDAs have to be filed immediately, Furmaniak should have been investigated for violating army regulations, whether by filing a SAEDA report delinquently or by making bogus charges against a fellow engineer.

Instead, this played into Simonini's hands, as he later used Furmaniak's discredited claims. Still, Furmaniak's SAEDA report led to the FBI opening a second PI, and this history of multiple PIs didn't look good to the investigators now.

When asked by the FBI why he waited nine years to file a SAEDA on Tenenbaum, Furmaniak responded, "I didn't want to appear anti-Semitic."[6] Anti-Semitism, it appeared, was spreading like a virus on the TACOM base. There was a "Jew" hysteria, but Tenenbaum was caught in a total catch-22. Part of his job was to strengthen US-Israeli relations. Meanwhile, his coworkers used that same skill as the very reason to wildly accuse him of treason. Or of invading their dreams.

Gilvydis was also approached by the FBI in 1994, but he retracted his previous allegations against Tenenbaum. Given Gilvydis's retraction and Furmaniak's baseless report, the FBI closed its PI and declined to investigate Tenenbaum any further at that time. But, of course, now they were back. And this time, it seemed like they were on a mission.

He was in the headlines, the world's press on his doorstep. He was concerned a crazy person would bring weapons to his home and start taking shots. It seemed so far-fetched. But the entire scenario was. He didn't know what to fear, where to look, or what to pay attention to. His life had become explosion after explosion. Tenenbaum froze behind the curtain of his wide front window. The veil of fabric wouldn't protect him. He didn't know if anything could.

THE ANXIETY OF TRAVEL

The list of what soldiers need can seem endless, but a contracting officer supported by the Office of Special Investigations had her job to do. The sand devastated computers, so she would find new batteries and refurbished parts. Wood, wire, trunks for storage, latrines—anything imaginable was up for negotiation if she could only make it to one of Afghanistan's bazaars.

Along the road in their transport caravans, every disturbed place in the road could be a sign of her upcoming death. The streets were constantly under construction, but the drivers and anyone else looking ahead knew that the disturbed gravel and dirt could be more than just roadwork.

When they reached the cities, crumbling buildings could be places of devastation or places that simply lay in wait for a line of US Humvees like theirs to pass. There could be a trigger. There could be none.

By her best estimate, one in every six Humvees met an explosion. She wanted to look at her hands, her supply list, or into her memories, but she didn't. She focused on her eight-person team, kept her jaw set and her eyes resolute. Because that was her job. They all looked to her. She never knew if the day would be survived, if this road would be the road that finally caught her, but until she knew, she prepared for the next negotiation.[1]

CHAPTER 13

THE POLICE STATE

*"I believe that none of this would have happened
had David not been Jewish."*

—DR. RICHARD MCCLELLAND[1]

Tenenbaum had repeatedly asked Marty Crandall, his attorney, if Crandall thought the government would "follow" him. Crandall had believed that given the vague, ephemeral nature of the suspicions against him, the idea that the government of the United States of America would spend their money putting a security detail on Tenenbaum, a quiet engineer with a yarmulke, a man with no record, and nothing more "suspicious" than a full knapsack and fluency in Hebrew, was frankly insane. The government had, in Crandall's own words, "far bigger fish to fry."

But then the government began to follow Tenenbaum. And every time he left his home, his nerves were put on edge.

Within days, government-issued sedans began appearing on the streets of his neighborhood.

Because Dr. Tenenbaum was on suspension from the base, he had a lot of time to kill. Much of his time involved the nascent beginnings of preparing for what he assumed might be an eventual court case. He had no idea if he would ever see the inside of a courtroom over his case. He had no way of knowing that his case would one day wend its way up through the IG's office for the Department of Defense (DOD-IG) and into the highest ranks of Congress. For now, he assembled what little information he had.

He had not been accused of a crime. Not a "real" crime. So far, as much as he could tell, his "crime" was being a Jew. Nonetheless, he tried to establish a routine. He rose, went to *shul,* went for a run, and tried to occupy himself establishing a defense against a crime he had not committed. He tried to avoid a nervous breakdown and frequently ended up calling Marty Crandall for updates and assurances, thus dwindling his retainer.

Tenenbaum would have *loved* to call Crandall daily, asking him what was going on. But that would have eaten into his billable hours, and he would've been bankrupt before he knew it.

Marty Crandall, meanwhile, was in regular talks with the United States government's prosecuting attorney, following the two factions that had formed within the case: Gugino's side argued, "Let's slow this down, this is way out of control"; Simonini's said, "We want this guy in jail." Gugino wasn't winning.

Crandall had a great admiration for Mike Liebson, respecting how hands-on he was while in charge of terrorism, drugs, and public corruption in leadership positions in the government. He kept Crandall advised through their secret dialogues, but not with specifics. Crandall was certain that Liebson would leave no stone unturned—and for his innocent client, that would be a good thing.

Tenenbaum was walking out his door on his way to his synagogue the Sunday following the FBI search when he saw the first dark sedan parked on his street. It wasn't directly in front of his house, but it wasn't hiding. He walked to his own car, sat down, and turned on the ignition, only to see the other car's headlights flick on.

He pulled out of his driveway, and the sedan set into motion behind him.

Within David Tenenbaum's neighborhood are numerous survivors of the Holocaust. Tenenbaum's late father was a survivor. He knew this history and the memories that still lingered not so deep under their skin. For these citizens, the now-constant presence of unmarked government cars, oppressive and omnipresent, was a painful and frightening reminder of a past time. They were a reminder of the darkest period of history in which these survivors had been first abandoned by, then harassed by, and ultimately *exterminated* by their government. This betrayal by the United States government now, harassing one of their own, was keenly felt. And it was gripping the community with a choking fear and a painful reminder of the world's continued anti-Semitism.

However, if the government believed that its presence would cause resentment toward Tenenbaum or that it would cause doubts in his neighbors' minds of his innocence, they were incorrect.

The effect was the opposite.

When Tenenbaum went for a run every day, he had a visible tail.

When he went to the grocery store, he had an FBI presence.

They parked on his street outside his home. Sedans were there every day.

Every night.

All night.

When he walked to *shul*, they followed him.

While he was in the synagogue, they parked outside. Visible for the whole community to see.

They were always there, down the block from the Tenenbaum house, around the corner. Stashed away in different parking lots, sometimes five or six at a time. It was like a procession whenever Tenenbaum left his house, the kind of procession that accompanies a high-ranking official. Or maybe a funeral, Tenenbaum often mused.

They even followed his wife as she waited in their daughter's carpool line.

Within his community, Tenenbaum had many close friends who supported him during this time. They were present for him physically, and they offered emotional support. One of these close friends, Jerry Abraham, had been a confidant of Tenenbaum's for decades.

"Right after David got his job with TACOM, we would walk and talk a lot," said Abraham. "And any time I would try to talk about what he was doing, he said 'I can't talk about it.' David was extremely ethical and aboveboard. Even though I knew him so long, he would not break any of the confidences he was supposed to keep in his position."[2]

Abraham had just started a new law practice in 1997. When he was driving home, he heard on the radio that someone Jewish was suspected of being a spy for Israel, another so-called "Pollard case." When the broadcast mentioned this supposed spy's name, he didn't believe it. It was ridiculous.

He approached Tenenbaum as soon as he could to talk.

"What's going on?"

His longtime friend looked exhausted, eyes puffy and face pale.

"They suspect me of espionage." Tenenbaum answered matter-of-factly, calmly, but Abraham could sense the levels of stress tightening just under his skin.

Based on Jerry Abraham's experience, in which Tenenbaum wouldn't reveal *anything* about his job, and knowing the man that David Tenenbaum is, he knew the accusations couldn't be true, but he listened as his friend explained the situation as best he could, disbelief mingling with fear and sometimes anger in Tenenbaum's voice.

The FBI surveillance was open and obvious to everyone in the community. Everybody saw what the government was doing. To Abraham, they were accusing someone everyone knew was *100 percent innocent*. It was an affront not to just Tenenbaum—but to the entire neighborhood.

"What can I do to help?"

Tenenbaum wished he had an answer.

Tenenbaum's wife playfully titled Abraham, a father of nine and a devout Orthodox Jew, her husband's psychiatrist. He was a sounding board, an advisor, and a true and loyal friend—for years before and in the years since, but especially during that dark period.

As the government kept up its omnipresence in the neighborhood, some of the older residents—the survivors—found it stirring memories that were far better left alone and in the patina of times past. These elderly citizens turned plaintively to Jerry Abraham too. Together with Stuart Snider and another attorney, the men decided that they would approach the US attorney's office.

They requested a meeting. The head of the criminal division, Alan M. Gershel, was a professor of Abraham's in law school. The appointment was set, and a group from the neighborhood went downtown together to discuss the impact of the government's behavior in Tenenbaum's case on the community. They went without Tenenbaum. He had enough meetings with attorneys. He didn't need any more.

Abraham dressed in a dark suit with a crisp and spotless white dress shirt. Tall and thin, flanked by pillars of his Jewish Orthodox community, he stood confidently in this powerful room surrounded by powerful men.

The group tried to be open as they explained how there were Holocaust survivors to consider. The situation was driving many of these neighbors to feel that what they were experiencing was a reoccurrence of what had happened to them in Europe.

"You have to realize," said Abraham, "for them, they had been in a situation where their own government had turned against them. And here they are, seeing numerous cars in our neighborhood, following people, this *presence*. It is stirring up very painful memories."[3]

The meeting went well from Abraham's perspective. The reactions seemed empathetic, if not supportive. It appeared as if the US Attorney's office understood that the Southfield neighborhood, as an Orthodox Jewish neighborhood, was unique.

The group understood, as they walked out of the building, that there was an accord. The government officials they had spoken to assured them they would be careful and that they would conduct their surveillance more discreetly.

When the group returned to their cars, they felt satisfied that the government had listened and was going to do something about it. However, that feeling didn't last long. A couple of days later, nothing had changed.

Not for the Southfield survivors.

And not for David Tenenbaum.

When Tenenbaum went jogging, there was a car always within sight of him. When he and the other men of his community were at *shul*, a black Lincoln was parked outside their synagogue. At all gatherings, whether personal or religious, at all hours of the day and all hours of the night, the government presence lingered.

CHAPTER 14

ENOUGH IS ENOUGH

"I deeply resent the implication that American Jews
would commit treason against their nation
because of their Jewish heritage."

—REP. NITA LOWEY (D-NY)

David Tenenbaum wasn't the only one weary of the "spy games" the US government was playing. His community was tired of it. Jerry Abraham was tired of it.

So, Tenenbaum's old friend made a decision one night, with a small grin spreading across his face. He decided to put *the government tails* under surveillance. The situation was ridiculous, he thought. This was Tenenbaum they were talking about. Abraham knew he wasn't a spy. And the community had let it be known that what the government was doing was not acceptable to them—to the survivors especially.

Abraham saw the usual dark government-issued sedan on the street. So, he got into his own car and parked behind them. The sedan immediately took off, and he followed. The government car went up one block and down then next, as if it was waiting for Abraham to fall back or to take a different turn, but Tenenbaum's old friend had a point to make. He stayed right behind them.

Then the government sedan hit the gas hard. They shot off through the residential neighborhood. Abraham let them go.

His pale eyes darkened when he saw them again the next day. On the way back from synagogue, the sedan was simply parked on the street. Waiting. Watching for Tenenbaum. Abraham was so furious the US Attorney's office did not do what they said they would do. The meeting had obviously been a false placating of the community's de facto leaders.

The days went by. Tenenbaum would jog to relieve the tension, but it never seemed to work. Winter turned to spring in Michigan. The buds emerged on the trees, hinting at a fresh start, but the mood of the community didn't match the changing season.

One day, Jerry Abraham had his kids in his car. They passed one of the surveillance vehicles, and he whispered to himself, "This cannot be our government." It simply made no sense. He was an attorney. He was educated. He once worked for the government himself, for the Internal Revenue Service. "If you have the case, *bring the case.*" He paused, tightening his grip on the wheel. "If you don't, what are you *harassing* a whole neighborhood for?"

Tenenbaum also had reached the end of his tolerance. Following his friend's lead, he also began thumbing his nose at the government's open surveillance. He had used his words; he was using his lawyer; he didn't know what else he could do to fight.

Tenenbaum began carrying his camera with him. He would, if he saw them, approach them openly and brazenly and take their picture. When he did so, the agents would always drive off, often over the speed limit, even driving in reverse through the quiet neighborhood.

Apparently, the men on the surveillance detail did not appreciate the neighborhood's new tactics. Or the traffic laws.

In Southfield, there are no rowdy neighbors. No wild parties at all hours. On weekends, without electricity use and cars, it's downright silent. So, a knock on the door just before midnight is even more frightening in the stillness. The knock on the Abraham family's door wasn't casual. It was hard and aggressive.

At that hour, in that neighborhood, someone might assume this ominous knock was a "death call"—a notification that someone has died in a horrible accident. Perhaps a long-distance relative or family member. Abraham had a feeling this was a visit for something else.

When the visitors identified themselves as from the Southfield Police Department, Abraham went out on the porch and asked how he could help. The Southfield police asked to come inside.

"No, you can't," he replied. "Do you have a warrant or documents?"

Abraham's children had come down the stairs—all nine of them, the oldest in her early teens. He asked the police what they wanted, what he could do for them, and why they were there.

But these police were not as courteous as the US Attorney had been in the earlier meeting. They were overtly hostile and angry. Their voices were not quiet, despite the hour.

"You know what you're doing. You know," they yelled. "And you better stop it—or we're going to arrest you."

Abraham, feet firmly planted on his porch, entire family behind him, was not one to be trifled with.

"I know my rights," he answered calmly. "And it would be in your best interests to leave my property. I'm an attorney, and I am not going to be intimidated by you."

The Southfield police did, indeed, leave that night. But the surveillance continued with no letup.

Other residents of Southfield and friends of Tenenbaum also refused to be intimidated. The actions against their community—and the Holocaust survivors they felt very protective of—emboldened them.

Other neighbors joined the peaceful fight. Simon Kresch, another community member and friend, joined Tenenbaum and Abraham in taking pictures. The action was legal. Every private citizen had the right to do so. But the action inflamed tensions. The FBI threatened Kresch. He complained to the police, but they just ignored him.

"Numerous people...and their surveillance cars; they even took pictures of another dark sedan with tinted windows flying down the street in reverse," said Kresch. The behavior was dangerous. What if a child had chosen that moment to cross the street?

Tenenbaum, who had done nothing wrong, was being treated like a criminal, as were his friends and neighbors. Yet the government and Southfield police were operating in violation of the law, driving recklessly and threatening those who stood up for their rights.

One particular Holocaust survivor, a survivor of Auschwitz named Manny Mittelman, was especially devastated by the actions of the police and the government. In Mittelman's mind, the entire community was under surveillance. And in fact, Mittelman was not incorrect.

The members of the synagogue were aware of the presence of government officers every day. Holy days, the Sabbath—it didn't matter; they were there.

If Tenenbaum took his young daughter to preschool, a car would be parked in front of the building. The presence of his young children or his wife or even his elderly mother did not make a difference.

Once, as Tenenbaum strapped his sixteen-month-old son into his car seat, little Yehuda Leib started saying one of the few words he knew at that time, the word "car." As Tenenbaum pulled out of the driveway, all his son kept saying was "caw, caw."

Tenenbaum grinned, a proud father, no matter what else was going on in his life.

"Yes, Yehuda Leib. We are going in a car."

But his son just kept repeating, "caw, caw." Finally, as Tenenbaum turned around, his son pointed to one of the surveillance vehicles and said, "caw." Tenenbaum realized at that point that even a sixteen-month-old child knew the "caws" that didn't belong in the neighborhood. From that time on, his son would constantly point out the various "covert" surveillance vehicles in the neighborhood and those that were following the family.

Maybe the FBI should consider hiring my son as a special agent even though he isn't even two years old yet, Tenenbaum thought to himself.

For six months, this went on unabated. Tenenbaum—despite the "billable minutes"—called Crandall to complain and to see if something could be done about it.

The most egregious episode took place when the Tenenbaums decided to take a trip to Ann Arbor to a children's museum located there. It was—he and Madeline hoped—to be a bit of a respite, a way to remove themselves from the pressures and stress of feeling like prisoners in their own home. Their lives had changed so much in the span of months. Every time they wanted to have a personal conversation, they would step outside into the backyard or just take a walk. Everywhere they went, they had a tail. It was no way to live. To this day, they still have private conversations outside the house, just to be safe.

On the drive to Ann Arbor, though, instead of a single surveillance car, there were five or six vehicles following them.

Tenenbaum stopped his car at a red light. He opened the door and climbed out, feeling a rage he was unused to. Enough was enough. He took out a video camera he had intended to use to film the children's joy at the museum and pointed it at the government surveillance detail.

His friend Jerry Abraham said, "This trip to the museum was outrageous. The whole thing was outrageous. The government's behavior was beyond the pale. Look at it this way, in this day and time—even those years ago—when there is so much technology, they could have *very simply* put a homing device on the Tenenbaum family car. If they were *that* worried he was going to take off, they could have done that. What was we [sic] he going to do, really? Go to Israel? Have Israel protect him? The government had already taken his passport!"

Tenenbaum and his friends knew this had nothing to do with fear that he was going to disappear. This was psychological warfare.

The government also claimed that Tenenbaum was a suicide risk. If they had really done their homework on Tenenbaum, they would have realized immediately how ridiculous that suspicion was. If anything, it seemed like the FBI was trying to drive Tenenbaum to do something rash, to either fight back to give them an excuse to put him behind bars or to give up and harm himself.

There was only one moment in the many months of pressure where Tenenbaum felt himself cracking. He was watching his kids play outside in the front yard when one of the surveillance vehicles of the FBI drove very slowly in front of his house as close to the curb as a car could drive. He saw the FBI agent leer at his children. Tenenbaum said to himself, "This is it." Enough. *Don't mess with my kids.*

When confronted by people in the community asking for some identification, the agents always refused to identify themselves. But in Tenenbaum's mind, in that moment, the men in the sedan were not FBI agents; instead, he acted like any other parent in a situation in which his children were being targeted. He grabbed a baseball bat from inside his house and went outside to confront the agent, but the sedan and its driver had already disappeared around the corner. Neither Tenenbaum nor his friends in the community were going to lie down and be passive. And the agents conducting the surveillance soon found out that they were messing with the wrong community.

STRANDED IN THE DESERT

Humvees came in to deliver supplies. They transported soldiers. They delivered mail. But they were always moving in Afghanistan, cutting through the heat with slow, steady determination. The vehicles traveled across roads made of gravel and sand that at times became so one with the desert that soldiers needed compasses to truly understand their routes.

There were few street signs or stop signs in many of the Afghan provinces. Drivers learned to turn at the second dune or at certain piles of rubble. Sometimes directions had to be asked of camel herders or roadside walkers, the price paid for the favor in food, water, or amoxicillin—the risk of speaking to strangers less than that of driving on into the unknown.[1]

Though when the convoys found the right roads, when the path and destination were clearly understood, they could feel just as stranded. The first Humvee in the line of vehicles was often the one targeted. Sometimes it was an IED that flipped the massive machine into a roll. Or sometimes, it was a thrown bomb made of soda bottles stuffed with rags and oil—oil was always in such abundance there. It was in that moment of the boom, in that moment that the fires started, that the heartbeat of every soldier present matched the rat-tat-tat-tat of the familiar gunfire. All the other Humvees in the line would be stranded behind the wreckage, on the wrong side of a bridge, in a narrow section of road, in the middle of an already devastated town.

They trained for this. They dealt with this. Doctors in the base hospitals were ready for this. But stronger vehicles could have allowed them to get through. Maybe not every time. But so much more often than they did.

CHAPTER 15

JEWS CAN'T BE TRUSTED

"If I had to refute all the other articles of the Jewish faith,
I should be obliged to write against them as much and for as
long a time as they have used for inventing their lies—
that is, longer than two thousand years."

—MARTIN LUTHER

The FBI filed a complaint with the US Prosecutor's Office. They claimed the community wasn't playing fair. They weren't used to this behavior in a community they had under surveillance. Put another way, they were upset that people were standing by their rights.

They were trying to split Tenenbaum off from his community, like lions splitting off a gazelle from the herd, but it had the opposite effect. His community was not going to allow that.

"What I see in today's day and age," said Jerry Abraham, "is a disproportionate number of political attacks by the government, and by its prosecutorial arm, against Jews—these are cases where people have done tremendous good for this country, and they come in as if they are the worst people in the world."

Tenenbaum didn't celebrate Christmas like almost everyone else on his base. He didn't travel or work on the Sabbath (and yet he willingly worked on Sundays while others would never think of such a thing on their day of rest). He kept kosher. He didn't drink alcohol. He didn't even drink coffee. He never went to the strip bars at lunch like some of his colleagues. He wore his yarmulke at all times.

"It's called profiling," Abraham said. "And you can't do it to Muslims, blacks, or Hispanics, but in the intelligence community, you can do it to Jews. Perhaps because of Israel, the Pollard case. Who knows?"

The situation was grueling, and it was wearing down Tenenbaum. For a driven man, a career-minded man, an intellectual man, to be without his employment, a prisoner in his own neighborhood, followed and made to feel like a pariah in his own community—despite their support—was destroying his health, both physical and mental. He felt stranded and stuck.

Even more, the events were shattering his faith in what the United States even stood for, what his life's work protecting America's warriors even stood for. He was hearing stories from overseas. He knew what American soldiers were up against. They were in vehicles ill-designed for the situations they were going into, and the government wasn't doing the best that it possibly could to protect them. Tenenbaum didn't understand how they could do anything less. But he didn't understand the United States government as well as he thought he once did.

As Dr. Michael Engelberg said, "Most people have blinders on. They think this is a free country, a democratic nation. But the reality is if the government turns on you, they wield so much power…they become, absolutely, a police state. And that is what happened with Tenenbaum. He was a victim of the police state."

The name "Pollard" was whispered again and again, but to Tenenbaum's supporters, he was the next Captain Alfred Dreyfus.

Dreyfus, a man of Jewish and Alsatian descent, was framed as a spy-traitor by the French military in the late 1800s through the early 1900s. Evidence was suppressed, and documents were falsified in a gross and twisted miscarriage of justice. At the same time, anti-Semitism was at a fever pitch. The French press would print libelous statements without any repercussions. The Dreyfus Affair, as it came to be known, would split French public opinion for decades—long after Dreyfus was exonerated and after the anti-Semitism behind his initial convictions was exposed.

In the United States, the scandal of the Pollard case was an embarrassing mark on the US government. Pollard, an intelligence analyst for the US government, pleaded guilty in 1987, as part of a plea agreement, to selling secrets to Israel. Because Israel is an ally, many felt that his given sentence of life imprisonment despite having entered into a plea agreement, which did not come with any such sentence recommendation, was grossly unjust, especially since lighter sentences had been given to others who spied for enemies such as the Soviet Union.

Tenenbaum's case was one of several that began in the 1990s in which the American loyalty of Jews who worked in the DOD, FBI, or other noteworthy government agencies was questioned. The connection with these questions and Project Scope, the FBI's exposed list of Jewish employees, is unclear.

David Tenenbaum had no idea that as he endured government tails and disruption in his daily life, Mark Mallah, a former special agent for the FBI, had also been a Jew singled out for a polygraph test and ended up accused of unauthorized contact with "foreign" officials from the Israeli government—espionage—in 1995. Mallah had cooperated through the grueling polygraph testing, the extensive search of his home, and the collection of his detailed financial records, appointment books, personal calendars, daily "to-do" lists, innermost thoughts expressed in personal diaries, personal correspondences, and numerous other items. He too was under surveillance in his neighborhood, where a small airplane circled above his home and tracked his movements.

While there were no findings of evidence against Mallah, his case remained marked "unresolved," even as he was allowed to return to work five months later with his "top secret" clearance level reinstated. In October of 1995, FBI Headquarters contacted him to disclose that he was "the subject of a security reinvestigation involving his inability to resolve issues relating to his associations with foreign nationals... as well as his susceptibility to coercion as a result of his concealment of these matters." After eight months of investigation, no evidence had been found against him, nor had any details about any specific foreign nationals been shared. Yet the case lingered.[1]

After finally being cleared in 1996, Mallah quit the FBI, stating, "I believe that in the wake of the Pollard situation, they probably believed, or at least suspected, that there were other Pollards out there and they did not want to get burned twice. So better to trample on any notions of due process, fairness, even objectivity in running the investigation than to risk being burned again by another Jew with perhaps questionable loyalties."[2]

Beyond Mallah, David Tenenbaum was also not aware that Adam Ciralsky, a Jewish lawyer and Peabody Award-winning journalist who worked for the Central Intelligence Agency, would be the victim of a discriminatory polygraph test when he was offered a position in the National Security Council (NSC).

Ciralsky was grilled about every Israeli he ever met from the time of his bar mitzvah. He was asked about every single person he had met in Israel and whether those Israelis he had met had ever tried to "pitch" him to work with Israel. He was even asked why he did not list his great-grandfather's first cousin, Chaim Weizmann, the first President of Israel, as a close and continuing contact, despite the fact that Ciralsky was born in 1971, nineteen years after Weitzman died in 1952. In addition, just like Tenenbaum's, Ciralsky's polygraph examiner was abusive, referring to Ciralsky as "that little Jew bastard." In the end, before he could accept the position, it was blocked by the CIA's Counterespionage Group (CEG), citing his "Jewish roots."

However, Ciralsky was nothing if not tenacious. He sued the government, ultimately forcing George Tenet, then director of the CIA, to testify under oath. Unprecedented in history, Tenet was forced to admit the conduct of the polygraph was "unprofessional," "insensitive," and "inappropriate."[3]

The offensive statement was made by a polygraph administrator identified as "Charles B" in the court transcripts; in a sworn affidavit, another CIA polygraph administrator, John Sullivan, said: "I was in B's office when he came and I asked him how the test was going. B's response was to refer to Ciralsky as 'that little Jew bastard.' I don't recall what B said after that but I believe that he said something to the effect that he, B, 'knew Ciralsky was hiding something.'"[4]

The lawsuit forced the government's hand on the issue of anti-Semitism with the hiring of the ADL to lead "sensitivity training." Whether this training made a difference or not is unclear.

At a later date, as his case dragged on for years, Tenenbaum would become acquainted with some of his fellow pariahs. All seemed to be targeted for a level of "Jewishness." As Tenenbaum delved further into the government's treatment of Jews in its employ, he learned that anti-Semitism was deeply rooted within the CIA, at least as far back as the Kennedy administration. James Jesus Angleton was the CIA's director of counterintelligence under John F. Kennedy. He was also responsible for being the liaison with Israel. Angleton had a love for Israel, yet he still suspected Jews who worked in the intelligence community or the Defense Department had dual loyalties to both the US and Israel. This, of course, was in an era when Kennedy's own presidential nomination came under suspicion because a segment of the voting public questioned if Kennedy had dual loyalties to the Pope and Rome as well as to the United States. In September 1960, a group of one hundred fifty Protestant ministers stated that he needed to "repudiate" the teaching of the Catholic Church in order to attain the presidency.[5]

As director of counterintelligence under Kennedy, Angleton had created what amounted to a matrix of CIA and other government officials that examined their "Jewishness," and who had access to classified material related to Israel.[6] (See Appendix 10.)

It seemed, several presidential terms later, that the "Jewishness matrix" still existed.

The Tenenbaum case was now added to the swirling undertow of anti-Jew mistrust and overt antagonism within the US government. And no one, it seemed, was willing to stop the persecution. The government charged ahead.

CHAPTER 16

THE LOSS OF LASS

"Anti-Semitism is the rumor about the Jews."

—THEODOR W. ADORNO

For eighteen months, David Tenenbaum was psychologically tortured—the thought of life in prison hung over his head. Almost none of his former colleagues would speak with him. The rare one or two who would take his call whispered they couldn't talk for fear of reprisal of their own jobs. He was an outcast and a pariah.

A man without a job. A man without a career.

He tried to cherish the small moments when his community stood so solidly behind him. He was respected. He was cherished. He had their full support.

Amid the months of surveillance, there was a celebration within the community. A convention was being held in Southfield for girls from a number of Jewish day schools around the US. They came from states across the nation, and they were all apprised of the local situation with the FBI surveillance of Tenenbaum.

On the Sabbath, dressed in their Sabbath finery, these girls found their own way to protest the close examination and distrust of an Orthodox Jew. Many had gathered together in Tenenbaum's neighborhood because they were staying at various people's houses. They were told about the FBI surveillance cars and decided to "have some fun." No music could be played on the Sabbath, but they kept traditional melodies in their minds as they held each other's fingertips and cross-stepped to the rhythm in their hearts. They circled the surveillance vehicles and danced around them, stepping with pointed toes. They moved together toward the center and back again, keeping up their rhythm to nothing more than the occasional birdsong or chatter from all those who had stopped to stare.

The agents hadn't a clue as to what was happening and what to do. What were they going to do? Arrest a bunch of fourteen- and fifteen-year-old girls? They were aghast, and they were surrounded.

Tenenbaum tried to find hope and strength in the solidarity of the members of his community, young and old, men and women. But with Tenenbaum on suspension, the Humvees he worked on also remained vulnerable. The LASS program—and the soldiers it was created to protect—were the other victims of Simonini's tunnel vision. Each new headline and accusation was a new improvised explosive in his own life. He just tried to keep going, like the soldier who kept driving, keeping an eye out for anything suspicious ahead, hoping he'd be prepared for the next boom.

The Tenenbaum family felt unrelenting pressure. Every month of early childhood sees so much change. Their two young children were growing, making new discoveries, forming new words, gaining new confidence and skills. Yet through so much of this time, Tenenbaum was lost to them. He couldn't focus on his family, even when he tried. He was focused on staying out of prison.

Tenenbaum can never get back that time with his children. The years of dealing with the unrelenting pressure left him exhausted and stressed. His children, for the most part, only knew their father as a hunted man—and whatever that did to his demeanor and temperament.

For months and years, the Tenenbaums understandably felt their lives were in danger. The government listed his case as one of active spying on their own website—even after Tenenbaum was later found completely innocent. His name, his hometown, and his address were easily findable with a simple Google search. They would receive phone calls from anonymous strangers. Once, Madeline answered only to hear someone yell the word "traitor" and hang up.

White supremacist websites focused on the case as well—listing Tenenbaum's name and location. Tenenbaum didn't know who was more dangerous to him: skinheads or his own government.

Yet as Tenenbaum's punishment off base dragged on, one of the most difficult parts of his ordeal was watching his family suffer. He was distracted and could not offer the kind of emotional support his wife needed. Knowing—and even expecting—at any moment that the FBI could swoop in, separate him from his family and community, and imprison him for life was never far from his mind. Sleep was elusive. Tenenbaum was frequently ill with meningitis, which his doctors said was no doubt stress-related. His finances were drained by legal fees. He filled his days by, essentially, preparing for a trial that may or may not come to pass at an unknown time. He tried to recall every conversation he had ever had with anyone who might help defend his innocence.

Tenenbaum called people he knew from work when he was on suspension. Contractors and colleagues—his friends, or so he thought. These were people who spent time with his family, team-mates who came to his home for dinner. But they wouldn't speak with him and asked Tenenbaum not to call them again. They may have been afraid, but the impression Tenenbaum received was that they thought he was guilty.

His marriage was on edge. The love was there, but his stress—and Madeline's—was creating two lonely spouses instead of a team.

His children suffered. After the FBI's raid and the confiscation of Tenenbaum's daughter's drawings and coloring books, Nechama was afraid to answer the doorbell. Whenever there was a knock or someone rang, the little dark-haired girl with the expressive eyes would scream, "No, don't answer the door. You don't know who it is!" It took years before Nechama became comfortable again in her own home. Something as simple as a delivery from the UPS would cause the child to tense.

Years later, after she graduated high school, she traveled to Israel for a year of post-high school seminary education. She called her father one night and started to ask him questions regarding the FBI raid that occurred when she was not yet in kindergarten. She was beginning to remember things, details and feelings she had suppressed for the past fourteen years. No doubt the raid itself made an impression, along with the pervasive tension in the home. The Tenenbaum children had grown up seeing their parents step outside for any deeply personal conversation. They had spent their formative years with a father the government was willing to lie about, smear in the press, and stop at nothing to paint as an Israeli spy.

Tenenbaum himself had to deal with insensitive people who just did not understand the constant, relentless, and intense pressure he and his family were under. Many would comment that he was essentially on a paid eighteen-month "vacation."

"At least you're getting paid," he was told again and again.

"Right," he wanted to respond. "But who is paying the thousands of dollars to my criminal attorney to defend me and keep me out of jail?"

He didn't know of any vacation that had the potential to end not in a bad sunburn, but with life in a supermax with murderers and career criminals as companions. He was living with the rubble of a mental war zone around him, and who knew what else was hidden, waiting to be triggered.

During this time, he was also approached by a few supporters who believed in him but felt that he would not be given a fair chance to prove not only his innocence, but that the government itself was being abusive. Their reasoning was hardly faulty—the government was behind the lies in the press, not sealing the search warrant, and harassing the neighborhood.

Someone even offered to smuggle Tenenbaum out of the country. Surely Israel would value his contributions, he was told. But America was *home,* and in his mind, leaving was *never* an option. Tenenbaum would stay and fight this out until the end.

He had done nothing wrong, and he was not about to run away.

The LASS project was dismantled—and not replaced. It was Tenenbaum's "baby." Without him on base and at the helm, it ceased to exist. The funding evaporated. The program was suspended. Simonini, under oath in later depositions, revealed his utter, sneering contempt for the program.

In Simonini's own words, "Mr. Tenenbaum was just another misguided engineer that didn't understand the foreign disclosure rules. And we had set him straight on what procedures he needed to follow, and we expected him to resubmit the LASS proposal and staff it properly, and we'd see where it would go."[1]

Simonini even commented to Tenenbaum in their meeting that he did not trust the Israelis and he did not trust Tenenbaum. Simonini was dismissive of Tenenbaum and Tenenbaum's program—yet Simonini was not an engineer and had little background to be able to judge. Dan Meyer, on the other hand, *was* a warfighter. He had experience in the Middle East Force of the US Navy. Meyer, the former director for whistleblowing and transparency (DW&T) to the IG of the Defense Department, would later say that Tenenbaum was, in essence, a visionary, developing LASS before anyone else in the military started addressing the problem of the Humvees.

Where it would go without Tenenbaum was nowhere, something his supporters and lawyers say no doubt caused irreparable damage to US troops in the Middle East. As one of his subsequent lawyers, the legendary Mayer Morganroth, stated, the entire ordeal "ended up costing American soldiers their lives."[2]

Tenenbaum, at the beginning, had no idea how deep the anti-Semitism and paranoia in his division was. As he was being harassed by the FBI, his community set on edge, somehow he held onto a hope that at least his program would go on—that America's fighting warriors would be held paramount. However, he would eventually discover that nothing of the sort was taking place at the TACOM base. Worse, he would discover that not only were the warriors not being considered, but that whispered innuendo had given way to outright anti-Jewish hysteria.

Tenenbaum had secured funding for LASS. One of the funders was a program manager, Terry Dean. He had believed in Tenenbaum and LASS enough to offer $100,000 for the program. Or so Tenenbaum had thought. But despite the hefty sum, Dean had succumbed to the thinking that Tenenbaum's "Jewishness" meant he was untrustworthy. Paul Barnard, the next-highest ranking security officer in counterintelligence, reporting to Simonini, testified later that Terry Dean had stated, in vicious gossip perpetuated on the base, that "Anything you give to Tenenbaum, he's just automatically going to go to the Israelis."[3]

He remembered the woman who patted his yarmulke looking for devil horns. He remembered the pork rinds left on his desk. He was completely blindsided by his treatment. He never saw it coming. Yet had there been clues all along?

FRANZ GAYL,
FELLOW WHISTLEBLOWER

Tenenbaum wasn't the only one vocal about the weaknesses of Humvees. Many dared to raise their voices, within their units, on their bases, and back home after the end of a deployment. But few blew the whistle louder than Franz Gayl, a civilian Marine Corps official and former Marine.

Gayl enlisted in the military the day after his seventeenth birthday in 1974. He first went into the infantry, then acted as a Marine security guard for US embassies before returning to school and later became an infantry officer. He achieved the rank of major before his retirement after twenty-two years of active service, but shortly after this retirement, Gayl returned to the work of serving his country as a civilian science and technology advisor to the Marine Corps at the Pentagon.[1]

During the height of the insurgency in Iraq, Gayl was invited to come to the war zone. There was equipment needed to better protect the soldiers, and, as Gayl soon found out, much of this equipment had already been requested but was held up in the Marine Corps bureaucracy. Various battlefield surveillance systems could save soldiers' lives, and "directed energy" non-lethal weapons could reduce the number of civilian casualties. Gayl was especially interested in Mine-Resistant Ambush Protected vehicles (MRAPs), which had the potential to replace Humvees in locations like the Middle East, where these legacy vehicles weren't suitable for the style of warfare, no matter how much up-armoring the soldiers or the military itself seemed to do.

According to Gayl's data, "Marines and soldiers riding in Humvees during IED attacks are more than ten times as likely to suffer death or maiming than if they were riding in MRAPs."[2] In addition, troops in MRAPs seemed dramatically less likely to suffer burn injuries.[3]

The Humvee's frame included too much aluminum, which was flammable. Its concave underside focused the blast energy on those inside rather than dispersing it. Because work on the LASS program had been halted nearly a decade earlier, so many of these problems lingered at the expense of American lives.

However, MRAPs were built for exactly these types of war zones. They were largely developed in the bush wars of South Africa, with a structure designed for the purpose of reacting to explosions. Their v-shaped hull dispersed the energy of a blast. They sat higher off the ground and were designed in modular parts that could break apart but protect the people inside. These modules were even able to be reassembled, depending on the extent of the damage. In Gayl's words, MRAPs were "designed from the ground up to protect the crews and passengers, protecting against all of the primary injury-causing aspects of an explosion."[4]

As a science advisor, Gayl was thorough in his research and then prepared a presentation to give to the Office of the Secretary of Defense (OSD) based on the issues raised to him by marines on the ground, including military commanders.[5] Yet shortly before his presentation, he was issued a written admonishment and told to delete all drafts of his presentation.[6] Whether the concern was the price of all of this new equipment, the interruption of existing contracts, or the display of the apparent mismanagement of bureaucracy in following up on these requests was unclear, but what was clear to Gayl was the danger the American soldiers were in.

He couldn't just be silent on the issue, even when told he had to be. American lives were being lost. There were ways to save them. Gayl still continued his research, and in 2007, back in the United States, he worked with the Government Accountability Project (GAP) and the Project on Government Oversight (POGO) to present his findings to Congress. In addition, he gave interviews with major media outlets, which put the Humvee issue in the spotlight for the American public more than it ever had been before.

FRANZ GAYL, FELLOW WHISTLEBLOWER

But in return for his efforts of trying to save soldiers' lives, his once-exceptional performance evaluations were downgraded; his security clearance was revoked; there was an attempt to suspend him without pay; and he was personally harassed.

MRAPs saved "thousands upon thousands of lives," according to then Secretary of Defense Robert Gates, but it wasn't until years later, in 2014, that Franz Gayl reached a settlement with the government that ultimately allowed him not only to keep his job but also to develop guidelines for how others who raise concerns about internal wrongdoing within the government are handled. Gayl was a whistleblower whose career was rocked by his drive to do the right thing for US soldiers. In many ways, David Tenenbaum fell into the same category. These were US government employees who wanted nothing more than to save the lives of their country's troops. But speaking up and having an uncommon initiative apparently had its costs.

CHAPTER 17

THE END IS NOT THE END

"Congress shall make no law respecting an establishment of religion, or prohibiting the free exercise thereof; or abridging the freedom of speech, or of the press; or the right of the people peaceably to assemble, and to petition the Government for a redress of grievances."

—US CONSTITUTION, 1st Amendment

Marty Crandall remained in constant touch with the US Prosecutor's Office, keeping his finger on the pulse of the investigation. The two separate factions remained in the decision-making process, with one new twist. While Simonini continued pressing for Tenenbaum to be arrested—and presumably locked up with the key thrown away for the rest of Tenenbaum's natural life—Special Agent Gugino suspected that Tenenbaum was innocent, a pawn in an elaborate chess match. Even if Gugino was not 100 percent convinced of Tenenbaum's blamelessness, he was at least certain that it all felt rushed and was based on the flimsiest of suspicions.

Gugino continued to double-check every detail he was told.

At one point, when there was an important briefing with the FBI and the various players, Simonini and Bernard attended and tried to micromanage and control the investigation. The FBI threw them out of the room. The tension was intensifying between the faction that wanted to brutally push an agenda against the unwitting engineer and the side that was doubting there was so much as a shred of evidence.

Special Agent Gugino discovered, fairly easily, that the "evidence" Simonini used to manipulate the FBI to open a criminal investigation— the only branch of the government in the Tenenbaum case that *could* open an investigation—was flimsy. Simonini had seized on the fact— which Tenenbaum does not deny—that sometimes he made travel arrangements to avoid traveling on the Sabbath and have kosher meals on flights. But Gugino, again under deposition, elucidated how utterly fallacious this "sinister" idea was.

"If someone is engaging in espionage-type activities, why do it so openly?" Gugino argued.[1]

In fact, Tenenbaum's travel orders and vouchers had noted his religious need for his travel arrangements and, as always, had been fully vetted and approved by his superiors. In addition, there was nothing sinister in making his own arrangements. Any employee at Tenenbaum's level, flying over water (i.e., to Europe or other continents, passing over oceans), is free to make their own arrangements—and countless government employees do so.

It was not until the discovery period when Tenenbaum filed a lawsuit against the army that he discovered documents which showed the ignorance of those involved in the case. One of these texts was from the *Jerusalem Post* from Monday, February 24, 1997, titled, "Alleged US Army Informant Considered Moving to Israel."

Above the *Jerusalem Post* article was a handwritten note by one of the FBI or Army investigators that stated:

FYI: Make or declare *aliyah* is something any Jewish person can do. Once in Israel they "make or declare *aliyah*, and they automatically become an Israeli citizen. A common practice but not for US government employees."

It's unclear who the article's source was, but it wasn't anyone in Tenenbaum's camp.

In fact, Tenenbaum had never considered becoming a citizen of Israel. Tenenbaum had been among the very first engineers to volunteer in the first Gulf War. He was American and proud of his citizenship. Instead, his supervisor urged him to use his talents as an engineer away from the battlefield to serve his country—something he had been trying to do with the LASS project. The idea that simply being Jewish meant that he would reject his own country offended him, not to mention that someone who had not interviewed him and who had no knowledge of who he was as a person was stereotyping him and jumping to outlandish conclusions. It disgusted him. Yet again he found himself, in some sad and poignant sense, grateful his father had not lived to see such anti-Semitism toward his son—his son who worked in service to the DOD. Now his very loyalty to his country was being called into question.

But despite all these prejudices, despite the web of deceptions used to push forward the FBI investigation, Marty Crandall at last informed Dr. Tenenbaum that he was *cleared*.

The FBI had gone through every file on his work computer, every file on his home computer, every bank statement for the last decade, and all his tax returns; they had interviewed virtually every person who ever worked with him; they had followed him—relentlessly—24/7, for months. They had analyzed music books and coloring books for "secret codes." Most likely, they had bugged his home—with or without a warrant, Tenenbaum had no idea.

In the end, and according to his lawyers, no doubt at the cost of *millions of dollars* to taxpayers (from the nascent beginnings of the investigation through its ending years later), they found *not one shred, not one scintilla, of evidence* that David Aaron Tenenbaum was a spy or had passed along any state secrets to Israel.

No evidence. No smoking gun. No personal enrichment from foreign sources. Not so much as a suspect email. No evidence at all. Period.

When Tenenbaum's property was returned by Gugino after he was cleared of any wrongdoing about eighteen months after his suspension, Gugino told him that there was considerable jealousy among Tenenbaum's coworkers: "You aren't the typical government employee. You were successful in developing programs. You did not wait for work to be handed to you but looked for and developed programs and obtained funding on your own. People were jealous. This brought out anti-Semitism. You didn't just make phone calls, but you went to meet with people face to face, including the Israeli liaison officer as well as the other liaison officers on the base. This gave your colleagues the impression that you were 'doing something wrong.'"[2]

The dream of a colleague.

A backpack in which he'd brought his packed lunch.

The fact that he preferred staying at hotels where kosher dietary customs were followed.

And most importantly, an intelligence and counterintelligence chief in Simonini who was "very anti-Jewish," "vindictive," and "bitter."[3]

All of these petty, vicious elements had conspired to destroy Tenenbaum. And now, the boxes of his personal effects were being returned without so much as an apology. On top of everything else, he was told that Simonini was retiring from the military.

It was over.

Except it wasn't.

CHAPTER 18

PARIAH

"The world is a dangerous place, not because of those who do evil, but because of those who look on and do nothing."

—ALBERT EINSTEIN

Tenenbaum was incredulous. His life was disrupted, millions of dollars were spent, and he—and his family, as well as his community and supporters—had suffered horribly. And now, there sat the boxes filled with the artifacts of his life. It was over. But how could he go back?

Along with the return of his bank statements, phone records, computers, and personal belongings, Tenenbaum received a letter from the US Prosecutor's Office dated February 1998. The letter stated that the FBI conducted an extremely thorough investigation and that if there was any evidence to be found showing that Tenenbaum had committed espionage or passed classified information to Israel, the FBI would have found it.

Special Agent James Gugino testified, "During the…investigation I did not interview one person or find anything in Tenenbaum's background that led to any evidence whatsoever that an act of espionage was committed by him."[1]

It was over. Only, in an audacious move, the FBI and the US Prosecutor's Office now wanted to interrogate Tenenbaum. They had publicly smeared him. His arrest had been front-page news in Detroit and had spread as far as the *New York Times* and international publications. They had wasted taxpayer money and destroyed a man's life. They had, in essence, made a glaring and public mistake. No doubt, in the old adage of "Heads will roll," someone up the chain of command wanted to know how this had happened. Tenenbaum, of course, mused they had only needed to walk down the hallway to Simonini's old office, where, as his former right-hand man attested, he had viewed the Tenenbaum case as a "festering wound."[2] It wasn't so much a "*how*" but a "*whom*."

The FBI and the prosecutor's office requested, through Tenenbaum's attorney Marty Crandall, to conduct an interview of Tenenbaum, which they "promised" could not hurt him in any way; they promised Tenenbaum that he could not incriminate himself. Considering that Tenenbaum had already been subjected to a Good Cop/Bad Cop ruse *and* a flagrantly abusive polygraph examination, he obviously had no faith or trust in the FBI and refused. As a matter of fact, Gugino even told Tenenbaum that he would not agree to be interviewed either if he was in Tenenbaum's shoes. In addition, Tenenbaum was by now quite aware that some of his colleagues—people with whom he had previously worked side by side and with whom he'd never shared so much as an irate word—had spouted bigoted and hateful statements about him. The entire base—the entire *system*—was corrupt as far as he was concerned.

Now they wanted him to "cooperate." He had agreed to "cooperate" by taking a polygraph. He had agreed to "cooperate" by allowing them to search his home and voluntarily giving up his passport. Where had cooperating gotten him? There was nothing to gain by agreeing.

Tenenbaum refused. In the past eighteen months, he had been enlightened that the behaviors of his colleagues—overt prejudices that would have led, no doubt, to human resources involvement and firings in the private sector—were being tolerated within the DOD. He was also wise enough now to know that *innocence* was no protection. Lady Justice was not only blindfolded; she was corrupt and bigoted. He would never, ever again speak to anyone on this subject without his attorney present—billable hours be damned.

The TACOM and the DIS investigators had not obtained what they wanted because there was nothing. Simonini, according to insiders, was seething.[3] The investigators had wanted Tenenbaum to be charged with treason. They had wanted a spy, and they considered Tenenbaum that spy. They had wanted the "next Pollard." They had wanted the kind of big capture that makes careers. In the words of one of the major players in the case, as spoken to Tenenbaum, "They messed up big time," and they needed to find a way to save face.[4]

And now what? Could Tenenbaum simply walk back on base? In Tenenbaum's mind, resigning and going into private industry was impossible. The internet was now burgeoning. One internet search of the name "David Tenenbaum" with the word "spy" would pull up *tens of thousands of results*. Unfortunately, as any high schooler could attest, *undoing* libelous statements on the internet is virtually impossible. Therefore, leaving wasn't an option in Tenenbaum's mind. His other reason had more to do with a sense of fair play and justice. He was simply not going to give them the satisfaction. Emboldened by the knowledge that there was not one scintilla of evidence attesting to the false and prejudiced accusations against him, he waited for them to make the next move.

TACOM, for their part, proceeded slowly, taking a number of months to decide what they were going to do with Tenenbaum. Even though the US Prosecutor's Office could not prosecute or convict him on espionage charges, they still would not give up and admit they made a horrendous mistake and apologize. Emails furiously flew back and forth between officials from the FBI, TACOM, and other agencies, which essentially said, "We can't get him on espionage—let's get him on false statements or something else."[5] Deliberations behind closed doors continued.

In April of 1998, Tenenbaum was ordered back to work by the army. But Simonini's camp—even seemingly without its ringleader now—had not thrown in the towel. There were many more tactics they had yet to utilize. The psychological warfare and pressures remained unrelenting, seeking to humiliate Tenenbaum at every step. He knew they had labeled him a "suicide risk" early in the investigation. Now he wondered if they were maliciously trying to induce him to kill himself, or at least push him toward divorce, financial ruin, or depression and mental illness.

The army listed Tenenbaum's name on its Aberdeen Proving Ground website as one of the US Army's espionage cases, even after he was completely cleared of any wrongdoing. The espionage article shows under US Army Espionage Cases:

David A. Tenenbaum, a mechanical engineer who worked for the Combat Vehicle Team at the US Army Tank Automotive and Armaments Command.

Tenenbaum is the only person listed on this website who was never charged with any crime whatsoever and was proven to be innocent. Yet, according to this army website, he was a spy. It is hardly as if the army's website is written and maintained by computer coders alone. All content must be approved up a chain of command. And Tenenbaum's name remained on that website for more than two years after he had been cleared and ordered back to work. (See Appendix 11.)

Someone wanted that website to proclaim he was a spy.

It was finally removed—but only after Tenenbaum's attorneys complained about the audacity to even place Tenenbaum's name on a website of government employees who were serving jail time for espionage.

The army website aside, TACOM/TARDEC were still not done with Tenenbaum. Their next aggressive tactic was to revoke his security clearance, which was at the level of secret. Even though Tenenbaum had only been working on unclassified programs prior to being placed on leave, the lack of a security clearance rendered him, essentially, a non-person on base. Engineers who were the movers and shakers would create their own programs, seek funding, and steer the course, just as Tenenbaum had done when he created LASS. Without a security clearance, Tenenbaum not only couldn't come up with his own programs—he wouldn't be able to work on anyone else's programs either.

More to the point, without a security clearance, the army could fire him if they wanted—and it seemed clear they did want him fired and gone as expediently as possible, preferably before he set one foot on base after his eighteen-month suspension. They seemed to want him to disappear.

Emily Bacon, chief counsel for TACOM, sent an email saying just that to Jerry Chapin, the director of TARDEC. His non-personhood could not be clearer in her writing:

Chapin asked if we had any legal reasons why the TARDEC engineer who was on administrative (paid) leave last February should not be brought back to work. I told him as far as we were concerned, if TARDEC can assign him work which does not require a security clearance, can make sure he has no access to that which does require a clearance, and can ensure that he is monitored, we have no objection to bringing him back to work. The engineer should be told that this arrangement (being assigned duties which don't require a clearance) is temporary; if he permanently loses his clearance, I don't want the Command in the position of being obligated to create a position which doesn't require a clearance. I told Jerry before he did that he should coordinate with the FBI agents to make sure they are aware. If the FBI objects then we should look at the basis for such objection and make our way from there. I agree with Jerry's assessment that this has gone on far too long.[6]

David Tenenbaum read and reread the letter from the US Prosecutor's Office as he tried to absorb how he was being treated. The letter had called the investigation thorough. If there had been evidence of spying, they would have found it, the letter said. Tenenbaum was cleared, but it was as if that hadn't happened. He was innocent, but TACOM/TARDEC, as can be seen from Emily Bacon's email to Jerry Chapin, was treating him as if he was a security risk who needed monitoring, and who could not be trusted with classified information.

He was Jewish. He was marked. He might as well have been wearing a yellow star.

Simonini, who to Tenenbaum's dismay had reappeared at TACOM as a high-level civilian after his retirement, waited the required six months and sent an email to Doug Newberry, one of the most senior and high-ranking civilians on base. The email stated that now that Tenenbaum would be returning, Simonini feared for his safety and the safety of his family. Simonini's family. Not to think about what had been done to David Tenenbaum's. Of a little girl who needed the lights on for months after the FBI came and searched every inch of her home.

Tenenbaum and the US Army appeared to be at an impasse. Dr. Richard McClelland was, at that time, the deputy director of TARDEC. McClelland called Tenenbaum at his residence to let him know he was being formally ordered back to work.

"I don't really want to go back. But it's not like I have a choice," Tenenbaum said into the phone.

"I think we should meet."

Tenenbaum's mistrust of those in power was deepening by the day. He told McClelland that he wanted to meet with him, first, in a "safe" environment before he returned to the base, and he suggested that they meet at Tenenbaum's house. McClelland agreed, and the two of them convened at the Tenenbaum home a few days later. They discussed where he would work, and McClelland seemed to be trying to allay Tenenbaum's fears and concerns as much as possible.

Compared with Emily Bacon, McClelland was treating Tenenbaum humanely and like a person—and not like "the Jew employee."

"When you return to work, come to my office first," the TARDEC deputy director said. "I'll show you your office space. I want to take this opportunity to apologize. You should never have been suspended. Simonini should have been fired."

McClelland conveyed his thoughts that Tenenbaum should have been allowed to continue working while the investigation was ongoing and should have just continued working until the investigation was completed. Tenenbaum had not been working on classified programs, after all. McClelland had access to all of Tenenbaum's files, and he was well aware that one of the SAEDAs was based on an employee's *dream*.

"Thank you for saying so," Tenenbaum answered when his boss finished, "but it would have been extremely humiliating to continue to work on the base while being openly investigated by the FBI. Not that I would want to go through these last eighteen months, but my story was international news. I don't think my coworkers would have appreciated being around an alleged spy."

McClelland soon left with assurances that this would all be made right.

Tenenbaum, however, continued with his sleepless nights. He was a little less concerned that every car behind him was a group of federal agents or that every doorbell ring or knock was the government coming to haul him away, but he couldn't imagine returning to the base, facing people he worked with, or having to deal with a bigot like Simonini, knowing that the man hated and distrusted him for nothing more than his religion. After eighteen months, the truth in the beginning was the truth in the end: no evidence, just a distrust of Tenenbaum's religion.

In some convoluted way, part of him was looking forward to seeing Simonini. There was a small victory at least in being cleared and returning to TACOM, even when some there seemed focused on putting him away for life.

He and Madeline whispered deep into the night as he prepared to return to work the next day in April of 1998. Madeline tried to reassure him that everything would be all right. Tenenbaum was less than convinced.

Madeline fell asleep. Her husband tossed and turned, then, fearing he'd keep his wife awake, he finally settled on his back and stared up at the ceiling. He listened to Madeline's breath. He forced himself to be still and listen to the creaks of his house. It wasn't over. Not by a long shot. Life would never be normal again.

THE MARBLE ER

The US Army Hospital in Baghdad was set up within what had been the Ba'ath Party's private hospital, "Ibn Sina." Ba'ath government officials once had their own rooms, each designed to fill visitors with awe of the occupant's wealth and glory, but they were now filled with countless hospital beds and groaning soldiers. The largest and most opulent of these rooms, which had been reserved only for fallen dictator Saddam Hussein, became the ER.

Crystal chandeliers hung overhead. The Italian marble walls and floors were frequently splattered with blood.

The helicopters were the doctors' first alert that new patients were coming. Their rhythmic thunder often mingled with the nearby bells that five times a day called Muslims to prayer. The doctors saw bullet wounds and concussions, but most frequent were the maimings, shrapnel, and burned flesh from IEDs.

Soldiers rushed in, carrying others on gurneys, teeth clenched in pain, desert camouflage uniforms standing out against the palace's white marble.

The doctors went to work, taking X-rays, discovering the shrapnel that littered the soldiers' bodies, examining the shattered bones, deciding if limbs could be saved, and acting to ensure as many lives as possible could be preserved.

Yet for so many soldiers, the option for saved limbs was lost because the limbs themselves were lost. IEDs blasted through the underside of the soldiers' Humvees, and no flak jackets, sandbags, or seat arrangements could protect them.

Blood dripped onto the floor, flowing from the wounds left by amputations from force, from surprise, from explosions that rocked vehicles and lives.

One soldier's foot used to be at the end of his leg, where it was supposed to be. He blinked, going in and out of consciousness, staring blankly at the grandiose columns that surrounded him and his fellow patients.

Another soldier raced into the room holding a five-gallon plastic bucket.

"I've got it!" he shouted to the doctors. "I've got it!" he repeated when no one turned his way.

"What?"

He stepped forward to show the huddled medics what his bucket held: the foot of the first soldier. He had found it down the road from the explosion.

Every man and woman in the room wanted to be surprised. But they weren't. Blood was everywhere. The sharp smell of it soaked into their skin, overwhelming almost any other sense of observation. This was Baghdad. This was war. This assistance from a soldier who would run down the street to find his buddy's foot was as good as it got.[1]

CHAPTER 19

THE RETURN TO BASE

"To err is human. To forgive is Divine.
Neither of which is Army policy."

—ANONYMOUS

nvoluntarily, Tenenbaum's eyes darted to the rearview mirror over and over again as he drove the short distance to the base the next morning. He pushed his foot on the pedal reluctantly, not sure if he wanted to speed or slow down to a crawl. If a car followed a little too closely, he squinted and wondered if it was an unmarked federal vehicle driven by an agent.

As he drove the streets, weaving through morning traffic, the familiarity was shadowed by trepidation. His hands sweated. He checked his mirrors again. The chain-link fence and security gate came into view for the first time in a year and a half.

Before he was allowed to enter his old building, building 200, where he had worked since he entered government service almost fourteen years of *loyal* service ago, he needed to get a new badge and parking decal to replace the ones that had been confiscated from him those many months ago. With all the stress inflicted on him, it felt like a lifetime ago. In all these months, the weight of the threat of life imprisonment had pressed down upon him. Even when there were light moments—when there were those suspended-in-time memories when his kids had made faces or had been silly, or when he had watched them sleep peacefully, the shadows of dreams fluttering across their eyelids— he had been unable to truly enjoy those feelings. Each happy moment had been suppressed, tamped down by the heart-palpitating thought that Snyder had been abusive and willing to blatantly lie and that Simonini would stop at nothing to save face—even if it meant Tenenbaum's imprisonment.

Tenenbaum arrived at the security building a few minutes before seven o'clock. He wondered if the base cop who had taken his badge and used it to scrape off his parking decal would be the one giving him the new decal and badge. He was thankful it wasn't. After picking up his badge and decal, he drove to building 200. First, he would meet with McClelland, and then he was to see the director, Jerry Chapin, who wanted to speak with him before he settled back into his job.

He parked his car and slowly made his way into the building. This was not going to be easy. He had been front-page news around the world, but nowhere more than the "ground zero" of Detroit. Once he was cleared, the army hadn't called a press conference to say, "Sorry, we made a mistake." As far as Tenenbaum and his supporters knew, only one Detroit paper had run any kind of story on the fact that he was cleared. It hadn't been on the front page, though. Instead, that newspaper buried the fact that he was not guilty of any crime against the United States of America right near the obituary section in less than an inch of space.

Tenenbaum entered the squat building and quickly made his way to Dr. McClelland's office, which was about a sixty-second walk from the building entranceway. He tried to walk casually, without artifice. He tried to relax the tension in his face, to look calm and comfortable. A narcissist, which he knew he was not, would have relished the attention, perhaps. Instead, he fought the feeling that everyone was staring at him. He was ushered into McClelland's office with its familiar military-issue shelving and chairs and desk, and a wall decorated with awards, diplomas, and military photographs.

"In a few days," McClelland said, "everyone will be used to you being back."

The deputy director of TARDEC did not tell him, however, that he had spent some of his time in the days prior to Tenenbaum's return visiting the desks and work areas in TARDEC where Tenenbaum was likely to interact. McClelland delivered the same speech over and over.

He advised Tenenbaum's civilian and military coworkers to welcome him back and "be nice."[1]

Tenenbaum wondered, when he later heard this, if this was a military installation or a sandbox.

Across the desk from a man who seemed to be treating him with respect, Tenenbaum's emotions bounced from once extreme to the other. He did not know how he would be looked at by his peers, or if he would be accepted back. He was furious as he contemplated what he had experienced over the last eighteen months. He knew that he would be seeing people, "colleagues," who had wanted him charged and convicted. There would be people he had shared conversations with or passed in the hallway who, behind his back, had called him "our little Jewish spy" or "little Jew bastard."

Emily Bacon's callous email to Jerry Chapin had made clear they would use the flimsiest of excuses to rid themselves of him forever. He knew that he was not wanted. He also did not want to be there, but he had no choice. What other job opportunities would he have? If he walked away, the internet would betray him, and no one in private industry would hire him. If he left, he gave up government benefits and healthcare and an eventual pension. It also meant they "won."

He wasn't going to let them.

Would they try to plant something in his desk to get rid of him? He would put nothing past them, not anymore, and he discussed this very idea with his attorney before returning.

When McClelland stood and his chair screeched against the floor, Tenenbaum flinched. He swallowed, feeling his heart beat rapidly in his chest as his hands went cold. The deputy director walked with him down the familiar halls that had once been a comfort zone for him. He knew they never would be again.

Behind every glance, every person whose hand he shook, and every movement he made, he wondered if others were whispering "traitor" behind closed doors. Or worse yet, "We're not done with you yet."

One associate shared that McClelland told the engineers to go over to Tenenbaum's desk and say hello and welcome him back. But many were afraid of associating with him because it could have been bad for their own careers. How could they be sure that he wasn't guilty? Maybe there just was not enough evidence to convict him. Maybe he was a traitor.

When Tenenbaum ran into engineers from his old group, each one ignored him and turned their head away from him. These were the engineers, his "colleagues," who told the FBI that he had done something wrong and that he couldn't be trusted. They did not know that Tenenbaum had read what they told the FBI about him.

Others told him, "You, being an Orthodox Jew with 'ties' to Israel, were in the wrong place at the wrong time."

Tenenbaum's new office space was on the opposite side of building 200 from where he used to work. The powers that be clearly wanted to keep him as far away from his original group as possible. By now, they knew via his attorney, Marty Crandall—who was essentially no longer needed now that Tenenbaum was not under criminal investigation—that Tenenbaum was completely aware of some of the ridiculous statements and accusations against him. Tenenbaum could think of no other person whose *backpack* was cited as reason for suspicion of espionage—not to mention the imaginings of a dream.

To keep things as neutral as possible until the situation settled down, Tenenbaum would report directly to Dr. McClelland. Although he would be using the desk area, he would not be answering to anyone within the group where he was placed. The manager of the group told him that the area where his new desk was located would be a perfect place for him because there was not a lot of traffic or people. It was a good thing people wouldn't see much of him, the man implied. He was put into hiding.

Like being in a witness protection program, thought Tenenbaum, *only who was being protected from whom?*

Tenenbaum could not help but recall Good Cop/Bad Cop, who had warned him of the "Gordie Howe" mushroom treatment. They had said if he didn't cooperate, he would be placed in a chilly, dark corner, dealing with only the foulest of manure.

I'm a mushroom now, Tenenbaum mused.

The group director told him maybe he should start "his new job" by reading *Army Science* magazine.

Tenenbaum was incredulous. *This* was what he spent years going to school for? To sit in a corner flipping the pages of a magazine with no interactions with colleagues? He was horrified. It was worse than he could have imagined because he had gone through eighteen months of pure hell—cleared his name—and it was meaningless on the base. He had come up with the idea for LASS, obtained funding for it, and now he was supposed to sit tucked away, reading magazines?

He was left alone in the silent cubicle. A magazine had been left on his desk. He ran his hands through his hair and rested his palm on his yarmulke, searching for strength, searching for composure.

A few minutes later, Tenenbaum was called into the Director of TARDEC Jerry Chapin's office. Chapin's administrative assistant was there, as well as a handful of others.

"Welcome back, David. We just wanted a brief meeting to avoid any pitfalls and to exercise cautions as to how we move forward." Chapin started off the conversation gently. "First, I just want to say that the accusations did not just affect you but the entire Research and Development Center. We don't want to put you at risk unnecessarily. All the charges have been dropped, and we will start you off like a new engineer."

Tenenbaum felt his blood pressure rising. Chapin opened his mouth to continue, but Tenenbaum interrupted. This was the "new" David Tenenbaum. The new David Tenenbaum had very little left to lose. The new David Tenenbaum was disgusted by the bigotry in the DOD. The new David Tenenbaum was not going to be victimized anymore. He raised his hand to stop Chapin mid-sentence.

"Hold on. Hold on just one minute here," he said in a firm voice. He looked directly at Chapin. "Let me make this clear: there were never any charges, just baseless, anti-Semitic accusations. Also, I am *not* a new engineer. I have been an engineer for over twenty years. And did you say it affected everyone...are you serious?"

He wanted to add, *and I created LASS to save lives, and you cowards dismantled it.*

"Well, yes," Chapin stammered. He seemed to struggle to regain his footing. He backtracked slightly. "I meant that we..." He let the thought hang in the air, appearing to think better of it. "Anyway, you will be assigned to work directly for Dr. McClelland. You can't go back to the Survivability Division. You can't go back to your old programs. We have either shut them down or given them to other engineers. You can't work with the Israelis anymore. And, oh, by the way, your security clearance is being revoked."

Tenenbaum looked at Chapin incredulously.

"Wow, and to think what would have happened had I been guilty."

In fact, Tenenbaum mused, he *was* guilty—of being Jewish. Horror of horrors, he kept kosher! It would all be funny if it hadn't destroyed his career, terrified his wife, children, and mother, strained his marriage—and drained his bank account.

There was silence. Tenenbaum scanned the faces of the other people in the room. Most just avoided eye contact.

"We will provide you a list of reasons as to why your security clearance is being revoked," Chapin began again. "There are two lists. One is classified and one is unclassified."

Later Tenenbaum began reading the list. He noticed that the classified reasons for which the army/TACOM had decided to revoke his security clearance were public information and had been written in various newspapers in one form or another over the past eighteen months. The reasons were not classified at all. Tenenbaum pointed this "mistake" out, and he was told that they would look into it. Eventually the army changed the classification to unclassified. Had the army refused to change the classification, it would have made it very difficult for Tenenbaum to work with attorneys and others to provide any type of explanation for the "classified" accusations.

However, this was a pattern that would continue—to this very day, as of this writing. Any time the DOD did not want to answer for their bigotry, they would label the events or information "classified." But the blacked-out "classified" information was never anything more than common knowledge.

Tenenbaum left the Chapin meeting utterly disheartened—and furious. He sat down again with Dr. McClelland.

"They should never have rehired Simonini," the deputy director said. Tenenbaum felt the muscles in his body tighten. He had heard about Simonini's retirement and had hoped that it would offer him at least a small amount of serenity, but he listened to McClelland explain how the lieutenant colonel had taken retirement then was rehired, double-dipping financially, one pension on top of another.

One of the highest-ranking civilians at TACOM, Doug Newberry, was a good friend of Simonini—and Newberry made the decision to bring Simonini back as a civilian after he did not receive his promotion to colonel and retired as a lieutenant colonel.

According to his former right-hand man, Simonini had never had his own command, and he was passed over for promotions repeatedly in an almost "unheard of" way.[2] Now, according to Dr. McClelland, it was Newberry's fault that they—TACOM—were stuck with Simonini, a slovenly dresser and poorly-regarded boss, who was faulted for his temper, abusive nature, and violent verbal tirades, including frequent threats to punch underlings "in the face." Again. Dr. McClelland expressed no respect for Newberry, but this detail didn't comfort Tenenbaum in the least.

"He allowed Simonini to create this mess. But this is where we are now," Dr. McClelland told Tenenbaum. "You should be aware that you will never get another security clearance. Your career is, for all intents and purposes, over. Without a security clearance, you will never get promoted. Actually, you will never again get promoted with or without a security clearance."

Tenenbaum clasped his hands in his lap so they wouldn't be visible shaking. McClelland reached into his desk and pulled out Tenenbaum's travel orders, submitted in November 1995 before a trip to Israel, and showed him the paperwork.

"Remember these? You were actually under investigation at the time you submitted these orders."

McClelland was not telling Tenenbaum this out of unkindness, as far as Tenenbaum could tell. And he considered himself a fine judge of character. He was explaining to Tenenbaum that all was not as it appeared; he was pulling the veil back on what the engineer was up against upon his return.

"Since you've been off the base, there is no longer an Israeli liaison officer at TACOM anymore."

"Why?"

"Simonini got rid of him." McClelland gave an almost impercep-
tible shake of the head. Tenenbaum later learned the officer had been
escorted off base by armed US military. "Look, David, you need to find
something to do. They are looking for an excuse to get rid of you."

"That's crystal clear. But how am I supposed to find work to do if no
one will work with me and I have no funds for any type of program?"
Tenenbaum blinked and tried not to let his mind wander to the battlefield, where, he was certain, soldiers experienced injury after injury,
death after death without LASS. He wasn't a doctor. This was the only
way he could think of to help.

"I can start you off with a small amount of funding. But for right
now, we put you in your new area to keep you away from your old
group and relieve tensions. One of your attorney friends also spoke
with me before you came back to TARDEC and told me that the best
person to work the Israeli programs is you, and that I would be crazy
not to use you. I did not disagree, but for obvious reasons, that will not
be happening."

Tenenbaum left McClelland's office even more disheartened. He
had tried to fight to get the LASS program reestablished but was told,
flat out, that he could not work with the Israelis anymore. No one could
give Tenenbaum a good reason why.

He returned to his "new accommodations" and began his "new"
career as a glorified file clerk. What a welcome back to "celebrate" his
innocence. He was given various types of technical planning documents, all unclassified, and told to make sure that they had the proper
signatures on them and to file them. He had once been nominated for
the prestigious SEEP assignment and advanced management track.
Now? A high school drop-out could have performed these tasks.
Actually, his five-year-old daughter could probably have done them
just as well.

One of his former colleagues, Ken, came to Tenenbaum's desk to
sign one of the documents. Ken had always struck Tenenbaum as a
decent, straightforward guy. Tenenbaum began to walk Ken back down
the hall towards his office, and he noticed that his colleague seemed
nervous, their small talk awkward and jumpy. They stopped walking
for a moment.

"Are you all right?" Tenenbaum asked. "You seem nervous."

"I don't want to be seen with you. People might get suspicious. I don't want them to do to me what they did to you."

Tenenbaum tried not to show his surprise, but he also did not want to make Ken nervous or uncomfortable. So, he just told Ken that he understood and watched as his colleague walked down the hall toward his own area. As he stood alone in the hallway, Tenenbaum's isolation was overwhelming. He hadn't thought returning to work would be easy—and he knew the stress of eighteen months of suspension had worn him down. However, he had thought once he was back at TARDEC that at least his work friends would be there for him. He had understood—or tried to—why they hadn't reached out during the months of suspension. Legal concerns would have prevented those communications. But he was back at work, back on base—with the support of Dr. McClelland. Surely now, some of them would rally around him.

They had once laughed and talked endlessly at shared dinners, mingling with each other's families. However, that seemed to be over. Ken was not the only one who was nervous around him. Tenenbaum ran into other people he knew and had been friendly with who either turned around and walked in the opposite direction or just ignored him and looked away from him or down at the floor. He was a pariah. He could have understood if he had been caught revealing classified information to Israel. But he hadn't. He had done nothing wrong.

He wanted to shout down the hall, "Your cowardly SAEDAs were lies! You're the ones who should be in jail, and our soldiers are going to be your victims!"

One of his other colleagues/former friends told him that if he was ordered to work with Tenenbaum, he would investigate Tenenbaum himself to see if Tenenbaum had the proper "need to know"—and even then, he would work with him reluctantly, if at all. Welcome back.

A small handful of past friends at TACOM, who were a little more talkative, told Tenenbaum that people were absolutely going to be very cautious around him. Most on base viewed Tenenbaum as guilty—but that there was just not enough evidence to convict him. Rumors floated that the Tenenbaum case had been mishandled from the start—just not for the obvious reasons Tenenbaum himself was aware of. Instead, his coworkers thought the army should have conducted more research first before they jumped the gun and accused him of treason—this would have avoided "tipping him off," and he might have been caught red-handed.

It's nice to have friends, Tenenbaum thought to himself.

One of Tenenbaum's colleagues told him that Jack Parks, Tenenbaum's old supervisor, held a meeting with some of the TARDEC employees he supervised and instructed them, "If you want to be cordial, be my guest and be cordial—but don't speak to him about work. Don't leave any papers or documents in the open where he could see them. We need to put cyber locks on the office doors so Tenenbaum cannot enter the offices."

Like the internet, which to this day offers tens of thousands of links professing Tenenbaum's guilt, squashing the rumor mill at TACOM would have taken motivated leadership willing to proclaim his innocence. There is a huge difference between declaring someone is innocent and stating "If there was evidence, the FBI would have found it" due to how thorough they were, versus they just don't have "enough evidence" to convict him. The latter seemed to be the prevailing TACOM rumor. They just hadn't been able to "catch" him. TACOM's leadership apparently was unwilling to give credit to the truth. The consequence was further humiliation for David Tenenbaum.

While Dr. McClelland was now considered his immediate supervisor, a different man was assigned to keep track of his time. Every morning like clockwork, Gil would come by Tenenbaum's desk, the one placed out of the way of people, where he could not be seen unless you were trying to find him. He would say good morning, but it was always clear he was checking up on Tenenbaum, making sure he was coming to work on time.

"Dave, I noticed that you were a minute late today," he said one day. "How do you want to take that…annual leave, vacation time, sick leave…?"

Tenenbaum at first thought he was kidding, but the man's straight face showed he was serious, matter-of-fact. This was just how he was doing business, how he was going to treat Tenenbaum. One minute. On a rare occasion. Everything needed to be accounted for in his mind.

Tenenbaum spoke about the awkward treatment with McClelland, but the zealous micromanaging didn't change. A number of weeks later, Tenenbaum was out sick for a number of days, ill to the degree that he was being taken care of by his close friend, Dr. Mark Meissner. Upon returning to work, his supervisor approached him and asked for a doctor's note, something for which Tenenbaum had never been asked before. Tenenbaum answered honestly that he didn't have one, but he was sure to deliver a note from Dr. Meissner the next day. He would not want to give anyone even a hint of suspicious behavior, and the communication was easy enough to obtain.

Yet, a few days later, his supervisor asked to speak with Tenenbaum in his office.

"What's up?" Tenenbaum asked as he took a seat in one of the chairs opposite the desk inside the small office.

"There is no such person, Doctor Meissner." His supervisor didn't hold his eyes.

Tenenbaum took a breath before he spoke.

"This is a joke, isn't it?"

"No, I looked him up. There is no Doctor Meissner."

"You actually looked him up because…"

"There is no Doctor Meissner."

"Do you want me to tell him that, or should we keep it between ourselves?"

"Doctor Meissner doesn't exist."

"You seriously think I made up being sick in bed for the past four days and I played with my imaginary friend Mark Meissner? You think I am lying?"

The clock on the wall ticked loudly in the space between them. Neither man immediately spoke.

"I looked him up, and I made a few phone calls."

"Doctor Meissner is not just a cardiologist; he is an electrophysiologist which is a specialty within cardiology."

He explained Dr. Meissner's specialty and their relationship to each other, going into detail which he knew was unnecessary, speaking slowly and wishing he had a recording device to preserve the absurd everyday conversations that now were the norm of his working life.

Tenenbaum found out later that, yes indeed, his supervisor did make a few phone calls. This supervisor, who was only in charge of keeping Tenenbaum's time, was playing not "*Where's Waldo?*" but "Where's Meissner?" The conversation was just one more area of his professional life where things had gone too far. He went to Dr. McClelland, told him what happened, and said in so many words that it would be best if he and his time management supervisor "broke up." The relationship didn't seem like it was beneficial in any direction. McClelland agreed, and he began to take care of Tenenbaum's time himself.

Tenenbaum's computer and personal items, as well as any other project notes he had taken before suspension (BS), had been boxed and placed in storage under lock and key. He was allowed access to his personal items now, but everything else was off limits.

Tenenbaum overheard Ed Lowe, the chief of the international office, say that the international office in their building was now considered a "restricted" area. All roads at TACOM having to do with anti-Semitism and suspicion of Tenenbaum seemed to lead to Simonini.

Walt Wynbelt, another executive at TARDEC, was surprised when Tenenbaum told him that his security clearance was in the process of being revoked. Wynbelt felt certain that Simonini was the person who was spearheading the revocation. Wynbelt, a supporter of the LASS proposal who had even discussed the LASS program with the Israelis when he was in Israel, wanted to know why the life-saving program had been suspended and—importantly—why it was never restarted when Tenenbaum was brought back to TACOM. He was not happy because he felt that LASS was an important program for the US Army. Important to the nation's fighting warriors.

After all, those slogans were painted on the walls to "protect our warfighters."

But they were empty words. Tenenbaum was beginning to see that too.

CHAPTER 20

A CRUSADER IS BORN

*"The only thing necessary for the triumph of evil
is for good men to do nothing."*

—EDMUND BURKE

Tenenbaum was a man with nothing to lose, and with nothing to lose, he decided to sue the United States government. He had to sue to keep his job. He wasn't looking for revenge. He was looking for vindication. He was looking for someone to say, "We messed up, and I'm sorry."

Based on information he had gathered, he knew that it was all a setup. The case against him was based in deep-rooted anti-Semitism within many levels of the government and its army. What he needed was an accomplished attorney who would handle a case of bias. Someone fearless and unafraid to go up against the government. A David willing to take on Goliath. And he found one in the person of Juan Mateo.

Tenenbaum knew that he was going to need a new attorney. The espionage case was over. He didn't need a criminal attorney to fight for him anymore. He needed someone who would stand up for his rights, the equality of his citizenship, and his humanity. He met a number of lawyers, seeking the right fit.

The basis of Tenenbaum's claim was that he was singled out for being Jewish. There was not one shred of evidence that should have raised any red flags. The reason to pursue him was solely, Tenenbaum knew and his attorney affirmed, that he was profiled.

Mateo took the case because, as a man of Hispanic descent, profiling was something, he told Tenenbaum, that he found personally abhorrent.

He took the case on a contingency basis—Tenenbaum's original criminal defense attorney had eaten up his life savings, as the original case was one of defense against criminal allegations—specifically espionage. Now, he needed an attorney who could go on the offensive. Mateo was a strong attorney who relentlessly deposed and questioned witnesses. His depositions were, in the opinion of many attorneys and supporters since, gifted in their crafting, homing in relentlessly on discrepancies and ideological differences.

In the beginning of Tenenbaum's lawsuit in 1998, Tenenbaum and Mateo had two years of discovery, which allowed them access to documents and the ability to depose under oath numerous individuals sworn to the truth in their testimony. The documents provided staggering information. The deposed individuals confirmed what Tenenbaum and his attorney already knew: Tenenbaum was profiled because of his religion.

During this time, Tenenbaum spoke with one of Simonini's security personnel, who was kind enough to provide Tenenbaum with advice on an attorney for his lawsuit. He said to Tenenbaum, "I know you have a sense of humor, so you must have a Jewish lawyer. If you want a good lawyer, get a guy named Goldstein or Goldberger…you know, a guy with the right name." He didn't seem to realize Tenenbaum's uncomfortable reaction, the internal wince at how his comment spoke to the core of the problem. Instead, he continued, "You should know that everyone is going to be on pins and needles around you. You are suing our office."

But suing the government was the only option Tenenbaum had left.

The stacks of documents and depositions would eventually fill boxes and boxes, filling the Tenenbaum dining room table and standing in stacks on the carpeted basement floor. None of it looked very good for the government. Tenenbaum hadn't taken any secret meetings. His bank account didn't suddenly swell because a foreign government was paying him for his betrayal. There was nothing about Tenenbaum that would convince any sane person in the private sector that he was a spy. There was nothing about Tenenbaum that would convince any sane person in the government that he was a spy.

But Simonini felt that Tenenbaum being a Jew—and only that—meant he was ripe for Israel's picking.

Tenenbaum had to give Dr. Richard McClelland credit. He told the truth under oath. According to testimony from McClelland, the director of TARDEC at TACOM:

Q: Do you think the fact that he [Tenenbaum] is Jewish and spoke Hebrew on base and wears a yarmulke [skullcap] on base was a factor in the thinking of the people who were investigating him and/or alleging that he was doing something improper with the Israelis?

A: Yes

Q: Are you aware of any similarly situated employee who was required to undergo a polygraph examination during an investigation that was being conducted by Mr. Simonini and others?

A: No…

Q: All right. There has been testimony on this record that Mr. Tenenbaum was simply subjected to a routine security clearance investigation. Is that your understanding of what happened to Mr. Tenenbaum or not?

A: No.

Q: What is your understanding of what happened with Mr. Tenenbaum?

A: That they told David that it was happening as part of his upgrade investigation, but without question, it was part of the investigation.

Q: Part of the investigation into his…?

A: Alleged wrongdoing.

Q: And the alleged wrongdoing having to be when Simonini alleged earlier to you in December that he had passed on either unauthorized or classified information to the Israelis?

A: Yes.

Q: Has any other similarly situated employee been subjected to this type of process that Mr. Tenenbaum was?

A: To my knowledge, no.[1]

Dr. McClelland, speaking honestly, was very straightforward in stating that Tenenbaum was singled out because he was Jewish. He was also very clear in his belief that Tenenbaum was pushed into applying for a higher-level clearance as a ruse to criminally investigate him for espionage. So why did Simonini and company suspect Tenenbaum of espionage? According to testimony from Gugino:

> He traveled without the group of colleagues and others that were traveling to foreign countries. He usually made his own airline reservations, which was outside US Army regulations or maybe even US government regulation, requiring that US airlines are used for flights to foreign countries. He did not participate in group activities with his colleagues. Generally, he spent time with foreign nationals when he was in foreign countries.[2]

The highly skilled Mateo was able to rip apart this line of thinking. In fact, the arguments were those a first-year law clerk could have handled. The government posited that Tenenbaum did not travel with colleagues when he traveled overseas. But the reason Tenenbaum traveled alone was that in all of his travels overseas except for one, he was sent alone—so there was no one from TACOM to travel with. On one trip to Israel where he traveled by himself but *could* have traveled with colleagues, he did not travel as early as his colleagues by personal choice, and he did not travel on a Saturday because it was the Sabbath. From sundown on Friday to sundown on Saturday, he is forbidden by the tenets of his Jewish Orthodox religion to use electricity or his car. He certainly could not travel via air carrier.

The government decried that he made his own travel reservations as opposed (supposedly) to almost all of his colleagues. Here again, Simonini had been deceptive in order to blatantly manipulate the FBI into opening an investigation. Tenenbaum had written authorization to travel on a non-US air carrier (El-AL Airlines, the Israel national airline) when he travelled to Israel because of safety issues. El-AL has an extraordinary record in the unstable Middle East. Whenever he traveled to any other country, such as Canada or any location in Europe, he traveled on the required US air carrier.

The idea that his lack of participation in group activities with his colleagues, such as going to restaurants, was somehow indicative of spying was too silly to even contemplate. Obviously, this item could be instantly stricken from the record because Tenenbaum eats only kosher food and was uncomfortable dining in a non-kosher restaurant, bringing his own food to eat when he absolutely needed to do so.

The government then complained that Tenenbaum spent time with foreign nationals when he traveled overseas to a foreign country. Gugino and others used the term "foreign national" like it was a dirty word. The point of Dr. Tenenbaum traveling to foreign countries—travel that was at the *insistence* of the American government he dedicated his career to—was to meet with and work with the people of the country to which he traveled. Colleagues from foreign countries are termed "foreign nationals." His travel orders stated that he would and should be meeting with specific foreign nationals.

Tenenbaum was astounded by the lengths certain players would go to in order to make him sound like a spy. It was mostly semantics. The government could try all it wanted to make it sound nefarious, but there was simply nothing there—just ephemeral accusations. However, he was heartened by how the case was going. Point by point, discovery by discovery, testimony by testimony, document by document, his lawyer was taking apart the government's case.

In addition, the judge they drew on the bench, Victoria Roberts, was a federal judge who, though new, was recognized by lawyers as fair. Mateo and Tenenbaum didn't win every point, but they didn't lose every point either. She was, Tenenbaum felt, neutral.

Then, as the case was drawing well past the halfway point, with no warning, the judge was removed. She was removed only after, by most legal analyses, the government was losing.

Suddenly, Robert Cleland, a federal judge who was based in Port Huron, "decided" he wanted to come to Detroit out of the clear blue.

Victoria Roberts had been a newly appointed judge. With little senior-ity on the bench, the case was reassigned to Judge Cleland.

After the change happened, one of the US prosecutors was over-heard in the hallway saying to a colleague, "We will *never* settle this case. We have got the best judge in the courtroom."

Tenenbaum was told that, in some circles, Cleland's reputation was that of the government's judge. So much for justice being blind.

Tenenbaum was stunned and nauseated by the developments. His own deposition had been contentious and grueling due to unwarranted personal attacks even after the persecution of the investigation, and the same held true for Madeline. As a couple, they had been put through the wringer. They were forced to discuss the intimacies of their marriage, their mental health, their children, and their relationship. In addition to the emotional fallout of the government's relentless persecution of him, he was aware that his earning potential was limited by the case. As McClelland had already told him, his once-bright future was doomed. No one would promote him or hire him. Plus, he was in danger of being fired—the government was looking for a way to be rid of him.

Shortly after the suspicious change of the judge on the bench, Tenenbaum and his attorneys were asked to go to a mediation confer-ence with Judge Benny Friedman presiding. Tenenbaum, his attorneys, and the government's attorneys sat in a room around a long conference table together trying to hammer out some type of settlement.

"We won't give you a dime," stated one of the more vocal attorneys from the US Prosecutor's Office.

Tenenbaum glared across the table. There it was. Rather than arriv-ing at mediation and finding a fair settlement for what he and his family had been subjected to, the prosecutors had all the confidence in the world that Judge Cleland was pro-government. As far as they were con-cerned, it appeared they already believed they had "won" the case, even though testimony had already been given that exposed the anti-Semitic agenda behind the investigation. What would be considered religious discrimination in private industry—and could even be considered a hate crime—was apparently business as usual for Uncle Sam.

MIKE HELMS, INSULT TO INJURY

As Tenenbaum knew, a government of the people, by the people, and for the people was not always made up of individuals who made choices that treated all of its people fairly. Sometimes judges were switched in the middle of a trial; sometimes whistleblowers like Franz Gayl were silenced and reprimanded; sometimes, the government's own rules and regulations weren't followed.

In 2004, when Mike Helms, a soldier turned civilian intelligence specialist, was deployed to the army's 902nd Military Intelligence Group in Iraq, he found himself authorized to act as a lead gunner. According to Helms, this military assistance was due to not enough trained military crew on the taskforce.[1] He had served three tours in the Balkans from 1996 to 2001, so he felt comfortable giving this assistance.[2] He worked with the soldiers, ate with the soldiers, and even entered conflict areas with them. Though a civilian, he was treated in every way like military personnel.

In June of that year, he acted as the gunner of the lead Humvee of a military convoy moving across Iraq's Sunni Triangle. The desert heat was brutal. Their line was steady, efficient, and a target on wheels. When they hit the IED, two thousand rounds of ammunition were blown from their vehicle.[3] The left side of their Humvee was mangled, and Helms lost consciousness, at first assumed to be dead.[4]

His brain trauma and severe shrapnel injuries showed little improvement after a week at the 31st Combat Support Hospital in Tikrit, so he was transported to a military hospital in Landstuhl, Germany. Yet, it was upon his release and return trip to the United States that his troubles worsened. Instead of traveling with the other battle-wounded leaving the hospital, he was asked to book and pay for his own commercial flight.[5] He was not a soldier, they said. He was not entitled to the benefits of those in the military service.

Helms went to Walter Reed National Military Medical Center in Bethesda, Maryland, as directed but was turned away. As a private citizen, his injuries fell under the Federal Workers' Compensation Program, he was told—even though DOD regulations clearly state that civilians deployed within a war zone are supposed to receive the same treatment as members of the military.

The civilian doctors who treated him had little experience with battle wounds. He was suffering from PTSD without an environment to support him.[6]

Helms struggled to become well—physically and mentally—knowing there were others who also fell in between the cracks, others who risked their lives in the support of their country only to be forgotten. In fact, between 2001 and 2007, roughly 7,500 civilians for the DOD worked in combat zones or in anti-terrorism capacities. Of these, seven died, and at least 118 were injured.[7]

"We must use government civilians…to fill out the force or we could not do our job right now," said Gary J. Motsek, assistant deputy under the secretary of defense for program support. Motsek called these civilians "unheralded patriots," but these words didn't always translate to fair treatment.[8]

When no army hospitals or other military personnel would assist him, Mike Helms went to the House Armed Services subcommittee, and later, the press.

Shortly thereafter, Helms's security clearance was revoked, and an investigation began around him concerning a server that he had created, which had a recent addition of malicious software and sexually explicit material. According to the IG, this material could have been introduced by any of multiple people who had access to the server.

"They interviewed no one but me, then busted me on having an illegal copy of Windows," said Helms, referring to the end of this process. "It should have been a slap on the wrist."

Yet it was the matter of his livelihood. And his health. And his efforts to help others in a similar position. Mike Helms was awarded the Secretary of Defense Medal for the Defense of Freedom, the civilian equivalent to the Purple Heart, but he still suffers from the lingering medical issues of the IED explosion.

Whether attempting to be proactive with the Humvees like Tenenbaum, trying to respond to a vehicle not working well like Franz Gayl, or ensuring equality of treatment after meeting an IED and injuries have been sustained, these civilian whistleblowers found themselves in a similar relationship with their government. They dedicated their lives and their voices to ensuring the safety and fair treatment of American soldiers and those in harm's way. They all continue to hope that it wasn't all in vain.

CHAPTER 21

THE VEIL OF STATE SECRETS

"It is by the goodness of God that in our country we have those three unspeakably precious things: freedom of speech, freedom of conscience, and the prudence never to practice either."

—MARK TWAIN

Judge Cleland did not disappoint the government.

When mediation failed to reach any result—with no middle ground whatsoever—the case dragged on. The taxpayers paid. The testimony continued.

Albert Snyder, Tenenbaum's abusive interrogator, swore that Judaism and religion were not even discussed in the polygraph. In a pattern that began behind the scenes in Simonini's and the various governments players' conduct, a pattern that would be repeated over and over again like a broken record, Snyder directly contradicted himself. He lied in either one place or the other.

For a polygraph examination that Snyder swore never even *brought up* religion, faith, or Judaism, his report to the FBI said that Tenenbaum's *number-one priority* in his life was his *religion,* then his children, and then his wife. So, either he spoke of religion, which meant Snyder lied when he said religion never came up, or he didn't speak of religion or faith, which means Snyder lied when he submitted his report. The fact that Snyder destroyed the notes he took extemporaneously complicated matters.

Lieutenant Colonel John Simonini himself had brought his biases into the Tenenbaum case. Here was a man in charge of the base's security who had been passed over for both his own command and promotion to colonel. A micromanager, he created stress in those who reported to him with abusive language and threats of violence. His discriminatory and biased attitude had an effect on others involved in the Tenenbaum case. As head of the Counterintelligence Division, Simonini was being relied upon to provide unbiased information to the base general and other executives at TACOM/TARDEC.

But Simonini's statements in court were an embarrassment. He felt free telling anyone and everyone who would listen to his strident voice that Tenenbaum's desire for a kosher diet and Jewish religion could be "exploited" by Israel. And with these blatantly anti-Semitic statements, TARDEC/TACOM not only protected Simonini but actually promoted him. What did that say about the executive leadership of a prominent army installation? Did they and do they still agree with his bigoted views?

The US government was not going to allow Simonini's statements to make the front pages—nor were they going to let Tenenbaum come out victorious.

Instead, the government invoked what is known as the state secrets privilege, claiming the case was about an issue pertaining to national security—a vague, easily exploited term. Criticized since its inception by the American Civil Liberties Union and legal scholars, the state secrets privilege allows the government to invoke a veil behind which no one can look.

It has been consistently misused.

The state secrets privilege was given its name in 1953 after the government attempted to invoke a privilege in response to a lawsuit by the relatives of civilian pilots killed in a military plane crash. The government claimed—without proof—that revealing elements of the case in open court would mean exposing state secrets that needed to remain classified. There was no way for the lawsuit to proceed, the government argued, because information that was fundamental to the case to counter the assertion that the plane was faulty was privileged.

Years later, elements of the case were declassified.

Tragically, what was also uncovered was that *nothing* pertaining to the case and the discovery sought by the plaintiffs' attorneys (representing the widows and families of the pilots) was a state secret. What *was* uncovered were faulty elements to the plane, which was *embarrassing* to the government—but not classified.

Initially, the state secrets privilege was invoked *rarely*. But according to the American Civil Liberties Union, in an article written by former White House counsel John Dean, the second Bush presidency invoked it at least twenty-three times in a five-year period. In contrast, from its inception in 1953 to 1976, it was invoked four times.[1]

With the invocation of the state secrets privilege, Tenenbaum's lawsuit could proceed no further.

In the blink of an eye, it was over. Paul Wolfowitz and John Ashcroft, household names and key players in the government, who supposedly represented the highest ideals of government service, provided sealed affidavits claiming that defending the government's actions would require the revelation of state secrets. They could do this without sharing a single word of what "state secrets" would be revealed. Tenenbaum could have held the secrets of the atomic bomb—or a recipe for chocolate chip cookies. It didn't matter. Once Wolfowitz and Ashcroft sealed their affidavits, the iron curtain came down. There was nothing Tenenbaum's team could do.

The counsel defending the government and the army attorney, Uldric Fiore, who signed off on the document invoking the state secrets privilege, successfully argued that the information within those affidavits could not be revealed during a public trial.[2]

Tenenbaum's attorney's hands were tied, and his legal team seethed at the injustice of it all. They could proceed no further. The abuse of Tenenbaum was "protected" by the government's claim that classified materials would have to be discussed in open court.

But that was a masterful piece of fiction.

The LASS program was not classified. Dan Meyer, who later served as the reprisal subject-matter expert to a Title VII religious discrimination investigation by the intelligence division of the IG-DOD took the position during the investigation that there was a "small" walled-off amount of information that might be considered classified, but in terms of the information required to adjudicate Tenenbaum's claims, Tenenbaum's attorneys knew that nothing involved in the preparation of the case and no questions they intended to ask fell into the category of state secrets.

To this day, if Tenenbaum is asked certain things about the case, such as detailed questions about the data that would have been provided, he is circumspect. But the heart of the religious discrimination and bigotry would reveal none of that. Classified information wasn't necessary to the conversation.

However, what they did want to discuss was embarrassing. So in addition to the anti-Semitism evident within the US Army and later the IG-DOD, the Tenenbaum case raised—and still raises—very real questions regarding the circumstances in which unregulated federal agency attorneys can use the state secrets doctrine, FOIA laws, and the Privacy Act to shield their clients from public oversight.

TACOM was hiding a thriving group of bigots and anti-Semites. From Simonini to others higher and lower on the food chain at TACOM.

According to a high-level DOD official, it wasn't state secrets but state *embarrassment*.

But Tenenbaum was not done.

CHAPTER 22

NEW PARTNERS IN THE FIGHT

"Darkness cannot drive out darkness; only light can do that.
Hate cannot drive out hate; only love can do that."

—MARTIN LUTHER KING JR.

A few years after Tenenbaum returned from suspension, as he found his way to work in an environment where trust was still remote, where camaraderie with his colleagues was never to quite reappear, he had a meeting on a different base in a different city, with someone who dealt directly with the casualties flown from Iraq and Afghanistan. She confronted him, anguish visible on her face. She was someone who saw the injuries from IEDs in an up-close-and-personal way, countless young lives cut down in their prime.

She faced Tenenbaum in tears, horror registering in her eyes. She saw death every day in her line of work. But not like this. Not corpse after corpse with the same sorts of devastating injuries. She did not yell. She did not scream. In fact, Tenenbaum almost felt that if she had yelled, it might have been better—it somehow might have assuaged both their unwarranted feelings of guilt, as well as pain. She just looked at Tenenbaum accusingly.

"It's your fault…It's your fault," she repeated.

Tenenbaum froze in place. What could he say to her?

"Why didn't you do something about it?" she asked him. "You design the combat vehicles. You are responsible for designing and developing those HMMWVs with the proper protection. You sent them into battle with nothing to protect them. Why? You are responsible for ensuring the safety of those boys. *Boys*," she kept repeating over and over again. "They are just boys. Why didn't you do it? Why did you let this happen?"

Tenenbaum just let her vent. The person she should have been verbally attacking was a man that Tenenbaum knew now sat in his office all day, festering in his fury about Tenenbaum. But he knew this woman was speaking from a place of pain—a pain he knew all too well. He didn't know what to say. What could he say? *She was right.* The DOD owed these warfighters better.

Her shoulders slumped when she finally fell quiet.

"I tried. I *really* tried," Tenenbaum answered in a hoarse whisper, forcing himself to see and acknowledge every tear on her face. "I did try, you know. But they stopped me."

Her mouth dropped open.

"Stopped you?"

How else could he put it? He nodded. "They killed my program, and then they tried to get rid of me. I fought for close to two years to stay out of prison, and they killed my program."

Her face registered confusion. He knew that sense of confusion only too well. He had thought they were all working for the same cause. To save soldiers' lives. But now he knew better. He knew the base was twisted with petty jealousies, with an unwillingness to address bigotry, to root it out and bring it out from the shadows into the light of day.

"They killed my program, you know. Simonini, he told me he stopped the LASS program. He told me. He said, 'I don't trust you, and I don't trust the Israelis.' LASS was going to model the exact kinds of explosions these kids would come across. And we were going to change the Humvees in a way that would protect them. I can't swear that we would have stopped all the casualties, but I am sure, as sure as I am standing in front of you, that I would never have rested until I discovered a way to keep them safe."

"He didn't trust you?"

"Apparently, this thing," Tenenbaum pointed to the yarmulke on his head, "must mean, to the Simoninis of the world, that I can't be trusted. Not to mention the entire state of Israel. And by the way, we had Germany on the LASS program too. We had other partners. But he wasn't going to let it move forward."

"Isn't he head of counterintelligence?"

Tenenbaum nodded.

"He's not even an engineer."

"You're right. He's not."

The woman's face was etched with pain and disbelief. "How could anyone be so stupid, or in his case—how could he let his own biases, his own racist, anti-Semitic views impact a program which may have saved countless lives. Unbelievable...just unbelievable."

She knotted her hands in front of her. Then she bowed her head, as if collecting herself. When she looked up again, her eyes were moist.

Tenenbaum knew she had every reason to be emotional and angry. She saw things very few people stateside have ever and will ever see. She was privy to the horrors of these young people returning limbless and dead. The corpses lined up in metal coffins, heading back, eventually, to small towns and to cities, to families who loved them, who would never get over the loss. Tenenbaum saw less than she did, in terms of death and casualties, but what he saw, he would always remember. The image of dead bodies burned in his mind indelibly, and he would always, always remember. Again, the line about the Holocaust came to him. *Never forget.*

But what could he say in that moment? In any moment. It wasn't a cop-out. He did try. His attorneys kept saying that the government had blood on its hands—and they were right. And now...now they were hiding behind the state secrets privilege, claiming national security.

The army ensured that they would not be held accountable for their bigotry. They ensured that they would not be held accountable for *their* soldiers' deaths. Tenenbaum knew he did his best. But that knowledge wasn't comforting, and it wouldn't take away the nightmares and the guilt that Tenenbaum felt every day. It was this emotion knotted inside his core that made him press forward with his case. It wasn't just about justice for him. This had to be made right. Tenenbaum approached the firm of Morganroth & Morganroth, PLLC to press onward.

Mayer (Mike) Morganroth is a legend who has defended such notables as Jack Kevorkian and John DeLorean, as well as political luminaries and many others. He is deeply principled and considered one of the nation's foremost litigators. He and his son, Jeffrey Morganroth, a powerhouse lawyer in his own right, ran their firm. Receiving Tenenbaum's inquiry, a young man in the law practice, fresh out of law school, was, in his own words, "ready to cut his teeth" on a case like Tenenbaum's.

Dan Harold, now a partner in the firm, is the grandson of Holocaust survivors. When asked about the case, his deceivingly boyish good looks and ready grin darken. In law school, he had interned with William (Bill) Marks, another legendary attorney who pressed Holocaust claims for Jewish families ruined and destroyed by the Nazis.

When asked his impressions of Simonini, the cordial and warm Harold did not mince words: "Honest to God, I thought he was a Nazi. He is not some stoic military figure of honor. He was a scowling figure who is full of self-importance and propaganda."[1]

In Harold's opinion, the Tenenbaum case, "put the entire country at a disadvantage because this is not America. We are a country founded on freedom of religion."[2]

Mike Morganroth echoed Harold. Of Simonini, he said, "I thought Simonini was evil. I thought he was a liar. He thought he could get away with it because of power."[3]

When it became clear that Tenenbaum's case pressing for a settlement was going to be blocked, Juan Mateo had bowed out. To continue would have been career suicide. Morganroth & Morganroth, PLLC stepped in on principle after meeting with Tenenbaum and hearing his story. They also had, at their disposal, an entire firm of paralegals and personnel to pursue such a complex case. Through this writing, they have, they estimate, spent almost three-quarters of a million dollars pursuing justice. In the experienced litigator Mike Morganroth's estimate, the government has spent *tens of millions.* He noted one need only consider the costs alone of a detail on Tenenbaum 24/7 for months and months at a time, no doubt on overtime—let alone the litigation costs, the government's team of lawyers and clerks, and so forth.

Harold was three months into his new job with Morganroth & Morganroth, PLLC when the case came across his desk. He was ready for a fight. Fortunately, he had the resources of the powerful firm behind him. They were able to construct detailed timelines of every element of the complex case.

Buoyed by the new energy surging into the case, they pressed on. The young attorney was relentless with the passion of youth—and fury.

"As the grandson of Holocaust survivors, this case scared me. It told me the challenges of the past remain," Harold explained. "If we don't remain vigilant, Jews are going to continue to be scapegoated and given inferior status. What's really scary is that this was happening in *America*, from 1988 to the present."[4]

Harold and Mike Morganroth were the perfect attorneys to press Tenenbaum's case. They were passionate to see it through to the end. In February of 2006, Tenenbaum and his new attorneys met with Senator Carl Levin, who was at that time the chairman of the Armed Services Committee. Levin was famous in the Senate for not backing down from challenges. His reputation was one of integrity and backbone. He would frequently go after the "fat cats" of the banking industry and those who abused loopholes in US tax laws to hide millions offshore. His reputation was fierce, yet fair.

Levin, from Tenenbaum's district, met with Tenenbaum, Morganroth, and Harold in his Detroit office. Tenenbaum's footfalls echoed along the marble corridor. US government symbols adorned the walls, along with pictures of Levin interacting with famous political players. If it hadn't all been so utterly painful, it might have been heady stuff.

They explained to Levin that the Tenenbaum lawsuit against the army was erroneously dismissed because, when the army realized that it was going to lose the case in court, it invoked the state secrets privilege.

Harold strongly felt—as demonstrated by the casual way in which people on Tenenbaum's base tossed around anti-Semitic biases as if they were common knowledge—that there is a group within the government and within the United States that was preconditioned to accept anti-Semitism. These people insist Jews cannot be trusted. And for this group, Jews are scapegoats. This group blindly accepts historical lies about "differentness" and "other." Why else would there be records kept, in the past, of Jews and their security clearances? There was mistrust of them in recent history.

Harold also brought up that the case involved an element of humiliation. Tenenbaum's life was picked apart on the front pages of America's newspapers. His life was destroyed. The government had no problems doing this. But when "fair play" was turned about, and the government was about to be embarrassed by the revelations that their counterintelligence officer had an issue with Jews in the American armed forces, and their "top" polygraph officer utilized abusive tactics—not to mention that the government was using polygraphs as a tactic when the private sector had dismissed it as junk science—they wanted to pull the curtain of state secrets and hide behind it.

As Levin carefully listened without cutting them off, Harold laid out his last—and perhaps most compelling—point. Soldiers were dying because of the United States government. Using under-armored, outdated Humvees and frontline vehicles in the urban theatre was a mistake. Tenenbaum was seeking to fix that, but despite Tenenbaum's vision, they shut down his program.

Harold invoked the Pat Tillman case. Tillman was an NFL player who turned down a lucrative contract offer of $3.6 million from the Arizona Cardinals to enlist in the US Army in the aftermath of 9/11. He was killed by friendly fire. It was alleged that the information regarding how Tillman died was covered up for weeks by the DOD to protect the image of the US Army. As horrible as that was, Tillman was a single soldier. His loss was horrific. And yet, in the case of Tenenbaum, thousands of volunteer soldiers might have been killed, maimed, and destroyed by the actions of the government against Tenenbaum. The LASS program was not replaced. No one else stepped into the void left when Tenenbaum was suspended. The government failed its duty to protect its warfighters with the right equipment in the wars it chose to enter.

In the hallowed office of this United States senator, Dr. Tenenbaum and his attorneys expressed shock and justifiable outrage that the army could not and would not be held accountable for the blatant anti-Semitism of nonessential military employees and even, by this point in the Tenenbaum case timeline, stood behind those very employees who spearheaded and directed the wrongful accusations and acts against Tenenbaum. Morganroth, Harold, and Tenenbaum counted on Levin's reputation as a fierce fighter against corruption. They asked him to become involved in the case and showed him the documents proving that Tenenbaum had been discriminated against for being Jewish.

Levin was incensed. He took one of the more powerful actions he could. Levin asked the Office of the Inspector General for the Department of Defense (IG-DOD) to conduct its own investigation and determine whether or not the army suspected and investigated Tenenbaum because of his being Jewish. He told them that an investigation by the IG-DOD should not take longer than six months. Tenenbaum and his attorneys left the senator's office with a sense of hope. Finally, someone within the government seemed to care.

NEW CONVOY OPERATIONS TRAINING

Eighty-five US soldiers died and 357 were injured in Humvee accidents in Iraq between March 2003 and November 2005, including sixty deaths and 149 injuries in rollovers.[1] This was just what happened in Iraq within just over a two-year span.

By 2006, soldiers were beginning to receive detailed training about how to prepare for IED blasts when in their armored vehicles. These were the best vehicles they had, so they needed to do everything they could to make the best of it.

Humvee doors needed to be "battle-locked," unless driving near bodies of water. Loose objects needed to be tied down, and keys were to be left in the lock that secured radios and other electronic equipment to expedite a complete evacuation, if necessary, without the loss of these materials. Seatbelts might have restricted movements, but with the danger of rollovers, they were unquestionably a necessity.[2]

In 2007, the Joint Multinational Readiness Center in Hohenfels, Germany, hosted forty soldiers from twelve NATO countries in a "train-the-trainer" counter-IED exercise.[3] Military personnel who had lived through fishtailing, rolling, or burning Humvees—many of whom had sustained injuries of their own—became the instructors ready to share their lessons that would trickle down to the soldiers who needed this safety knowledge in war zones.

American soldiers were in harm's way, but so were men and women from so many other countries. They relied on shared, unclassified intelligence and teamwork to enable lives to be saved and injuries to be prevented. It was a process Tenenbaum agreed with. If only it were a process they had let him continue.

CHAPTER 23

THE INSPECTOR GENERAL

"Get your facts first, and then you can distort them
as much as you please."

—MARK TWAIN

On March 14, 2006, only a few short weeks after the meeting with Senator Levin, Tenenbaum and his attorneys received a letter from him. In it, Levin stated:

> I believe that Mr. Tenenbaum's allegations are serious enough that they must be addressed on the merits. For this reason, I have referred this matter to the [Office of the] Inspector General of the Department of Defense for an independent review.[1]

At last, confirmation that the senator would do as he had promised. Tenenbaum and his attorneys felt victorious. If the Office of the Inspector General (IG) was fair and impartial, it would have to make a finding of discrimination. How else could someone explain singling out Tenenbaum for the destructive treatment he received?

The role of the IG is investigative. In the United States, it investigates the actions of government agencies, military organizations, or even military contractors. The IG is an oversight agency examining waste, fraud, misconduct, and criminal activity. There are multiple inspectors general, one for each different branch of government. The Tenenbaum case would make its way to the IG for the DOD.

The IG usually works at a glacial pace. Oversight of tens of thousands of cases of government wrongs is a massive undertaking, and of the numerous inspectors general, perhaps none are more important than in the DOD, where soldiers' lives, not to mention hundreds of billions of dollars in government military contracts, are on the line. Each case must be thoroughly handled.

The IG-DOD takes cases in the order that they are received, and Tenenbaum's case was way down the line, about number 998. However, its position changed after the meeting with Senator Carl Levin, who lived up to his reputation and was outraged. Thanks to his intervention, the case of Tenenbaum against TACOM was bumped up to number two on the list. In fact, Tenenbaum's work to understand the threat to American warriors became the subject of an investigative series including reviews of whistleblowing by Franz Gayl, Mike Helms, and other well-known whistleblowers.

John Crane, the former assistant IG for communications and the liaison for the DOD, who eventually won the Joe A. Callaway Award for Civic Courage, believed in the protection of whistleblowers—in fact, the Callaway Award was given to him precisely for that reason. Crane lived his life, eerily, by the same quote Tenenbaum used in his doctoral dissertation:

First they came for the Socialists, and I did not speak out—

Because I was not a Socialist.

Then they came for the Trade Unionists, and I did not speak out—

Because I was not a Trade Unionist.

Then they came for the Jews, and I did not speak out—

Because I was not a Jew.

Then they came for me—and there was no one left to speak for me.

—MARTIN NIEMÖLLER

Crane liked to update the quote. He would often cite it, substituting "gays," or "African Americans," or "Muslims," or any of dozens of minority races, religions, gender identities, or sexual orientations. He was precisely the liaison the case needed.

Crane, tall, with an aristocratic face and a trim beard, was in charge of Capitol Hill affairs, so he automatically handled situations like this and was among the first in line to receive the letter drafted by Peter Levine, general counsel for Carl Levin, after the meeting among Tenenbaum, Morganroth, Harold, and Levin. To him, the question was how to respond.[2]

Crane was no fool rushing in. He was thorough and meticulous, the type who questioned *everything*. And therefore, that question of response was not one he would take lightly—then or since.

The letter arrived when Uldric Fiore, who had previously served as chief of the Army Litigation Division, where he had initially raised the state secrets defense, was now the general counsel for the IG-DOD. Fiore did not reveal his previous handling of the Tenenbaum case, nor did he recuse himself. As the case dragged on over the years, the names changed, but the government's dogged reluctance to make things right didn't. That was something that seemed to rankle Crane, for whom doing the right thing as a public servant was a higher calling.

His office didn't get a lot of letters talking about the State Secrets Act, and they didn't get a lot of letters from whistleblowers who alleged reprisal. Senator Levin had not precluded looking behind the shroud of the State Secrets Act. It would obviously be difficult to investigate an issue while portions were hidden from the very investigators struggling to come to the truth.

Clearly, Senator Levin, flack and pushback be damned, wanted the IG's office—in this case, in the figures of Crane and his team—to get to the bottom of the Tenenbaum case. Levin seemed quite indignant that signs pointed toward anti-Semitism.

Then Dan Meyer, a doggedly determined thinker with tremendous personal integrity within the IG-DOD, was assigned to the case. He had turned the case down twice, stating that it was outside his directorate's mission area. But Richard Thornton Race, the deputy IG for investigations, called him to the corner office overlooking the Potomac River and delivered the verdict, "Sorry Dan, Senator Levin said to find a better attorney than our deputy general counsel, and you're it. Get going."

Working hand-in-glove with Race and Acting IG Thomas F. Gimble, Crane had hand-selected the relentless investigator. The agency was sucking wind due to a failure of senior legal leadership in vetting the case, and they needed someone with Senate Armed Services Committee (SASC) credibility. Dan Meyer was a whistleblower to the SASC regarding the explosion onboard battleship *USS Iowa* (BB-61) in 1989; he would later blow the whistle to Senator Grassley regarding investigative misconduct related to Afghanistan's Dawood National Military Hospital's patient abuse as well as the leak of classified information by CIA officials promoting the film *Zero Dark Thirty*. Ethically centered, unlike the Washington swamp-creatures opposing him, he had strong credentials and excellent bona fides. In fact, Crane had helped create Meyer's very position. At the time, Meyer was the director of civilian reprisal investigations. It was a job for which Crane himself had created the title and written the description, providing a force multiplier in congressional and public relations. (See Appendix 12.)

For many years, the IG-DOD wrongfully applied the more stringent military whistleblower reprisal standards to civilian cases, cheating DOD civilian employees of their rights before the US Office of Special Counsel. Crane created the position as an advocate internally for an end to the practice. In essence, there were different standards—with the civilian threshold being higher for management—and they needed a civilian case investigator who fully understood the differences.

A few weeks after Meyer arrived, he completed a review of the civilian cases and confirmed John Crane's hunch. A meeting of senior leadership without the IG-DOD attorneys was convened with IG Joseph E. Schmitz. Meyer delivered the verdict: the IG-DOD needed to change its practices to abide by the law.

When Schmitz asked Meyer whether he needed to call the US Special Counsel, Meyer was clear, "No, I already have."

Meyer was permitted carte blanche with oversight and law enforcement authorities by seven subsequent defense or intelligence community inspectors general. He would use those powers again and again to protect sources and lawfully disclose wrongdoing between 2004 and 2018, though he would ultimately be fired by the director of national intelligence after doing so.

Working for Race, Crane, Assistant IG for Administrative Investigations Donald M. Horstman, and finally, IG of the Intelligence Community Irvin Charles McCullough III, Dan Meyer was given wide latitude to break through the dikes put up by agency attorneys. Meyer's newly created position was made for cases precisely like Tenenbaum's.

Meyer was given complete discretion to accept or decline cases for investigation, a fact that was problematic for the IG-DOD's Office of General Counsel. The three biggest weapons employed by federal agency lawyers against the American people are the ability to not docket a case, the ability to narrow or expand the scope of an investigation to manipulate the findings, and the ability—through the legal sufficiency determination process (deciding whether a case has enough legal merit to continue)—to "slow-roll" an investigation. Slow-rolling allows the lawyers to wear down the wronged employee and diligent investigators until the proponents of investigative integrity leave, retire, or in some cases, die. Dan Meyer was permitted by Deputy IG for Investigations Richard Race to select cases thematically instead of selecting cases based on a need to fluff his proverbial Rolodex or ingratiate himself to deep state functionaries within the bowels of the federal bureaucracy.

Meyer had a string of cases regarding avionics safety; he developed a string of cases regarding the morale and welfare of US soldiers, airman, sailors, and marines in Southwest Asia, and he developed a line of cases regarding the intelligence community.

To Tenenbaum, the case was about religious discrimination. Meyer would do a religious discrimination case because that is what the IG and Carl Levin, chairman of the Senate Armed Services Committee, agreed would be done. To Meyer and the Civilian Reprisal Investigations division, the Tenenbaum case was an opportunity to study both the federal government's failure to timely address the light-armor survivability vulnerability and the health of the counterintelligence capabilities of the US Army, including the DOD's polygraph program.

Meyer used his docket to get his head under the hood of the federal government. This worried the attorneys on the top floor of the IG-DOD. However, it provided all sorts of opportunities for John Crane and Richard Race to use Meyer's investigation as a tool to manage the IG-DOD's attorneys.

Fiore was also involved right away. And with his involvement, the games began. Without revealing his history with the case, according to what Crane told Tenenbaum, Fiore prepared a response for Crane to sign and give back to Senator Levin.

Without having interviewed a single person, without having investigated a single element of the case, Fiore was ready for the case to go away. But signing this drafted letter and shutting down a case that seemed to have merit was not something the principled Crane was prepared to do.

The US Army Litigation Division had successfully used the courts' national security deference to prevent an examination of the anti-Semitism vented by Tenenbaum. But Tenenbaum's case presented a unique congressional oversight moment. John Crane told Dan Meyer that the Senate Armed Services Committee, under Republican leadership, had signaled to Crane that oversight of the DOD was not a priority. However, when the Senate flipped to the Democrats in 2006, a new activism followed the change of leadership and sparked a renewal of whistleblower protections that lasted through the Senate loss by the Democrats in 2014 and continued until 2017. David Tenenbaum was a constituent of the new chairman of the Senate Armed Services Committee.

Three trends emerged: Senate control, an activist chairman, and personal constituent status. Crane sensed the opportunity to do the right thing and pushed for Senator Levin to ask for the investigation. Levin then erected a firewall against Army command meddling: first Crane's influence over the IG, then Meyer's reputation for aggressive investigations, then the protection of Meyer by Richard Race, a legendary former secret service agent with service back to the Nixon administration, and finally, Meyer's acquisition of talent within the civil reprisal investigations directorate who did not regard their IG service as a lackadaisical "second career" that simply provided a second paycheck. All this combined to restore the IG-DOD's sense of ethics; bigotry now could be targeted.

Fiore's drafted response was written as if it was the *final* report—the last word on the case—without Crane having placed so much as a preliminary phone call. According to what Crane told Tenenbaum, Crane didn't understand how the general counsel seemed to have so much knowledge about the case and seemed so swift and steadfast in its actions. Because of the supposed state secrets, no one should have known anything about the case except for Crane himself.

The idea was chilling. It aroused Crane's suspicions. He didn't like being handed a position on a case without doing any investigating himself. He wondered just why Uldric Fiore, or the Office of General Counsel, was so involved in the case.

Attorneys are not allowed to handle a case more than once. Since Fiore handled the case while he was a Judge Advocate General (JAG) officer for the army, there was no way he should have handled the case as the IG-DOD general counsel. But he inserted himself in there anyway.

The original declaration of state secrets went up to US Deputy Secretary of Defense Paul Wolfowitz. Tenenbaum's case was the type of issue that rose to the highest levels. Tenenbaum waited for updates on his case in faraway Michigan as Wolfowitz signed off on—rubber-stamped—the fact that there was blocked information and that the shroud should be pulled across all the facts.

While David Tenenbaum walked the familiar halls of his base, where he'd spent years of his life problem-solving, analyzing data, and reimagining the possibilities of armor that protected US soldiers, John Crane learned more about the Rhodesian design of V-hull trucks like MRAPs that dispersed the energy of IED explosions. He discovered how the light-skinned Humvees being used in Iraq had been designed for northern Europe, in a time and place before IEDs. He came to understand the religious issue at the core of the case. It was not the type of whistleblower discussion that he would typically be a part of.

In Michigan, while he waited, Tenenbaum began training as a paramedic, knowing that in ambulances, he'd experience fear, urgency, and the pressure to work at higher speeds that might be helpful in his research, if he was ever able to continue any form of research. He was in the process of designing and developing safer ambulances for both the army and the civilian sector. And if not, at least he was being given the chance to help save lives. He just wanted to help someone. He wasn't so sure it could be himself.

Crane was meticulous. As he explained to Tenenbaum, Crane, in Washington, examined the issue of a polygraph being used as a retaliation tool. He examined the home-search details and the further surveillance of the FBI's investigation. Despite Fiore's best efforts, Crane's personal integrity was to a higher calling: the truth. Or, more to the point, to the law.

According to one anonymous investigator, "The law is you can't investigate someone, or administer a polygraph, just to retaliate against them." He was baffled by Tenenbaum's assumed loyalty to Israel over the United States with no evidence to this fact. "That would be like saying that anyone who speaks English, who has read Shakespeare, would actually compromise national security information to the British simply because they had Shakespeare in common."[3]

This was chilling, a very dangerous road.[4] If this was OK, the government could make affiliation based upon any ethnic background, religion, cultural matter, or all kinds of things. These were sweeping assumptions based on stereotype, bigotry, and prejudice—*not* on Tenenbaum as an individual.[5]

Joe Schmitz, the IG from March 2002 until September 2004, had different reactions to the Tenenbaum case. Schmitz was very proud of his German heritage. He had an obsession regarding Baron von Steuben, George Washington's IG at Valley Forge and a German who had served in the Prussian Army and become the drillmaster for General Washington. However, the Von Steuben Society in the US, during the Second World War, was thought to be a fifth column for the Nazi government.

There was controversy over Schmitz's insistence of visiting the Potsdam Garrison Church, where a new plaque was placed in Von Steuben's honor, in brass, with both English and German translations. His trip was supposedly to benefit German-US relations, but the location was popularly considered a neo-Nazi shrine site because this was where the Nazis initially formed their government.[6]

Later, 2016 Republican presidential nominee Donald Trump would resurrect Schmitz as a viable foreign advisor, and Schmitz's name graced above-the-fold headlines across the world.[7] He allegedly commented to those close to the Tenenbaum investigation that the figures related to the Holocaust—the millions of men, women, and children slaughtered in the name of the Nazis—were false. The Nazis could not have killed that many Jews because "the ovens" were not big enough.[8]

At the time of Tenenbaum's case arriving in Washington, Schmitz had made the move to hire Uldric Fiore, a man who was believed to share his passions, and who had previously provided legal counsel to Schmitz after at least two Jewish IG employees had been removed from their positions under his watch. (See Appendix 13.)

But it was Dan Meyer, not Schmitz or Fiore, who provided leadership for the investigations of the case, implementing and ensuring accountability in the protection of employees—military and civilian, as well as contractors—who disclose violations of laws, rules, and/or regulations.

Meyer considered the Tenenbaum case in line with a series of intelligence community cases which would lay the basis, during the first decade of the new century, for President Barack Obama's creation of the first regulatory and then statutory system for the protection of intelligence community whistleblowers. It was during the Tenenbaum case that Meyer realized the directive that eventually emerged as PPD-19, Protecting Whistleblowers with Access to Classified Information, would have to have a second section devoted exclusively to personnel security actions, including polygraphs.

Meyer had been involved in the Able Danger case, a sixteen-month investigation to determine whether the United States had advanced warning of the identities and plans of the 9/11 masterminds, which was disproved by the Senate Intelligence Committee. Meyer was determined to do everything in the Tenenbaum case "by the book" and acted with an abundance of caution. And Meyer was not partisan on this matter. It fit into a very specific set of priorities of his when it came through the door, in his own words, "a really meaty intelligence, counterintelligence case."[9]

Not a subject matter expert in religious discrimination, Meyer was fascinated by the LASS project. As a former warfighter with experience targeting and destroying light-armor vehicles through the naval gunfire support program, the idea that David Tenenbaum's LASS program had been shuttered, leaving the warfighters without the necessary equipment and tools to fight, was something that Meyer felt passionately about. Meyer studied under navy strategist and tactician Captain "25-Knot" Larry Seaquist, USN, commanding officer of the battleship *Iowa*

(BB-61). Seaquist taught Meyer disdain for the navy's Jurassic fixation on open-sea, blue-water battles between aircraft carrier groups and focused him on the emerging littoral warfare needs of pre-Desert Storm Near-East security. Meyer understood the shift of combat toward asymmetrical "gang warfare" and away from traditional Napoleonic armies meeting on the battlefield. And if this was the new normal, light-armor survivability systems were essential.

Meyer was impressed that Tenenbaum was aware of and working against the IED threat in the mid-to-late 1990s, well before the two wars in the Middle East. His supporters called Tenenbaum a visionary when it came to LASS. As the DOD investigation would later reveal, Simonini had, under oath, called Tenenbaum no more than a "misguided engineer."[10]

If they were fighting the war, they needed to look at the needs of the people carrying out the work. Meyer knew the resources of the IG should be dedicated to protecting US warfighters. It was essential to him that they examined the services and support being provided to the men and women doing their missions on the ground.

Meyer's expertise also was involved in some well-known IG cases, including the "Gina Gray case, at Arlington National Cemetery, which reviewed what was done with the men and women of the armed services when they died, when they were interred, and real abuses at Arlington National Cemetery." [11] (The Gray case, which recommended compensation to Ms. Gray, occurred at the same time the Tenenbaum case was drawing to a close.)

In addition, in early 2010, Meyer supported a whistleblower, William Zwicharowski, at the Dover Port Mortuary.[12] The case involved accusations, later proved by the US special counsel, that the morticians' special rules regarding the respectful way of treating bodies were not being followed.

Meyer felt a passion for these whistleblowing cases but was unsure of his place in Tenenbaum's religious discrimination case. It was Richard Race who stepped in at this critical moment.

"I'm not letting you out of this." Race said to him. "You're being put on this at the express request of the Hill. We need you on there because they think you have integrity. They know you will do a good job. There won't be any monkey business."

Understanding the necessity of having someone with a passion for right and wrong at the helm, Meyer finally agreed. The strong support within the leadership of the IG-DOD, regardless of his decision, persisted all the way through.

In short, Meyer was not one to be swayed, not one to be bribed, not one to be pushed in one direction or another. He was dedicated to impartiality. The investigation was to remain untainted by influences from the outside.

CHAPTER 24

CUT AND PASTE

"At his best, man is the noblest of all animals;
separated from law and justice,
he is the worst."

—ARISTOTLE

David Tenenbaum had his job at TACOM, but for a long time, he was little more than a glorified paper pusher. Ever since he had been cleared and brought back from suspension, he wasn't able to truly work as an engineer. No one wanted to work with him, and his ideas never gained approval.

So he poured his passion into his volunteer work as a paramedic. In the back of his mind was an idea about designing better ambulances—both for civilians and the military. He was there when bones were broken, when drugs induced overdoses, and when hearts had stopped. He was there when a man tried to commit suicide by slicing the skin of his wrist.

He was a student paramedic at the time. The cut was deep and bleeding profusely. Tenenbaum put pressure on the injury, trying to stop the flow of blood. He held the man's hand tightly as the man lay on a gurney in the back of the ambulance; Tenenbaum hoped the ligaments were strong enough to keep him connected. The vehicle hurdled toward the hospital. This wasn't like any work he'd ever experienced. His own heart beat rapidly. Standing in the back of the ambulance that day, he was working with a husband-wife team of emergency medical technicians. They worked with a speed, skill, and professionalism that awed him. They knew how to take the broken and so often save their lives.

The vehicle swerved suddenly. They had been traveling with the lights and siren on at around forty-five miles an hour. A car had cut them off. Tenenbaum was tossed into the side stairwell of the ambulance, and the female medic flew, arms outstretched like superman, into a metal drug box.

Banged up from the collision, Tenenbaum looked down at his hand. He was still clasping it tight, and in that moment, he feared it wasn't empty. He feared their patient's hand had severed completely from his arm and that Tenenbaum was still clasping it in his own.

Thankfully, his hand was empty. Their patient was still strapped down in his place, sliced wrist bleeding again but still fully connecting his arm and hand. The experience inspired Tenenbaum to try to make ambulances safer—it was just how his brain worked.

In Washington, D.C., Meyer plowed ahead, still hesitant about the religious discrimination focus he was going deeper and deeper into. Every day, the blatant anti-Semitism became more and more clear.

"Hey, if you want me off this, I'm fine by that," he said one day to Race. They had already had this conversation, but he needed to raise it one last time. "I'll step down. I have no pride in my role. You can have a special agent come on if I am becoming problematic." Meyer was seeing just how racist some of the people with TACOM were toward Tenenbaum. He was becoming more and more disgusted, and his updated reports on his investigation of the Tenenbaum case told the truth. He saw the anti-Semitism of Simonini and Albert Snyder as well as others. He saw how the LASS program that could have saved lives had been terminated. He saw how Tenenbaum's career was destroyed by bigots within the Department of the Army, and he had no problem letting those in the IG-DOD know what his investigation was turning up.

Race listened, his face giving no hint of his opinion on the matter.

"Give me forty-eight hours," he finally answered. And Meyer was left wondering if perhaps he *shouldn't* have offered to step aside. He was being fair, after all. He was investigating everyone, absolutely everyone, trying to examine every aspect of the case from every angle as thoroughly as possible. Not everyone would be as meticulous, he knew.

When Race came back the next day, Meyer was nervous. He wanted the case to have the best possible chance for the truth.

"Nope, I talked to everybody," Race said matter-of-factly. "We think you're doing a great job."

Meyer nodded his head. There was no question left in his mind. He would sort it all out. Justice would be fair. Justice would be thorough. The US warfighters and the US people deserved nothing less.

John Crane was very supportive all the way through as Meyer, proving once again to be a stand-up investigator, waded deeper into the Tenenbaum case with an open mind and an eye for objectivity.

But cases like Tenenbaum's were often very difficult, involving deep-seated prejudices, secrets, and hidden surprises. In addition, the culture of the IG-DOD was just past a very difficult time, fraught with tension. Only the year before, the most senior Jewish executives had been walked out of the building. It was commonly believed that the IG at the time, Schultz, declared the action his greatest achievement—making his building "Juden-free."[1]

Now, there is a proactive Equal Employment Opportunity (EEO) outreach program for the IG-DOD employees, in part because Dan Meyer insisted on it after Tenenbaum's case. Meyer helped build it.

Meyer looked again at the congressional correspondence around the Tenenbaum case, reviewing exactly what question they were setting out to answer. Senator Levin specifically wanted the investigators to look at state secrets, but when they took that part out of there, the religious discrimination case was going to be equally challenging.

While passionate about the case, Meyer, at his core, was also a man of facts and figures. Regardless of what he would find, he would eventually have to hand over to the IG a factual report. He needed hard facts, so he used a matrix similar to the one he used in whistleblowing contexts.

He had to learn about Title XII law, where language is very important. Considering the Tenenbaum case as a whole, language was certainly a part of it. What people *said,* in addition to what they did, mattered. Meyer conducted interviews with the main figures in the case and continued his questioning, both aloud to his interview subjects and in the back of his mind.

When Meyer spoke with Tenenbaum, there were no doubt left in the engineer's mind about discrimination. What had once been disbelief and fear had hardened into realization and a base level of ire that lingered just beneath Tenenbaum's skin. He was always gracious, always calm, always polite to the lead investigator on his case, but Meyer could see the exasperation and indignation in Tenenbaum's eyes.

Meyer knew he needed to understand the root of the feelings of discrimination and what it was like on a daily basis to live in a world that seemed to insult you without even realizing it, so he turned to two of his law clerks with a social experiment.

Of these two clerks, one was Italian American and one was Jewish American. Meyer guessed the Jewish-American clerk might find things offensive that the Italian American clerk—or others—might not consider rude or inappropriate at all. There was a cultural misunderstanding that needed further exploration, and this was the best way he could think of to figure it out.

"Part of the reason I am doing this, pairing you two together, I'm letting you in on the secret," Meyer explained to the clerks. "The tension between you two is what will help me to discern if discrimination was involved here."

He turned to the Jewish-American law clerk, who, from what he had seen so far, was quite convinced this was a case of discrimination. Meyer said to her, "You need to monitor the comments of your coworker, when he pushes back, and if he says it's not discrimination, I want you to discern where it is coming from. Is it the *law,* or is it that he's a white guy who is Italian American and there is some bias there?"

Meyer walked away from the pair and the burgeoning social experiment thinking of the culture of the IG-DOD. He had recently had a case where a woman with a disability was having difficulty answering questions in a group setting. She had a peer who, if she spoke and missed something in that setting, would say, "Jane, you ignorant slut," from the *Saturday Night Live* sketch. He thought of other cases that had been given shorthand names around the office like the "Dirty Santa" incident, a name used for a case in which alcohol was introduced at holiday parties and an attorney groped an investigator, or other events that led to conduct that had no place in the workforce. He was, it seemed, cleaning up the discriminatory climate one case at a time.

The interplay between his two clerks worked exactly as Meyer had hoped it would. The dialogue between the two of them was powerful, but eventually they reached an impasse. Tensions and offenses were out in the open and examinable, but they needed a next step to bring these ideas into the matrix of the case.

As Meyer was at an office supply store getting some computer paper, he walked by a display for kids prepping their science fair projects. The tri-board posters stared back at him. Calling back to a different era, pre-internet and pre-computer, he realized that was exactly what they needed. He bought the tri-board and lugged it from Hagerstown, Maryland all the way across Washington, D.C. to the IG's office near the Pentagon City Metro Station.

Arriving at his office, he approached the two clerks and explained exactly how they would present the discrimination findings of the case to IG Claude "Mick" Kicklighter, who took over as IG-DOD in April 2007 from acting IG-DOD Thomas Gimble. Gimble had been appointed as interim IG-DOD when Joe Schmitz was forced to resign in September 2005.

"I want you to cut and paste the elements for a reprisal, for a discrimination case, paste those elements down the center."

If there was any reaction to this project taking the clerks back to the cutting-and-pasting days of elementary school, they were respectful enough to keep it off of their faces.

"Make Xeroxes of *all* the transcripts," Meyer continued. "You put all the statements that are discrimination and match it to the center in the board. Here are the statements where we see discrimination. Boom, boom, boom." He tapped the board as he spoke. "Now, here's the kicker. On the right-hand side, I want you to take the statements made about Mr. Tenenbaum. And instead of Jewish, I want you to put in 'Black' or 'African American.'"

These fake quotes on the right side were what he was counting on. In other words, they were simply the Tenenbaum quotes converted to racial discrimination. He walked away from the clerks, but he hadn't gotten very far before he heard, "Oh my God," from over the cubicle.

He laughed slightly, knowing they had it.

When the quotes were converted to pertaining to race, discrimination was as plain as Meyer's face in a mirror.

After the clerks finished their project, he asked them, "Why is discrimination when it's an African American but not a Jewish person?"

None of them had a real answer.

"It was a real challenge, maybe because we're not trained, we're not socialized in this way," Meyer mused. "We don't see religious discrimination in the same way we see racial discrimination."

He then gave the clerks a week to write up their analyses. Meyer took the board as a prop along with the analysis and brought them both to his boss.

He said to him, "If you don't see it on the Jewish side but do see it on the African American side, you have to ask what's going on in your head."

His boss immediately saw the discrimination. He told Meyer to take the analysis and the work from the tri-board and to put it into a PowerPoint presentation for the IG. The tri-board remained in a corner cubicle, in plain view of African American special agents of the defense criminal investigative service. The new deputy for investigations, Charles "Chuck" Beardall, asked Meyer to come see him, closed his door, and asked what was going on.

"Take that damn thing down. We will get complaints from our black special agents," Beardall said as soon as the door was closed.

Enjoying the moment, Meyer quipped, "But not from our Jews; Chuck, by the way, where are all our Jewish special agents? Didn't we used to have some?"

Because the acting IG was now Claude Kicklighter, whom Meyer understood to be an evangelical Christian, he thought it would be interesting to see if this viewpoint would have any bearing on his reaction.

Meyer presented his findings to IG Kicklighter, read his briefing, including the PowerPoint presentation, and showed him the actual tri-board that the clerks had put together for the case.

IG Kicklighter, wearing his customary fishing vest, sat back in his chair and looked out over the Pentagon. He then turned to Dan Meyer at his left and looked him right in the eye.

"This is discrimination," he said.

Meyer nodded, knowing he had a case, knowing what nobody else did in that moment—that he had the support and backing of the IG. In the IG world, if you have cover and backing, you have a finding. According to Dan Meyer, Tenenbaum had two members of the Senior Executive Service on his side, two on the fence, and three bitterly opposed to giving a finding to "the Jew."

Meyer knew that such a finding would not go over easily. He said to Kicklighter, "If at any point, if your thoughts, if they change, let me know, because I'm proceeding knowing I have the backing of the front office."

Even having this 100 percent support of the IG, Meyer wasn't going to tell anyone. They both understood this.

"Now that you've got a finding for your Title XII figured out," IG Kicklighter continued, "take it outside the building."

Meyer also checked with Kicklighter's principal deputy, his former supervisor Richard Race.

"Dan, take it out of Washington, not just out the building. Remember, that is a draft; the attorneys will freak if they find out we circulated a draft for review outside the building."

Meyer then checked in with his future supervisor, John Crane, who joked, "Welcome to the Order of 'Other Duties as Assigned.'"

Circulating drafts is problematic because they change; they document where the decision-making is at a particular time. Sometimes findings change for legitimate reasons, as in when new evidence is gathered or old evidence is impeached. But findings can change for political reasons as well. A senior IG executive tips off the Secretary of Defense or White House, and political pressure pushes the "delete" button. By taking the draft out of the building at his chain of command's request, Meyer was their agent in throwing sea anchors over the side, restricting what the senior leadership of the IG-DOD could do when pressured wrongfully.

Meyer nodded again. The reason for this, of course, was the recusal process. The general counsel was recused. The issue with Fiore, for example, made keeping this kind of finding "in house" a little complicated. Meyer, his boss, his boss's boss, and a John Crane concerned with strong congressional working relations wanted nothing to interfere or intervene with the *truth*. And this was not all altruistic. The Pentagon routinely only supplied two-thirds of the needed budget for the IG-DOD. Crane was tasked with monitoring the Senate Armed Services Committee's interest, particularly in light of the Committee's control over the National Defense Authorization Act (NDAA). Every two years, Committee staff would sit down and ask the IG, "What good works have you done over the past twenty-four months?" The implication was clear: IGs who punch clocks and watch Fox News all day get no supplemental funding. By fiscal year (FY) 2012, Crane and Meyer's work in whistleblower protection, including the investigation regarding David Tenenbaum, was covering one-third of the salaries at the IG-DOD. One slip, and a third of the Mark Center staff would suffer a reduction in force, or "RIF." Pink slips. No job.

So, David Tenenbaum's case was more than a security issue. It was a blend of renewed ethics, hardcore oversight politics, and a probe into a hostile work environment as well as the substantial and retaliatory actions that came out of this environment. For years, the DOD said it did not profile by "religion." Meyer proved in the Tenenbaum case that the Department did, in fact, target at least one Jew. To make this finding, Meyer had to have "cover" from John Crane, Richard Race, and IG Kicklighter.

Meyer has been quoted as saying investigations should be "all about transparency." According to him, "we shouldn't run from letting the people know what we federal employees are doing. In fact, if we had more transparency, we would have fewer problems. More government transparency allows more senior executive and congressional oversight, and oversight allows for the correction of government failures."[2]

When describing the IG's reprisal investigations, Dan Meyer stated, "We don't call them as we see them; we call them as they are. I have no concerns at all for protecting the wrongdoer. At the end of the day, the business of government is the people's business, not the wrongdoer's business."[3]

When Tenenbaum had sat across the desk from Meyer and Intelligence Special Agent David Ingram, another investigator, he came across to both men as a sincere person, a family man, and a dedicated engineer. He had told them about LASS and about his motivations for consulting with US allies to save soldiers' lives. After Tenenbaum's sworn testimony, Ingram, who'd had his reservations, did a complete turnaround and realized that Tenenbaum had indeed been wronged by the intelligence community and that there was something *not right* with his being suspected and investigated for espionage. Nothing about this screamed out anything but earnest ambition to help America's fighting warriors. Ingram and Meyer both realized that the only thing—literally the only thing that caused Tenenbaum to be investigated—was his religion. There was *nothing else* to account for the suspicions and aspersions cast upon him but prejudice: pure, unadulterated anti-Semitism from bigots within the DOD.

And now Meyer had proven it.

PHOTOGRAPHY OF THE ARMY DEAD

For eighteen years, the United States government banned the photographing of military casualties on that long flight home, when our young men and women rightfully and sacredly return to US soil from far-flung counties in flag-draped coffins.[1] Some criticized the ban, insisting it had long hid the sacrifices—the real sacrifices—of a war fought by an all-volunteer army. The combined wars in the Middle East added to the chorus demanding the real costs of war be shown. Then, in 2009, the images began.

First, Americans saw the flag-draped caskets lined up inside the maws of massive military planes, the red, white, and blue stars and stripes crisply protecting simple silver metallic transfer cases. Then soldiers, acting as pallbearers for their fallen comrades, unloaded the cases from the planes and to the tarmac as other soldiers saluted or stood at attention.

For army tank engineer David Tenenbaum, the images were gut-wrenching. He could only watch from the sidelines as the death tolls in the combined wars in Iraq and Afghanistan mounted. Tenenbaum had made it his personal and professional mission to prevent the deaths of these young men and women, fathers and sons, mothers and daughters, nieces and nephews, brothers, sisters, and soldier kin—those united not by blood but by bonds forged in battle. Each flag-draped coffin was, perhaps, a young man or woman Tenenbaum could have saved. The scenes on the evening news of those returning without limbs, with traumatic brain injuries, reduced, at times, to drooling, vacant-eyed hollow shells of former selves ripped through him even more.

219

CHAPTER 25

EXPERIENCE AND DECEIT

"Being different, they were suspected,
envied and reviled by their neighbors."

—BEREL WEIN

Tenenbaum was informed that he was needed at a meeting with the national automotive center on base at TACOM with high-level senior executives and military personnel. He was only being called in to help, but anytime anyone told him that he was required to attend something unexpected, his skin still turned cold.

"What's this meeting about?"

His colleague explained how they were examining the safety of gunners within a Humvee and what happened if the vehicles stopped suddenly or if corners were turned fast. The gunner was often either ejected from the vehicle or crushed when the Humvee rolled. Instead of using the LASS program and rebuilding the vehicles the right way, the engineers had been just adding more armor. They didn't seem to fully comprehend what this did to the suspension, to the wheels, and how it affected the whole.

"Weren't you working on this?" Tenenbaum's colleague asked. "They want to know if you'll get involved."

McClelland had supported the program Tenenbaum had been working on (preventing medics in the back of ambulances from being thrown around inside the vehicle as they were standing up and working on a patient), but the person who took over after he left said that it wasn't important, or "sort of useless." She refused to continue funding the program, but the research had been well underway.

Soldiers were getting killed in similar situations. Tenenbaum knew that the theory and technology could be applied to military vehicles where soldiers stood up, such as HMMWVs. There had been so much press attention on the issue during this time that it went up to the congressional level quickly.

Tenenbaum attended the meeting. He heard the concerns of the other engineers present, took his own notes, and responded thoughtfully when anyone asked him questions about specifics. He thought about his work as a volunteer medic in the ambulances and his idea for restraints that would have been so helpful. He returned from the meeting to Building 200, where he met his boss.

"What do you think?" his boss asked.

"I think they're doing it because it's political."

"I know it's true, but you should never say that," his boss screamed at him before taking a breath. "Can you do something about this problem?" His boss asked in a calmer voice.

"Yes," Tenenbaum answered.

A general at the meeting had told him, "Okay, Tenenbaum, you are now running the gunner restraint program. Pick your team, and money is no object." This was a phrase that was rarely uttered in the government.

As he stood with his boss, though, Tenenbaum knew he was right. It was a political issue more than a concern for saving soldiers' lives. But he would do it. He would help, even if his focus wasn't the one everyone shared. The irony, he thought, was that the very same person who refused to continue funding the program the year prior was at the meeting as well. There was a sudden urgency for developing a solution, but the new solutions would be a year later than they had to be—a year too late for some of those HMMWV gunners.

A team was assembled; some members were chosen by Tenenbaum and others by the government. To Tenenbaum, there were mainly two of them who took the lead. They made quick progress, even when he contracted meningitis—due to stress, said his doctors. He was not technically allowed to work, but in bed at home, he still did. He wanted to test the new restraint system designed to pull a soldier in rather than letting him fall out or holding him in the place where the weight of the heavily armored Humvee would crush him.

Tenenbaum had talked to gunners as they'd been assembling their research. He asked nineteen- and twenty-year-old kids how they were taught to react if they felt themselves going out.

"Well, as soon as it starts to turn over, we're told our buddies will pull us in."

Tenenbaum blinked, pausing before answering.

"Do you know what centrifugal force is?"

"What do you mean?"

"There's no way your buddies can do it."

"Then when we fall, we should hit the ground and roll."

"You might be going forty to fifty miles per hour, with thirty-five pounds of extra equipment. You're supposed to hit sand or hit the pavement and roll?

"That's what my sergeant told me."

When he questioned the soldier, the soldier said he wouldn't wear a restraint system. But Tenenbaum knew that it was his job to develop the protective system for the gunner and the army's job to make sure the soldier wore it.

Media attention on the subject of soldier safety intensified. Tenenbaum pushed through his recurring meningitis, and his team developed a system that they were proud of. Within four months, it was ready for testing. Within five months, the system—between twelve and fifteen thousand units—was sent overseas.

Tenenbaum gave a lot of credit to his team for working so well on the solution, though he found it interesting that when the project was discussed, when names were mentioned, "Tenenbaum" never seemed to be included.

Back in Washington, D.C., despite Meyer's finding, there was not a clean, straight line from a finding to an IG report. Right up until the last minutes before the release of the report—signed late at night, with minutes to spare before its deadline—Fiore and others who wanted to *change* the finding had minions working to do just that.

Tenenbaum was told that the general counsel and some of the deputy IGs were attempting to undermine and sabotage the report.

As they were gaining traction, Tenenbaum drew a lucky break. Someone wanted the truth to be told. Tenenbaum had been in touch with an organization called the Project on Government Oversight (POGO). POGO is a United States independent nonprofit organization that investigates and exposes corruption and other misconduct to achieve a more honest, open, and accountable federal government. POGO investigates federal agencies, Congress, and government contractors.

Tenenbaum had described his case to POGO and asked them to get involved. They had heard of his case and said that they would look into it and would get back to him after they had conducted some research of their own. POGO was already looking into allegations of corruption within the IG's office for the DOD, but they did not have a "smoking gun."

Many IGs—in this case, the IG for the DOD—have to answer to Congress as well as the DOD itself. POGO, and many others, felt that it was impossible for the IG-DOD to be fair and equitable in their investigations of the DOD or army if these organizations also acted as their "boss." Just like Fiore, there were significant reasons why this was too cozy.

A week or so passed from Tenenbaum's first call to POGO to when he decided to follow up with another call. The person to whom he spoke thanked him for sending them the documents related to his case.

"We're just going to need time to comb through all these documents. There are stacks of them. We appreciate you sending them, but it will still take some time."

"What? What are you talking about?"

"The documents relating to your case."

A long pause followed.

Finally, Tenenbaum, throat dry, said hoarsely, "But I didn't send you any documents."

POGO replied that they had been sent a large number of documents that dealt with the IG-DOD and had his name on them; POGO had assumed they were from him. They thanked him again.

Tenenbaum asked if perhaps they could fax the documents to him to shed some light on their origin. The documents were sent to

224

Tenenbaum at about 4:30 p.m. that same day. They were documents from within the IG-DOD—inside documents that Tenenbaum had no access to—which included, among hundreds of pages of other items, internal PowerPoint presentations and internal emails regarding Tenenbaum's case. These documents and emails proved how Uldric Fiore was interfering on a case in which he was required to recuse himself. He was making a concerted effort to ensure that the IG-DOD ruled against Tenenbaum, and that the IG report would *not* find for discrimination. And he was not the only one.

Fiore's underlings in the Office of General Counsel, as well as deputy IGs, were attempting to "hijack" the report, changing the findings to show there was no discrimination and "protect" the Department of the Army from being held accountable for their anti-Semitic actions.

POGO had this to say about Tenenbaum's case:

> Mr. Tenenbaum filed a lawsuit alleging discrimination on the basis of his religion, but the case was dismissed when the "state secrets privilege" was asserted as to evidence Tenenbaum wished to submit. It is important to note that the memorandum recommending that the Army approve the assertion of the state secrets privilege was written and signed by Uldric L. Fiore, Jr., Col., JA, Chief, Litigation Division, of the Army's Judge Advocate General.

Further:

> By 2006, the attorney serving as the General Counsel to the DOD/OIG, was the same Uldric Fiore, now retired from the Army. Again, it was Fiore who had previously served in the litigation branch of the Army and had recommended the assertion of state secrets privilege which resulted in the dismissal of Tenenbaum's lawsuit. Fiore had further been involved in briefing the Secretary of the Army on the case.[1]

Fiore should never have been allowed to work on Tenenbaum's case as this was a clear case of a conflict of interest. A first-year law student would know that Fiore needed to recuse himself.

Fiore never revealed his relationship to the case to Senator Levin. Uldric Fiore also failed to notify the IG-DOD that he had previously worked on Tenenbaum's case as chief counsel for the army. When he was found out, he refused to recuse himself from the IG-DOD case, and when he was finally forced out of it, he still had his people working on the case and was kept fully informed of its happenings.

Henry Shelley and Bryan Yonish were Fiore's men on the job. Fiore's fingerprints were all over the case—interfering, advising, and most of all, trying to control the outcome. The very man who invented the ultimate lie to prevent the government from having to answer for its crimes was now controlling the investigation of those crimes. Once he was off the case, there were still those beneath him ascribing to the same "party line," who kept up his efforts.

But Dan Meyer and justice were prevailing. The finding was irrefutable.

In addition to the interviews Meyer conducted, he and the handful of IG staff and attorneys who supported civil rights investigations and were interested in doing the right thing, and who wanted to conduct a fair and impartial investigation, however few they were, had discovered an antiquated system, a network of the good old boys and white men of privilege who had no intention of joining the modern century where discrimination is not only frowned upon but illegal. Meyer was able to construct a detailed timeline, including the "October briefing," in which numerous lies were propagated by Simonini in order to involve the FBI. That briefing was where everything seemed to start for Tenenbaum—it was the birth of the false concept that he desired to gain higher and higher security clearance because he wanted access to top secret programs so he could feed them to the Israelis. Except that Tenenbaum had never pushed for higher clearances. His own words had never been strong enough to dispel these ideas—not until now.

The army was guilty as charged in the David Tenenbaum case. They had set out to ruin a man's life. These documents, along with stacks of copied emails and more, were the "smoking gun" that POGO needed to show the internal corruption within the IG-DOD, and they had arrived perfectly on POGO's doorstep. At the time, POGO did not even realize the importance of those documents. As was later seen with WikiLeaks and the Panama Papers, receiving piles of documents and data without background information and clarity on their origins does not make them easy to interpret.

Tenenbaum explained the significance of what these papers were to his contact at POGO. In actuality, the case—while tragic—was not complicated; without any shred of supportive evidence along with Simonini's anti-Semitic comments, it was not difficult to establish the crimes committed.

POGO realized what it now had in its possession. In today's language, the Tenenbaum case would be considered a hate crime. Someone had tipped them off, and for this, David Tenenbaum would always be grateful. POGO next published the documents on its website and sent letters to members of Congress with this damning information.

Fiore wasn't done, though.

Neither were Yonish, Shelley, or Deputy IG-DOD Chuck Beardall. According to an email sent on April 16, 2008, a "Tenenbaum meeting" was expected to occur. According to POGO, "Bryan Yonish will be spotlighted for a progress account of his re-tooling of the report based upon Army input and changing the discrimination finding."[2]

"His re-tooling."

"Changing the discrimination finding."

In the words of Martin Luther King Jr., all that was needed for evil to triumph was the *silence* of good people. The IG report—crafted after millions of dollars, countless interviews, late nights of Meyer and others writing reports, Tenenbaum's own sacrifices, and his lawyers' collective work—was going to say what *anyone* would have said years before. Anyone with eyes, ears, and a heart could see that this entire fiasco was driven by bigotry.

But it also, according to Meyer and POGO, exposed a fundamental problem with the IG's office. A portion of the funding for the IG's office, and those working within it, is covered by the very agencies it is bound to investigate. The fox, in essence, is guarding the henhouse. The executive director of POGO, Danielle Brian, released the following and sent it to members of Congress:

> We believe there will always be a basic conflict of interest between the agency general counsel, whose job is to protect and defend the interests of the agency, and that of the inspector general, who must expose waste, fraud, abuse and other misconduct committed within that agency.[3]

Among the several questions that she argued need to be raised were:

- Did anti-Semitism in an Army engineering office prevent the development of armor that could have protected the U.S. military in the field?
- Has an internal Defense Department Inspector General investigation been hijacked and its conclusions altered because of internal conflicts of interest?
- Does the general counsel to the Inspector General at DoD actually consider the IG his client, or is he instead beholden to the General Counsel of the Department, who has the best interests of the Secretary and the Department in mind?

The document continued:

Tenenbaum is a civilian mechanical engineer with the U.S. Army Tank Automotive and Armaments Command (TACOM) in Warren, Michigan, where he created a program designed to upgrade the armor on the Army's light armor vehicles, including Humvees. In the early 1990s, some of his colleagues and supervisors suspected that he was a spy for Israel. Tenenbaum was suspended, his security clearance revoked, and the FBI launched an investigation of him. But the U.S. Attorney's Office closed the case without bringing any charges. Tenenbaum returned to TACOM, but not to his previous position. In fact, the Army not only restored Tenenbaum's security clearance but it upgraded his clearance from secret to top secret. He then filed a religious discrimination lawsuit but the case was dismissed on the basis of "state secrets privilege"; the Army attorney who recommended the assertion of that privilege was Uldric L. Fiore, Jr.

In 2006, at the request of Sen. Carl Levin (D-Michigan), the Deputy IG for Investigations was asked to examine whether Tenenbaum had been treated unfairly and been discriminated against because of his religion. After an investigation, the finding reached was: "Mr. Tenenbaum experienced religious discrimination when his Judaism was weighed as a significant factor."

The questionable conflicts of interest arose when the investigators' findings had to be okayed by the IG's general counsel. But lo and behold: the IG's general counsel was one Uldric L. Fiore, Jr., who did not initially disclose his former involvement in the case. When it was discovered, he initially refused to recuse himself. Once he was recused, the legal "scrub" was assigned to his staff members.

The documents received by POGO show that those staff members have now apparently decided to ditch the investigators' original finding of discrimination. An internal email obtained by POGO says that at an upcoming "Tenenbaum meeting," one of those staff members "will be spotlighted for a progress account of his re-tooling of the report based upon Army input and changing the discrimination finding."

A man has a backpack at work. He's a Jew. Clearly, he's smuggling out documents for Israel—this despite the man in question *creating* a program to save soldiers' lives and limbs.

A man tests "deceptive" on his own polygraph. "I must have been having a dream" about that Jew Tenenbaum.

A man makes hotel reservations to reserve a room in a hotel that serves kosher meals. Clearly, he is a traitor.

If someone wrote this into a movie, Tenenbaum knew, no one would believe it.

But at last, unnumbered deaths later, and after a man's life and career and finances had been ruined, the IG-DOD found, unequivocally, that anti-Semitism was at the root of it all. Not only was it at the root of it all, but anti-Semitism was the *only* factor that existed against Tenenbaum. All that the evidence gathered after months and years of FBI and IG investigations proved was that Tenenbaum was the victim of religious discrimination.

However, even at the zero hour—with the actual report signed under cover of night because of the interference on this case—Chuck Beardall sent a secret email, a copy of which came across the fax machine at Morganroth & Morganroth, in which he stated that the "finding" of "discrimination" needed to be changed. Beardall wanted it "rewritten." (See Appendix 14.)

Tenenbaum's attorney sent a letter to the deputy IG for investigations threatening them with litigation. Mr. Morganroth, Tenenbaum's lead attorney, wrote a letter to the IG:

> I want to assure you that there will be no finality regarding Dr. Tenenbaum until the original Investigation Report is released and justice has been obtained for Dr. Tenenbaum and his family. In the event of any tampering with or re-writing the Investigation Report, we will not hesitate to commence litigation, on behalf of Dr. Tenenbaum, against each and every individual who participated in any such activity which would clearly constitute obstruction of justice and a violation of the Inspector General's required neutrality and proper oversight. Furthermore, tampering with or re-writing the Investigation Report would be an insult to the families of the thousands of soldiers who were killed and the tens of thousands of soldiers who were wounded and maimed due to insufficient vehicle armor which might have been corrected with the LASS program which was another casualty of what the Investigation Report concluded were acts of anti-Semitism and other unlawful conduct perpetrated against Dr. Tenenbaum.[4]

The letter was sent out on April 24, 2008. Tenenbaum and his attorneys also sent the POGO information to members of Congress. There was a tremendous debate occurring in the offices of the IG. Meyer and Ingram, who had conducted the investigation and had done the interviews of those involved in the case and heard from those involved in the anti-Semitic rhetoric, wanted to do the right thing and render a formal finding of religious discrimination.

The general counsel and his team were trying to protect the army by having the finding changed.

Letters were sent to IG Claude Kicklighter, the IG himself, from a number of organizations in support of Dr. Tenenbaum. Tenenbaum found out from Dan Meyer that John Crane told him that many of the letters were faxed to General Kicklighter but were intercepted by Patricia Brannin, the deputy IG. Brannin took those letters and shredded them before Kicklighter could see them. When it was found out what she had done and she was confronted, she said, "I don't have to answer to *those people*"—were "those people" Jews, perhaps?[5]

The audacity was chilling. Kicklighter was being deceived by his own deputy IG. Fortunately, in the persons of John Crane, Dan Meyer, and others, there was a dogged determination to wade through the deception and ensure the truth was told.

CHAPTER 26

THE LIGHT SHINES ON THE TRUTH

"All the great things are simple,
and many can be expressed in a single word:
freedom, justice, honor, duty, mercy, hope."

—WINSTON CHURCHILL

The IG report was published in July 2008. The IG ruled that the polygraph Simonini utilized to try to take down Tenenbaum was a ruse to criminally investigate Tenenbaum. Even more so, the report stated that Tenenbaum was suspected and investigated because—and *only* because—he is Jewish. This was all stated in the IG report that was published, but there was another draft of this IG report that was prevented from being published by those who tried to change the report findings. This "draft" report was even more damning to the Department of the Army. (See Appendix 15.)

But in short, the United States Army illegally discriminated against Tenenbaum because of his religion. For no other reason.

The government didn't even address Snyder not taping his interrogations or his abuse toward Tenenbaum. They didn't address many things that Tenenbaum and his supporters said and still say must change. They did not address the fundamental issue of the IG's office receiving funding that finances the very salaries and careers of the people it investigates—a problem that remains to this day.

But in this case, the report of the IG states—without wavering—that Tenenbaum was the victim of ethnic and religious bigotry. Tenenbaum finally felt at least partially vindicated. The local as well as national newspapers wrote about the IG report. The newspaper stand on the base at TACOM sold out within hours of the *Detroit Free Press*, with the IG report story on the front page.

Tenenbaum wondered how the people at TACOM would react. He thought that they would finally see that he was completely innocent of any wrongdoing whatsoever and would congratulate him.

He was ready when one woman who he worked with approached him with the *Detroit Free Press* article about the IG report. But she just looked at him and said, "See what you have done? It's all your fault. You are to blame."

Tenenbaum just looked at her. He was too stunned to say anything. She thought he'd brought shame upon the base.

Apparently, for some, the shame of prejudice was acceptable. It was the negative spotlight that was the problem. Perhaps the old patterns of thinking were too entrenched. It takes real leadership to change the culture of a base, of a ship, of a boardroom. It is true regarding religious discrimination and so many other things.

Around the time Meyer worked on the Tenenbaum case, there were increasing concerns of sexual harassment within multiple government sectors. Women were moving into the military and up through the ranks. Some might have shrugged remarks off with "boys being boys," but in one case, a commander came to Meyer and asked for advice on dealing with a recent rise in sexual harassment within his command. Meyer was known, in his own words, as "the Ivy League guy, the stuffed shirt," so it was him the commander asked what to do. Meyer pointed out that around the officer's lounge, his senior and junior officers would frequently deride fellow officers with the word "cunt." Meyer pointed out that if the officers were using that term, dropping it casually, the attitude that underlay that word would be conveyed to the men and women in the ranks. "Candid language is great. It's cathartic. I swear like a longshoreman all the time. But when I do it, I am mindful that words have long tails littered with culture, and some of the culture is demeaning and wrong. You need to choose your words wisely, and know their impact. Leadership leads with words, almost exclusively. Sailors will pick up actions, but it is words that tie everything together."

It affected how the men looked at women—not as equals, but as exploitable anatomical parts.

The commander thanked Meyer, and the very next time the word was dropped among the officers, he stood up and said use of the word "was conduct unbecoming of an officer," a prosecutable offense. He took the leadership, took the reins. Eventually, the word was eradicated. Over time, women were more accepted. Harassment cases diminished. That navy captain became a three-star admiral.

What TACOM needed was *that* kind of leadership. No one should have felt that Tenenbaum was at fault. Yet Simonini remained in charge of counterintelligence. And Tenenbaum was still a pariah.

And the army wasn't done with its tricks.

A few days after his vindication, Tenenbaum was called into his supervisor's office and told that he needed to undergo a drug test.

"It is common for someone at your security clearance level to have to undergo a 'surprise' random drug test," his supervisor said. "You were randomly chosen."

Tenenbaum—this new Tenenbaum who wasn't going to cooperate with them anymore—leaned back in his chair, a bemused and disgusted smile on his face.

"Really? I was randomly chosen. How? All of a sudden after five years of having a top secret clearance I have been randomly chosen? I would like to know who ordered the test. Show me the federal regulation which you say mandates random drug testing."

Others involved in the negative aspects of the IG report were also "coincidently" ordered to undergo a drug test. Tenenbaum was skeptical at best.

Tenenbaum sent an email to his supervisors explaining his position:

Pursuant to my attorney's instructions, please provide me with a formal written request to submit to a random drug test signed by the head of the department requesting such test or, in the event that no department is requesting such test, the person requesting such test. Given the circumstances of my case and the fact/coincidence that other individuals involved in the Inspector General's investigation and report concerning my case were also requested to submit to a random drug test, I require a formal written and signed request in order to ensure that the test is being properly requested and administered.[1]

Tenenbaum never heard from his supervisor again about a drug test.

About a week later, Tenenbaum had to undergo required training. He was one of the last to arrive at the conference room where the training was being held and had to sit at the head of a very large conference table. He sat next to his supervisor. There were close to forty people in the conference room. One person was teleconferencing in from Washington, D.C. The training hadn't yet begun, and the person calling in from Washington was obviously not privy to who was in the conference room. He was shooting the breeze with one of the people in the room who sat at the other end of the table from Tenenbaum.

In the midst of the conversation, the man asked, "Hey what's with this spy guy, Tenenbaum?" The room fell silent, and then everyone looked toward David Tenenbaum. The voice on the phone continued, "Hey, is he still working there? What did he do?"

No one said anything. They just kept staring.

Finally, Tenenbaum was the one who spoke.

"If you have any questions to ask, why don't you just ask me?"

"And who are you?"

"Me? I'm Tenenbaum."

There was a very uncomfortable silence which permeated throughout the room. Everyone was quiet. Then, Tenenbaum's supervisor, Ralph, spoke up.

"I think it's time we started the training."

Tenenbaum looked to his left where the caller's supervisor was sitting and said, "You need to speak to Joe."

"I'm not speaking to him."

"You can't let him say that."

"I'm not speaking to him."

Ralph looked at the caller's supervisor, who also happened to work for Ralph and said to him, "See me in my office after the training. You need to speak with him."

Leadership and character remained absent. No one was taking the lead to change the culture that allowed Tenenbaum to be treated this way.

It seems that in some ways, things became worse for Tenenbaum after the IG report was published.

THE RESTRICTION AND REPLACEMENT OF HUMVEES

Between 1985 and 2010, AM General, the company that came up with the initial design of the Humvee as a replacement for older-styled army jeeps, produced roughly 240,000 of the military vehicles.[1]

In July of 2010, knowing the weaknesses of Humvees and seeing the possibilities of other, more effective vehicles for such volatile war zones, Major General John Campbell, commander of Joint Task Force-101, ordered that specific approval would now be needed by a colonel for Humvees to be used outside of a military base.[2] Colonels are one of the most senior field-grade positions in the military. The Humvee issue was finally being taken seriously.

It was a vehicle that was never designed to be used in the heat of combat. With its protruding grill and muscular frame, it was the assistant to the heavily armored tanks of the first Gulf War. Just like the jeep before it, the Humvee became a symbol of strength, ingenuity, and ruggedness that is recognizable by military and non-military Americans alike. It was the perfect all-terrain vehicle, as was needed in the deserts of the Middle East, yet its weaknesses outnumbered its strengths in war zones dotted with IEDs.

MRAPs, the same mine-resistant ambush protected vehicles that Franz Gayl had spoken so highly of, had been chosen to be the replacement for much of the Humvee fleet in Iraq and Afghanistan by the US Marine Corps in 2007, and by the time of the Humvee restriction in 2010, they were beginning to arrive for the soldiers there. MRAPs could protect the men and women inside them far better than the Humvees, though their maneuverability paled in comparison.[3]

As of the time of this writing, a Joint Light Tactical Vehicle (JLTV) program is in the works to build a vehicle with the strength and protection of an MRAP but the ease of mobility of the Humvee.[4] Frontlines of the battlefield aren't as clear as they used to be, and the military is adjusting. IEDs usually detonate unexpectedly. No one can be prepared for everything that comes their way, but if nothing else, they can ensure everyone's given as fair a chance as possible.

CHAPTER 27

AFTERMATH

"There may be times when we are powerless to prevent injustice,
but there must never be a time when we fail to protest."

—ELIE WIESEL

A few years after the IG-DOD published its report, Tenenbaum was called into the office of one of the associate directors for TARDEC. When he arrived, he saw Simonini leaving. The man's presence still made him uncomfortable, but before Tenenbaum even had the chance to sit down, the associate director who summoned him started talking.

"Who are you working with? What programs are you working on?" She blurted out.

He was taken aback. It was not an unusual question, but it just came from out of the blue. Before Tenenbaum even had a chance to respond, she continued.

"I'm livid…I am livid…who are you working with?"

Tenenbaum kept himself collected, but he felt his brow furrowing. "You mean you're angry with me?"

"No," she said, taking a deep breath, "but I need to know what you are working on and with whom."

Tenenbaum shifted in his seat.

"I'm working with Boeing. I am looking at applying aircraft models and survivability technology to ground combat vehicles." It was a project he was really enjoying, and they were making good progress. It was good to feel proud of something, to know his work could really make a difference. "There are enough similarities to utilize the way aircraft are designed for safety and survivability and maybe, just maybe apply it to ground combat vehicles. We can partner up with the airline industry and perhaps save time and money."

She nodded before continuing.

"Well, let me tell you what happened." She laced her fingers together on her desk. "Did you recently have a conference call with a number of Boeing personnel across the US?"

"Yes."

"Apparently one of those Boeing engineers decided to Google-search your name. They found a great deal of information which worried them. They called someone in their security division who called our security division"—Tenenbaum knew this meant Simonini—"who called me and wanted to know what is going on. I am livid. How dare they check into one of my engineers as if he has committed some type of crime?" She flattened her hands on the desk. "For an instant, I just sat there with nothing to say."

Tenenbaum's core tightened in a way that was too familiar. Would there really never be a day he would be past this?

"I am attempting to develop a program and save us time and money by utilizing technology and science which exists now," he said, "and I am being scrutinized and questioned because no one from the army ever apologized and can't stand up for me. And it goes right back to Simonini, who was the primary 'screwup' who has the ability to tell them not to work with me, the fox guarding the henhouse. He could tell them to back off and instead comes to…what…complain to you?"

"I am writing them a letter. How dare they suspect one of my engineers."

Tenenbaum left her office with the understanding that he would receive a copy of that letter, though he never did receive a copy, despite asking for one.

Old feelings lingered. Discomfort. Distrust. Disturbances in the work atmosphere that no amount of work ethic or perseverance could seem to erase.

Then, in approximately January of 2013, Tenenbaum, against his wishes, was transferred to the Ground Systems Survivability Division

(GSS)—his old group, where he was suspected of being a spy. Tenenbaum was appalled that he was being transferred back to the group.

Although many of the original people no longer worked in that area, the black cloud still hung over Tenenbaum's head. He did not want to go back. In the over twenty years since he was originally accused, he had rarely returned to the part of the building where the GSS was located. Even when he had to go there, he cringed and only went if there was no other choice.

As one of his supporters stated, "It's like post-traumatic stress disorder. Imagine if your colleagues lied, painted you as a traitor. Now imagine as it went up through the chain of command, every higher-up was willing to cover up what happened in order to keep the momentum going. Your family was threatened. Your life and career dismantled. Then, one day, they want you to go back and see those same faces again. It's disgraceful."[1]

Some improvised explosives were devices in the war zone. Some improvised explosives were crafted by lies and actions lacking any moral fiber. Both had an impact at the boom. Both could tear a man's life apart.

Usually, if Tenenbaum had to meet with someone in that area of the building, he asked them to meet with him in a different area. But now he was being told that he had to move not just to that building, but to the area housing the GSS.

No longer willing to be silent when he felt he was not being treated fairly, Tenenbaum repeatedly vocalized his concerns. After numerous discussions, he was told that he could remain in the area in which he currently sat but that he would have to work for the GSS. However, after a very short period of time, his new "supervisor" threatened to suspend Tenenbaum for refusing to sit in the GSS area despite Tenenbaum producing physician's letters that were clear that Tenenbaum must not sit in that area. Tenenbaum's supervisor began docking Tenenbaum's pay, at which time Tenenbaum filed with the Equal Employment Opportunity Commission (EEOC).

At the hearing, the presiding judge looked at the evidence before him, then looked at Tenenbaum and his attorney and said, "Is there any way you would settle this right now?" in obvious disgust with what the "GSS supervisors" were doing.

The GSS/TACOM had no choice but to agree with Tenenbaum and his attorney. Interestingly, right before the EEOC hearing, Tenenbaum received a letter from his supervisor's supervisor stating that Tenenbaum deserved to be suspended from duty and that there were very serious charges against him…but he felt that Tenenbaum could be rehabilitated. Eventually, though, Tenenbaum ended up being transferred to the robotics section, where he is still attempting to develop programs.

Despite his security clearance, Tenenbaum no longer had the ability to get a program started. LASS didn't exist, and any attempts by Tenenbaum to begin a discussion on the Humvee situation was hampered by the fact that no up-and-coming engineers or career personnel within the TACOM base were going to risk career suicide to work with someone who had, in the minds of most, a black mark on his record.

His security clearances were all restored. In fact, his security clearance now was higher: top secret. But he was forbidden to ever work with Israel, a US ally, again, meaning that his background, the background that was once considered an asset, was somehow construed as potentially dirty or potentially dangerous to the government.

No one would work with him on projects, even after his success with the restraint system for the Humvees that also translated to a new system for ambulances in the civilian world. He knew his work was doing good, but again, he heard others taking credit for the designs. His name was stricken from final engineering reports. He didn't need glory, but he wanted to exist.

Dr. David Tenenbaum is essentially still in no man's land. A pariah.

Simonini left the DOD in August 2016 without ever being punished for what he had done. In fact, he issued a stern warning to everyone beneath him that they were forbidden to speak about the Tenenbaum case and the writing of this book.

Thomas F. Gimble, the acting and later principal deputy IG who negotiated the Tenenbaum report's completion also supervised a report finding that the Pentagon had unlawfully conducted intelligence operations in violation of Executive Order 12333. This finding was unpopular with the Bush administration, and thus Gimble was not chosen to be the permanent, statutorily confirmed IG. He served as deputy under IG Kicklighter until he retired.

John Crane was forced from the building and left government employ in 2013. The reason is somewhat shrouded in secrecy as there is ongoing litigation, but mainly it appears to be because he knows too much. His congressional disclosures regarding Zero Dark Thirty and corruption within the IG-DOD may have also contributed to the force-out. In a McClatchy article, he neither confirmed nor denied he was the person Joseph Schmitz referred to in his Holocaust denials. He neither confirmed nor denied he was the person who knew Uldric Fiore's obsession with Nazis. However, he has stated on the record that when the time comes, if he is placed under oath, he is willing to testify to the dehumanizing conditions in this book.[2]

Dan Meyer's career is still tainted by the "finding of the D-word." He, too, a champion of whistleblowers, sued IG-DOD Jon T. Rymer in 2016 for discrimination he received as a gay man in his governmental career, ultimately settling the case as Rymer departed and a new inspector general, Glenn Fine, took over. Continuing the tradition of aggressive oversight under the protection of IG Irwin Charles McCullough III in the intelligence community, the spirit of the Tenenbaum investigation continued in the community until McCullough and his boss, James Clapper, retired in 2017.

Within a year, Meyer was on his way out of federal serving and back in private practice. Fast-tracked for senior executive service selection in 2010, he was bumped aside after Race's conviction for violating US banking laws. The same year, he had led the list for President Obama's selection as US special counsel after Elizabeth "Beth" Slavet stepped aside. When Carolyn Lerner was eventually selected over him, Meyer was told, "You are too independent." McCullough, who (horrified) watched all of this from the National Security Agency and Office of the Director of National Intelligence, resolved to have Meyer promoted to the Senior National Intelligence Service during the spring of 2017. Retiring three weeks before the board decision, McCullough believed he had ensured Meyer's selection, but instead he watched as Meyer was not only looked over, but also as the IC whistleblowing initiative of

President Obama and Director Clapper was brought to an end over the next eight months.

Most of the other players who were part of the persecution of Tenenbaum were promoted.

Patricia Brannin, who allegedly referred to Jews as "those people," was nominated for a monetary award—which she was awarded—by the DOD.

And Dr. Tenenbaum is still waiting for justice.

Over the past few years, Tenenbaum has been sent additional information that only serves to add more fuel to the fire. Based on the positive report of the IG-DOD in July 2008, Tenenbaum should have been given a remedy for the blatant anti-Semitism perpetrated by the US Army as well as the continuous retaliations, which have not stopped as this book is being written. What happened? Per a sworn statement by a high-level government official:

> In regard to the Tenenbaum case, Mr. Shelly [who was the general counsel for the IG-DOD as Uldric Fiore was fired, and was Fiore's right-hand man] repeatedly raised the Jewish backgrounds of Mr. Levine and Chairman Levin as the only reason they supported Mr. Tenenbaum. Mr. Shelly repeatedly used the term "Jewish conspiracy" and "the Jews" when referring to the congressional support Mr. Tenenbaum received. Mr. Shelly was particularly adamant about a "Jewish conspiracy" when outside civil advocacy groups wrote letters to General Kicklighter on behalf of Mr. Tenenbaum.[3]

It seems that Henry Shelly, at that time the general counsel for the IG-DOD blocked any remedy attempts for Dr. Tenenbaum. And it also seems that he blocked FOIA requests put into the IG-DOD for further information on the Tenenbaum case.

In the preparation of this book, one of the interviewees who remains on the base asserted, "I don't know if David is guilty or not."[4] Despite millions of wasted taxpayer dollars, an unwavering IG report and more, it appears Jew as Other—as dual-loyal scapegoat—remains.

In short, *nothing* has changed.

AFTERMATH

Though at the current time there are up-armoring efforts on Humvees and a reexamination of where they should be used, the persecution of Tenenbaum meant the government lost *years* of a head start on doing so—with the human tolls of death and dismemberment as a result.

They also lost the visionary who was trying to help US soldiers long before any such programs existed.

They lost time.

They lost limbs.

They lost lives.

They lost the way of truth and fairness.

CHAPTER 28

ARE WE THERE YET?

*"Those who cannot remember the past
are condemned to repeat it."*

—GEORGE SANTAYANA

"Tenenbaum is trouble. Stay away from him," his colleagues have been warned.

Search engines like Google remain a constant adversary, spreading rumors and old news stories without their corrections or amendments.

Circa 2016, Tenenbaum set up a meeting at a university in Washington, D.C. with a number of researchers and professors in the area of traumatic brain injury (TBI) research. A few weeks before the meeting, one of the professors sent him an email stating that he saw (by searching Tenenbaum's name) that he had some problems with the government and that he needed to explain himself before this professor would be willing to meet. He sent this email to everyone with whom Tenenbaum was supposed to meet.

Tenenbaum asked the TACOM attorney to follow up with an email explaining that he had never done anything wrong, but the attorney refused. Needless to say, the university refused to work with Tenenbaum.

On November 2, 2017, a letter from Senator Claire McCaskill, a Democrat from Missouri, and Senator Gary Peters, a Democrat from Michigan, was sent to the secretary of defense asking him to right the wrong in the Tenenbaum case. (See Appendix 16.)

In a meeting held between the senators' staffers and officials from the Department of the Army who represented the secretary of defense, the army would not even acknowledge that Dr. David A. Tenenbaum was the victim of anti-Semitism by its own leaders. They said the IG-DOD report was not comprehensive enough (after two years of an intensive investigation), that there was no anti-Semitism (despite all of the interviews, anti-Semitic quotes from government personnel regarding Tenenbaum, and an IG-DOD report stating that the investigation was anti-Semitism), and that they were not going to do anything.[1] As of the writing of this book, the case is still being "worked" through the "system."

EPILOGUE

This book is the true story of how the US government spent millions of dollars on a criminal investigation, not to determine whether or not Tenenbaum was guilty of treason, but to prove that he was guilty. Innocence was never in the cards as far as the government was concerned. The theme was guilty until proven innocent. And even after it was proven that Tenenbaum was completely innocent of any wrongdoing whatsoever, the army and its various intelligence agencies still refused to apologize, and, on the contrary, solicited the support of the judicial system to ensure that this case never goes to a jury trial and the facts of the case never become public.

The state secrets privilege should strike fear in the hearts of all Americans. If they can do this to Tenenbaum, they can do it to anyone. Indeed, if even religious discrimination is considered a matter of national security, then national security has no boundaries or limits over civil rights. There cannot be a free society when national security trumps all. There is no freedom without liberty and justice, and liberty and justice cannot exist when national security can trump them.

Those who think this is a democratic society, home of the free and the brave, should consider the middle-of-the-night knocks on the doors of Dr. Tenenbaum's friends and a community of Holocaust survivors who felt, yet again, like their government was not just abandoning them but victimizing them.

They should consider the now-adult Nechama Tenenbaum, whose girlhood was marred by the thought of men with badges and guns coming for her father.

They should consider the ever-faithful Madeline Tenenbaum drawing the shades as the media accosted her and her children.

The power of learning from our own history should be made very clear to us. But the pattern of anti-Semitism continues to this day despite the economic and cultural contributions Jews have made throughout history. Even our own government abuses its rights and privileges and has been found to religiously profile Jews who work for the DOD because, like other countries before them, they believe, as the 1995 DOD memo suggested, that Jews carry dual loyalties with a stronger loyalty towards Israel. Yet, rather than admit their abuse, the government allows for it to happen, protects those who are guilty of it, and then allows the perpetrators to hide behind the cloak of national security to ensure that they can continue to religiously discriminate against those who are different. Their objective, it seems, is to continue their profiling based on how Jewish someone is and, at the same time, to make sure that what they do does not become public.

AUTHOR'S NOTE

The wars in Afghanistan and Iraq have killed over three thousand soldiers and injured over thirty-three thousand. Over 2,550 soldiers have specifically died from IEDs.[1] In unprecedented numbers, young men have returned from the war theatre with their genitals blown off. Gone. From IEDs.[2] Over 1,500 US soldiers have returned without a limb.

But even those who appear unscathed often have the hallmark issue of Middle Eastern warfare—traumatic brain injury. Even milder blasts can cause concussions, headaches, dizziness, and mental confusion. Worse, sometimes these blasts are compounded and the brain suffers neurological damage. Stateside, these soldiers often face depression and post-traumatic stress disorder that sometimes lead to suicide.

A decade before the start of the wars in the Middle East, as a US Army civilian engineer, I began developing my Light-Armored Systems Survivability (LASS) program with a goal of finding a way to improve the US Army's light-armored combat vehicles—like HMMWVs—and make them less vulnerable to the devastation of roadside bombs. I relentlessly insisted there had to be a better way to equip these vehicles for the realities of urban combat for the purpose of saving soldiers' lives. There had to be a way to make the vehicles safer, stronger, and able to withstand the shrapnel of improvised devices. Our idea was to combine the knowledge and expertise of three countries—all US allies—with real battlefield experience along with experimental ballistic knowledge in the area of explosive devices and combat vehicles. These allies, working together, could save lives—and limbs, and brains.

I had many years of experience working with both the Germans and the Israelis over the course of my career. In fact, I also worked with the British, Canadians, Dutch, French, Italians, Swedes, Swiss, and

251

Singaporeans. My skills at navigating the delicate cross-cultural relationships between the US military and other countries had once meant that I was fast-tracked for upper management. It was these skills in part that enabled me to gain a secret security clearance at the US government's TACOM base in Warren, Michigan.

I was comfortable working with engineers and the military around the world, and in the case of the LASS program, a program I cocreated and headed, I felt Germany and Israel could strongly contribute to the program and save US combat troops' lives because of both their past experiences as well as their advanced technology and computer modeling expertise in the areas of ballistics and survivability.

Based on the now-discredited testimony of a Jew-hating lieutenant colonel in the counterintelligence office of TACOM and one of the nation's top military polygraph experts, who appeared to think nothing of manufacturing "confessions," I was framed as an Israeli spy and accused of one of the most horrific crimes a US government employee could be accused of: espionage against the United States government. A crime that carries the death penalty.

Before my ordeal was over—though it is still not fully "over"—the US government would expend *millions* of dollars on a bogus investigation; higher-ups in the IG's office would resign in protest; US senators and high-ranking government officials would demand an investigation; my family's lives would be placed in danger; my career would be destroyed; my personal finances would be decimated; and my fellow Orthodox Jews in a neighborhood that was home to Holocaust survivors would be harassed and threatened by the police. In addition to the destruction of lives and of my career, the LASS program, which I fully believe would have prevented the grievous bodily harm and death of US soldiers in the wars in the Middle East, would be dismantled.

Perhaps even more surprising and egregious than the anti-Semitic personal bias of key figures in the US military is that no one within the Inspector General's Office for the DOD or TACOM would ever be held accountable for their racist and criminal actions. TACOM attorneys and high-level senior officials stood behind a proven anti-Semite and conspired to attempt to fire me even though it was proven that I was completely innocent of all allegations. These high-level officials within

TACOM and the IG-DOD were not only complacent, but were active participants in the "Jew hunt."

After millions of dollars and years of investigations and lawsuits, I have been completely cleared. I try to hold onto the words of Claude M. Kicklighter, who wrote to the Honorable Carl Levin, the chairman of the Armed Services Committee at the time:

> It is also my opinion that the initial personnel security and counterintelligence investigation process was poorly handled and managed, although the appeal process ultimately exonerated Mr. David Tenenbaum. It is my belief that Mr. Tenenbaum is, and has always been, a dedicated, loyal and professional civil servant in the service of our Nation. (See Appendix 17.)

But my life and reputation are still a work in progress.

As of this writing, I still have not received reparations, or even an apology, from my country to which I devoted my life and career.

APPENDICES

Appendix 1

Jews have long been depicted in past as well as present literature in a less-than-flattering light. In Daniel Defoe's novel *Roxana: The Fortunate Mistress* (1724), he portrays the blackguard Jew dealer the following way: "...whose face contorts into that of the devil at the sight of the heroine's jewels and whose skullduggery is reflected in the stream of wicked epithets—such as 'villain, cursed, rogue, dog of a Jew, traitor'— that are used to allude to this nameless fiend." Many of these tags are still used nowadays for Jews.[1]

Appendix 2

According to AR 381-12, 4-2: "DA (Department of the Army) personnel will report those threat-related incidents specified in paragraph 3-1 to the supporting CI office within 24 hours after learning of the incident. Persons who report threat-related incidents, behavioral indicators, or CI matters which are intentionally false or fabricated may be subject to disciplinary or administrative action."[2]

Appendix 3

Simonini, through the instant motion and through his October 31, 2001 deposition testimony, completely reversed himself and admitted that he suspected Tenenbaum of being a security risk because Tenenbaum is Jewish. Simonini testified as follows:

> Q: Then the statement that says, "I also felt he had natural religious and ethnic sympathies" would still have been written in here?

A: Sure. Because it's very hard from the Jewish cultural perspective to separate religion from their heritage. It's a big element of their heritage.

Q: So because he was Jewish, whether he was Orthodox or Conservative, wouldn't have mattered to you because it's linked with a cultural aspect?

A: Absolutely. Correct.

Q: And when you say ethnic sympathies, you're talking about Jewish sympathies, correct?

A: Sure.

Q: The natural religious was the Jewish religion, whether he was Orthodox or not doesn't matter?

A: It's hard to separate Jewish history without their religion. Other societies and cultures are a little bit different.

Simonini's comments about Jewish history and other cultures drew gasps from the other participants in the deposition.[3]

Appendix 4

Gugino was asked about these events in a sworn deposition.

Question: Did you ever come to know an allegation made by Simonini before the criminal case was brought up that Tenenbaum had admitted to Simonini himself in the presence of Paul Barnard that he had been passing unauthorized information to the Israelis?

Gugino: You know, that's possible. I don't remember that specifically. If you have something I can refer to, I would appreciate looking at it because I just can't remember.

Question: Well, I know it's in your 302, but what I'm looking at right here is in the DSS file.

Gugino: You know, I read all those 302's [sic], and there may have been some statement I recall to that effect, but anyway, it didn't mean anything to me because it wasn't concrete enough.

Question: I understand it's not concrete enough, but it would be significant if the Director of Intelligence and Counterintelligence at TACOM is telling you Tenenbaum had made another admission that could have led somebody to believe he's passing classified information to the Israelis.

Gugino: Well, I had a few people give me the same information over and over again that they had information that would be helpful to an investigation that Mr. Tenenbaum was passing information to a foreign government representative, but I didn't have anybody who ever, witnessed such an act, could tell me when it happened, how it happened, where it happened, to whom what information was given…As a matter of fact, every time I made another investigative inquiry, as to the possibility that Israel or one of their allies was making some advancements in tank technology that paralleled in the research and development at TARDEC, nobody in the United States government could give me an example.

At the very least I was skeptical. So people would make statements like that to me, and even if Mr. Simonini had made that statement to me, I would not have been satisfied until that point in time that I could have sat down with Mr. Tenenbaum and his attorney and gone for days asking detailed questions.

Question: Simonini had led the DSS people to believe that Paul Barnard was also present when Tenenbaum allegedly made that comment.

Gugino: Right.

Question: And according to the DSS memo, Barnard says he recalls the meeting on July 16 [where Simonini claims that Tenenbaum admitted passing classified information to Israel] however, does not recall subject i.e. Tenenbaum making any direct admissions regarding unauthorized disclosures to the Israelis.

Gugino: Yes, I read that.

Question: Do you recall Simonini generating a report about this alleged comment made by Tenenbaum July 16, 1996?

Gugino: No, and if I read it, I skimmed it, and I don't remember it, but I don't remember it.

Question: Do you think that it would have been a reasonable precaution by someone in Mr. Simonini's position that had Mr. Tenenbaum made that admission, he would have made a report about it and at least done something about that allegation?

Gugino: Oh, I think so. If such a statement were made, an incriminating statement like that, I think that he would have at least thought about bringing that to the FBI because we are in power to conduct investigation into espionage activities.[4]

Appendix 5

Why in the world would someone—i.e., Simonini—give a higher-level clearance to an engineer who he had already judged to be a spy—not only a spy, but one who has and could have caused so much damage, "a nuclear bomb," to the Armed Forces of the United States of America? This first question was also asked of Mr. Paul Barnard, Simonini's second-in-command, who was just as surprised and perplexed as Tenenbaum and his attorneys. Gugino responded as follows:

Question: Okay, did Simonini ever inform you that he thought unequivocally that Tenenbaum was spying for the Israelis?

Gugino: Ask me that again.

Question: Did Simonini ever tell you unequivocally that he thought Tenenbaum is a spy for the Israelis?

Gugino: You're asking me to recall conversations I can't recall, but I clearly had that indication that that was his belief.

Question: His opinion was, hey, the guy is, quote, guilty?

Gugino: Yeah, dirty, guilty, something like that. I remember reading that or hearing it, yeah. This was the beginning of the Yourchock and Riley set up of Tenenbaum for the eventual polygraph.

Appendix 6

Even Gugino did not feel that Tenenbaum should have undergone a polygraph. He even commented on his reservations about polygraphs in general:

> There was a lot of interest from various parts to resolve this issue once and for all and I had a key desire to get it resolved once and for all because generally I am not a big believer in polygraphs [sic] examinations. I've used them during my career as an FBI agent and they have been a beneficial tool, but I did not really believe that a polygraph would have been extremely useful at this point in time because personally I didn't feel like I had enough information on which to base a polygraph examination. In other words, as an investigator it would be my responsibility to sit down and write out the detailed questions that should be asked during a polygraph examination. Prior to the DIS Interview, of Mr. Tenenbaum, which occurred I believe on February 3rd, I didn't have enough information to do that and I didn't know if anybody did.[5]

Appendix 7

Gugino had entered TACOM thinking that he was going to catch this traitor, and suddenly, things were not moving along as smoothly as he expected. Tenenbaum was cooperating and giving him conflicting information to that of the polygraph examiner. According to Gugino:

> It became quickly evident to me that questions I was attempting to ask were not quite squaring with Mr. Tenenbaum. In other words, I was attempting to ask some questions, I don't remember the specific questions, about answers that had supposedly been given by him to Mr. Snyder during the polygraph examination and his body language, his demeanor, his verbal answers to me indicated that was not correct.[6]

Appendix 8

Gugino's remarks on this include the following:

> Question: Isn't one of the other reasons you had reservations on February 14, 1997 [the day the search was conducted on the Tenenbaum home] is that you expressed concerns about the reliability of the information you were getting from the polygraph examiner, Mr. Snyder?
>
> Gugino: I did.
>
> Question: Are you saying that the only time, the first time you began to suspect Mr. Snyder's results in the polygraph was when you were interviewing Mr. Tenenbaum on February the 14th and he suggested or was surprised by some of the remarks that you made that Snyder had indicated they covered.
>
> Gugino: Yes.
>
> Question: Weren't you expressing concerns with Snyder's representation even before you interviewed Mr. Tenenbaum on February the 14th?
>
> Gugino: That was a personal thing.
>
> Question: Well, didn't you tell Agent Riley that you had "reservations regarding the accuracy of Snyder's account of the interview of February 13, 1997"? Didn't you tell that to Riley?
>
> Gugino: I'm sure I did, especially if you have a record of it, because I know I was thinking it and I probably said it.
>
> Question: As of the 14th, before you talked to Mr. Tenenbaum, you have reservations about Snyder's accuracy, don't you?
>
> Gugino: Yes.
>
> Question: What were those reservations?
>
> Gugino: I don't know how to talk to that issue. I really don't know how to explain it. I just had a feeling that something wasn't adding up, and I don't know what it was.

Question: When you expressed these reservations with Mr. Riley, did you then have a phone conversation with Mr. Snyder?

Gugino: Yes.

Question: And what did you discuss in that phone conversation?

Gugino: I asked him to reiterate and confirm topics that we had discussed after the polygraph examination, and one reason was to make clear in my own mind that I understood correctly what I thought he had said and to try and ascertain if for some reason I was being given misleading information.[7]

Appendix 9

Gugino testified in his August 19, 1999 deposition that he did not want to search Tenenbaum's house and he made it quite clear to Tenenbaum and his attorney Marty Crandall that he was uncomfortable doing the search. Again, he wanted to close this investigation but apparently was overruled by FBI Headquarters in Washington.

Question: But as early as the same day you opened the investigation you had reservations about conducting the criminal investigation?

Gugino: Oh yeah, sure I did.

Question: What led you to those reservations?

Gugino: Mostly no new information had ever developed. I worked on this particular case, on the investigation of David Tenenbaum, practically every day the cases were opened, the two preliminary investigations and then after February 14th of 1997, the criminal espionage investigation, and I never developed any new information.

Question: And you concluded that on February the 14th?

Gugino: Well, that was on my mind, and I am sure I expressed if not in words at least in body language and sympathies to Mr.

Tenenbaum and his attorney at the time, [the time Tenenbaum's house was searched] Marty Crandall.

Question: Even though you had those reservations, you still went through the process of raiding his house.

Gugino: We were already there.

Question: Did you at some point in time early on in the investigation consider closing it out?

Gugino: From a personal standpoint, I would have been very happy to close the investigation as soon as I could have. I just did not have the sense that they were ever going to find any kind of evidence that anything had been compromised...I would have done it because the information that Yourchock and Riley were uncovering was information that I had already investigated. They interviewed people who had the same vague recollections, assumptions and innuendo to pass on that they had previously passed on to US Army Intelligence and Security Command (INSCOM) representatives supposedly and to colleagues of mine within the FBI and to me. It had not changed. There was nobody that could offer any evidence that Mr. Tenenbaum was acting against the best interest of US National Security.

Appendix 10

According to Seymour Hersh (1991) who won a Pulitzer Prize in 1970 for International Reporting:

Intelligence community investigators were surprised to discover at the end of the CHAOS inquiry a cache of Angleton's personal files, secured with black tape that revealed what obviously had been a long running and highly questionable study of American Jews in the government. The files showed that Angleton had constructed what amounted to a matrix of the position and Jewishness of senior officials in the CIA and elsewhere who had access to classified information of use to Israel. Someone in a sensitive position who was very active in Jewish affairs in his personal life, or perhaps had family members who were Zionists, scored high on what amounted to a Jewishness index.

One government investigator, talking about the Angleton files in a 1991 interview, recalled his surprise at discovering that even going to synagogue was a basis for suspicion.

"I remember the First Amendment," the investigator added sardonically. "You know, Freedom of Religion."[8]

APPENDICES

Appendix 11

Aberdeen Proving Ground MID
A Company 308th MI Bn, 902d MI Group,
USAINSCOM

Department of Defense

Defense contractor was fined $1 million for illegally giving away plans for sensitive U.S. military technology.

Three people, including a former Pentagon analyst and her husband, were charged with spying for East Germany and Russia in an espionage operation that began in 1972.

U.S. Army Espionage Cases

Robert Lipka, former U.S. Army clerk charged with selling defense secrets while working at the National Security Agency.

Eric Jenott, U.S. Army soldier charged with spying and breaking into military computer system.

David A. Tenenbaum, a mechanical engineer who worked for the Combat Vehicle Team at the U.S. Army Tank Automotive and Armaments Command.

U.S. Navy Espionage Cases

Robert Kim, former U.S. Navy computer specialist charged with giving defense information to a foreign government.

Kurt Lessenthien, former U.S. Navy nuclear submarine crewman sold military secrets to Russia.

Convicted spy Jonathan Pollard, former U.S. Navy intelligence officer claims he was an agent of the state of Israel.

Federal Agencies Espionage Cases

Earl Pitts, former FBI counterintelligence agent accused of spying for Russia.

Harold Nicholson, a former CIA station chief plead guilty to spying for Russia.

back to Aberdeen Proving Ground Military Intelligence Detachment Home Page

Web master:(apgmid-2@juno.com)

http://www.apg.army.mil/tenants/902dmi/ESPIONAG/Espionag.htm   7/24/00

Appendix 12

The position was originally posted as a "Whistleblower Affairs Officer," or "WHAO," senior officials within the IG-DOD did not want the "W" word in a formal position, so Civilian Reprisal Investigations was the negotiated middle ground. When he was forced out of CRI due, in part, to the Tenenbaum investigation, the new office was called the Directorate for whistleblowing and transparency (DW&T) to stick the "W" word back in the face of the program's detractors within the IG-DOD. Subsequently forced out of DW&T over *Zero Dark Thirty* and Dawood, Meyer's new protector, Inspector General of the Intelligence Community Irvin Charles McCullough III, insisted on the "W" word after recalling all the fighting over it during the previous decade.

The word "transparency" wasn't a favorite with Director of National Intelligence James Clapper, so the new IC Whistleblowing Program was housed in the Intelligence Community Whistleblowing and Source Program, or IC-WASP. "The Wasp" was the new buzzword and its catchphrase "Don't Sting; Don't Be Stung" was a reminder to supervisors, managers and employees of the intelligence community to not play games with sources or investigations.

Even though Meyer has returned to private practice, first with Compass Rose, PLLC, and now as a partner at Tully Rinckey, PLLC, an Albany-based international law firm, the IC-WASP still survives in an albeit reduced form supervised at a lower managerial level than intended. From his office overlooking Washington's central Farragut Square, Meyer now supports Tully Rinckey, PLLC's Military Law and Federal Employment practice groups, defending national defense and intelligence community employees as he has done, in fact, since 2000.[9]

APPENDICES

Appendix 13

Morganroth & Morganroth, PLLC
Attorneys At Law
3000 Town Center
Suite 1500
Southfield, Michigan 48075
FAX (248) 355-3017

URGENT   URGENT   URGENT   URGENT

Material Regarding:

David Tenenbaum

Three pages

URGENT   URGENT   URGENT   URGENT

265

ACCUSED OF TREASON

Morganroth & Morganroth, PLC
3000 town Center
Suite 1500
Southfield, Michigan 48075

May 30, 2008

Mr. Morganroth,

Your letter of April 18, 2008, was a bright ray of sunshine to so many employees of the Office of the Inspector General (OIG). Since May 2005, when Mr. Uldric Fiore was appointed as General Counsel of the Office of Inspector General by former Inspector General Joseph Schmitz, an atmosphere of fear has descended upon the entire agency. It is the sort of fear that Jews throughout Europe probably felt as the Nazi's spread across Europe – to feel defenseless and powerless as the courts and attorneys who were charged with protecting the minority are corrupted and turned into the instruments of their demise. The destruction of the Jewish community throughout Europe was, afterall, perpetrated through the manipulation of law that legally stripped citizens of their rights as citizens and who without rights became stateless people who could be sent to concentration camps.

You can imagine the shock of employees when Uldric Fiore who was intimately involved in the purge of the Jewish members of the Senior Executive Service in the OIG was appointed General Counsel! Mr. Joseph Schmitz, the son of prominent Holocaust denier Congressman John Schmitz became Inspector General in the spring of 2002. In August 2002, Joseph Schmitz in an anti-Jewish pogrom marched out of the OIG building located at 400 Army Navy Drive both Ms. Carol Levy, Director of the Defense Criminal Investigative Service and Mr. Joel Leson, Assistant Inspector General for Administration and Management. Many have described that day as a scene out of Nazi Germany. Carol Levy was without warning confronted by Security in her office, ordered to surrender both her weapon, badge and cell phone and physically escorted out of the building with no charges. Carol simply disappeared. Joel Leson while not a law enforcement officer was marched out of the building in a similar manner and disappeared. In one afternoon, the two Jewish members of the Senior Executive Service were gone with no explanation.

The personal attorney selected by Joseph Schmitz to defend himself against suits by Ms. Levy and Mr. Leson was his personal friend, then Army Colonel, Uldric Fiore! The same Uldric Fiore who litigated against David Tenenbaum while in charge of Army Litigation and who then tried to first shut down the Tenenbaum case as IG General Counsel and when challenged regarding his conflict of interest then instructed his attorneys to ensure there was no finding of discrimination.

What is especially chilling is that the selection of Mr. Uldric Fiore as General Counsel by Mr. Schmitz is widely regarded as a pay off for providing legal counsel to Mr. Schmitz in planning the pogrom of Ms. Levy Mr. Leson. It should be noted that Mr. Fiore, even while serving as a Colonel in the Army litigating against Mr. Tenenbaum, found the time to personally represent Mr. Schmitz against Ms. Levy and Mr. Leson. It should also be noted that Ms. Levy and Mr. Leson were successful in their lawsuit against Mr. Schmitz. There were absolutely no grounds found for the actions of Mr. Schmitz and defended by Colonel Fiore. The Government reached a financial settlement with the plaintiffs representing several years of income and creditable service that carried them to the minimum age for Federal retirement. Their lives, however, had been permanently altered, and their associates and peers knew they had been forced out of 400 Army Navy Drive under armed escort and made to disappear. Their careers in the Federal Government had ended and their reputations had been irrevocably damaged.

To give context to the actions of Mr. Schmitz and the atmosphere at 400 Army Navy Drive since the appointment of Mr. Fiore, it helps to review other actions of Mr. Schmitz beyond the pogrom of Ms. Levy and Mr. Leson. Mr. Schmitz was obsessed with all things militaristic, Fascist and in particular German. Mr. Schmitz used Baron von Steuben who had served first with the Prussian military and who then served with General Washington during the Revolution as a stalking horse for his extreme right wing views. A manifestation of his obsessions was a ceremony honoring von Steuben in Berlin, Germany on the 60th anniversary of the death of Adolf Hitler on April 30, 2005. Part of the celebrations was to be a visit to the Garrison Church in Potsdam Germany where in 1933 Chancellor Hindenberg and Adolf Hitler joined forces to overthrow the Weimer Republic and start the reign of Nazi terror. Imagine, an appointed American official spending tens of thousands of taxpayer dollars to visit a neo-Nazi shrine site on the 60th anniversary of the death of Adolf Hitler! Then Deputy Secretary Paul Wolfowitz learned of the bizarre nature of the plans of Mr. Schmitz and on the day Mr. Schmitz was to leave, ordered Mr. Schmitz not to attend his own celebration. The details of these events were reported on the Federal page of the Washington Post in April 2005 and publicly pursued by Chairman Charles Grassley.

For further insight into Mr. Schmitz you should simply use Google to search for Congressman John Schmitz , the father of Joseph Schmitz, who was expelled from the John Birch Society for extremism in urging the overthrow of the U.S. government to be replaced by a Prussian style Pinochet dictatorship. The father of Joseph Schmitz also publicly sponsored Holocaust denial seminars.

In that context, you can understand the above stated shock when Mr. Schmitz appointed Mr. Fiore to be General Counsel. It was especially surprising because, as is general knowledge, Mr. Fiore had applied to be a GS-15 in the Office of General Counsel, but was found to be unqualified. Mr. Schmitz then selected Mr. Fiore who had been found to be unqualified to work in the office of General Counsel to be a member of the Senior Executive Service and to be General Counsel.

In light of the above, it is urgent that you inform Chairman Levin and Senator Grassley before Mr. Fiore has an opportunity to use his direct influence to derail the case of Mr. Tenenbaum. All indications are that General Kicklighter has never been informed of the full extent of the relationship between Mr. Schmitz, the pogrom and now the actions against Mr. Tenenbaum. General Kicklighter is universally viewed to be an

267

honest and honorable man who has to fight everyday against the Office of General Counsel headed by Mr. Fiore. Many also believe that it is long past time to fully investigate how Mr. Fiore was rewarded with a position for which was not qualified.

The eyes of so many at the DoD IG are on you to ensure that there is no injustice in the case of Tenenbaum and that the unethical activities of Mr. Fiore are publicly revealed. An investigation may also remove the climate of fear caused by Mr. Fiore that make OIG employees fear for their jobs and careers in publicly stating the truth. Your effort to support David Tenenbaum may be that bright ray of sunshine that helps to illuminate the dark corners in the Office of General Counsel and remove the stain brought upon the OIG by both Mr. Schmitz and Mr. Fiore.

APPENDICES

Appendix 14

-----Original Message-----
From: Beardall, Charles W., OIG DoD
Sent: Wednesday, April 16, 2008 8:18 AM
To: Young, Shelton R., OIG DoD; Crane, John R., OIG DoD; Meyer Daniel P., OIG DoD; Ingram, David, OIG DoD; Yonish, Brian., OIG DoD; Horstman, Donald M., OIG DoD; Ragley, Donald A., OIG DoD; Shelley, Henry C., OIG DoD
Subject: Tenenbaum meeting

Sorry that I didn't get to the Front Office quickly enough to control the frequency and number of attendees at Tenenbaum meetings. Frankly, I can update the IG by myself as to the status of the report, but for this time at least, the addressees that should attend are Dave, Dan, Bryan, and me. And, Bryan will be spotlighted for a progress account of his re-tooling of the report based upon Army input and changing the discrimination finding. I previously advised the IG that Bryan was redrafting; we would vet internally; and we would have a new draft by the time he returns from his trip.

Chuck Beardall
Deputy Inspector General
for Investigations
Department of Defense

Protecting America's Warfighters

Appendix 15

Specific statements in the draft report were "left out" of the published report, such as:

- "TACOM discriminated against Tenenbaum through the actions of its supervisors and its managers."
- "The evidence collected by the OIG-DoD in this review proves a case of discrimination."
- "Mr. Simonini is not only prejudicial against someone with a religious orientation, but prejudicial against a Jewish person specifically."
- "It appears that Tenenbaum's covert and devout religious practice as an Orthodox Jew was one of the factors the group weighed in considering whether he posed a potential risk of disclosing classified information to Israel, a country known for attempting to exploit such devotion."
- "Knowing the foreign espionage offices will target American employees of the Department of Defense in recruitment campaigns, we have regulations which balance our Constitutional right to the free exercise of religion with the same document's mandate to provide for the common defense. These Department regulations permit profiling of potential spies based on demonstrated cultural affinity; they prohibit the profiling of the same based on their race or ethnicity. Lacking sufficient evidence in the SAEDAs to proceed with a counterintelligence investigation, the TACOM leadership violated these Department regulations when they decided to have DIS proceed with a single-scope background investigation (SSBI) of him for TS clearance as a means of generating the necessary sufficient evidence."
- "The October 21st meeting and its aftermath raise several concerns regarding the integrity of Department supervisors and managers at this Command (TACOM), albeit many years ago. First it seems questionable for TACOM, its Director of IC (Simonini) and the 902nd Military Intelligence Group to allow an SSBI of Tenenbaum for a TS clearance to proceed

given that their security concerns about Tenenbaum led them to take preventive measures against him, including restricting his access to Secret information. Second, it seems that the SSBI was being used as a substitute for a counterintelligence investigation (CI), which would have been the regular course of action in light of any legitimate security concerns that the group identified. It has been argued in responsive comments that Tenenbaum's supervisor, Dr. Jack Parks, may have made false or misleading statements on a form to initiate the clearance process."

With the above-cited standards in mind, we reviewed the evidence and found that Mr. Tenenbaum was the victim of religious discrimination.[10]

Appendix 16

On October 26, 2017, Senators Claire McCaskill and Gary Peters wrote the following letter to the Honorable James Mattis, the Secretary for the Department of Defense:

RON JOHNSON, WISCONSIN, CHAIRMAN

JOHN McCAIN, ARIZONA
ROB PORTMAN, OHIO
RAND PAUL, KENTUCKY
JAMES LANKFORD, OKLAHOMA
MICHAEL B. ENZI, WYOMING
JOHN HOEVEN, NORTH DAKOTA
STEVE DAINES, MONTANA

CLAIRE McCASKILL, MISSOURI
THOMAS R. CARPER, DELAWARE
JON TESTER, MONTANA
HEIDI HEITKAMP, NORTH DAKOTA
GARY C. PETERS, MICHIGAN
MARGARET WOOD HASSAN, NEW HAMPSHIRE
KAMALA D. HARRIS, CALIFORNIA

CHRISTOPHER R. HIXON, STAFF DIRECTOR
MARGARET E. DAUM, MINORITY STAFF DIRECTOR

United States Senate

COMMITTEE ON
HOMELAND SECURITY AND GOVERNMENTAL AFFAIRS

WASHINGTON, DC 20510-8250

October 26, 2017

The Honorable James Mattis
Secretary
Department of Defense
1400 Defense Pentagon
Washington, DC 20301

Dear Mr. Secretary:

We write to bring to your attention a matter that has long required redress by the highest levels of Department of Defense (DOD) leadership. Dr. David Tenenbaum, an Army civilian employee and engineer with the U.S. Army Tank-Automotive and Armaments Command (TACOM), was the subject of a series of espionage allegations. The Department of Defense Office of Inspector General has determined that these allegations were false and initiated with discriminatory intent.[1] This matter is 25 years old and, despite the findings of the Inspector General, Dr. Tenenbaum has received no relief and no one has been held accountable for the discrimination which led to these egregious actions. We request that you personally review this case and direct DOD to take appropriate action to provide Dr. Tenenbaum redress.

This case began in July 1992, when TACOM employees made espionage allegations against Dr. Tenenbaum. These allegations led to DOD investigative activities and two Federal Bureau of Investigation (FBI) preliminary inquiries. Dr. Tenenbaum sought relief against these actions, but was stymied by national security claims raised by DOD, which remain unclear and unverified. Finally, in 2006, Senator Carl Levin requested that the Inspector General conduct an investigation into the matter.[2] After reviewing both classified and unclassified material, the Inspector General released its findings in July 2008. Specifically, the Inspector General found that Dr. Tenenbaum was "subjected to unusual and unwelcome scrutiny because of his faith and ethnic background, a practice that would undoubtedly fit a definition of discrimination." Furthermore, the Inspector General concluded that the "personnel security and counterintelligence investigation process was poorly handled and managed" and that Dr. Tenenbaum "is, and has always been, a dedicated, loyal and professional civil servant in the service of our Nation."[3]

[1] Department of Defense Office of Inspector General, *Review of the Case of Mr. David Tenenbaum, Department of the Army Employee* (08-INTEL-10) (July 13, 2008).

[2] Letter from Senator Carl Levin, United States Senate Homeland Security and Governmental Affairs Committee, to Department of Defense Office of Inspector General (Mar. 14, 2006).

[3] Department of Defense Office of Inspector General, *Review of the Case of Mr. David Tenenbaum, Department of the Army Employee* (08-INTEL-10) (July 13, 2008).

APPENDICES

The Honorable James Mattis
October 26, 2017
Page 2

The false allegations against Dr. Tenenbaum have not only caused him personal hardship, but also disrupted his professional progress and credentials. In 1997, in addition to being temporarily suspended from work, Dr. Tenenbaum lost his access to classified information. In 2000, his security clearance was revoked. Subsequently, the revocation was found to be based on unsubstantiated allegations in 2003 and, even in the face of the other allegations, his clearance was restored and upgraded, which emphasizes the dubious nature of the claims against him. Dr. Tenenbaum has been in a professional stalemate since this ordeal began and has been unable to seek other opportunities within DOD or elsewhere.

The Inspector General's report was an overdue step in the right direction, but DOD's lack of a remedy in accordance with the Inspector General's findings sends a message that DOD is not concerned with even the most egregious cases of discrimination and employee retaliation. This inaction may also discourage employees from reporting other concerns, which has serious implications for waste, fraud, abuse, and national security. Furthermore, this case has lingered for a considerable number of years and requires serious and prompt attention from DOD leadership. We ask that you direct the cessation of any retaliatory action towards Dr. Tenenbaum and take action to resolve this matter once and for all. In doing so, we also request that your staff inform our offices of the steps you plan to take to address Dr. Tenenbaum's case on or before November 22, 2017. Thank you for your attention to this matter. Please contact Saundrea Shropshire at saundrea_shropshire@hsgac.senate.gov or Joseph Lindblad at joseph_lindblad@hsgac.senate.gov. Please send any official correspondence related to this request to Lucy_Balcezak@hsgac.senate.gov.

Sincerely,

Claire McCaskill
Ranking Member

Gary Peters
U.S. Senator

cc: Ron Johnson
Chairman

Chuck Grassley
U.S. Senator

Appendix 17

INSPECTOR GENERAL
DEPARTMENT OF DEFENSE
400 ARMY NAVY DRIVE
ARLINGTON, VIRGINIA 22202–4704

1380

SENATE ARMED SERVICES
COMMITTEE

98 JUL 18 PM 2: 16
JUL 13 2008

The Honorable Carl Levin
Chairman
Armed Services Committee
United States Senate
Washington, DC 20510

Dear Mr. Chairman:

Attached is our independent review of the case of Mr. David Tenenbaum requested in your letter of March 14, 2006. I carefully reviewed the Tenenbaum case for many months, including many classified and unclassified documents, and received a large number of briefings. It is my opinion that Mr. Tenenbaum's ethnic background, and his deep devotion to and the practice of his faith were factors in the many investigations. Mr. Tenenbaum was subjected to unusual and unwelcome scrutiny because of his faith and ethnic background, a practice that would undoubtedly fit a definition of discrimination, whether actionable or not. The attached report supports these views.

It is also my opinion that the initial personnel security and counterintelligence investigation process was poorly handled and managed, although the appeal process ultimately exonerated Mr. David Tenenbaum. It is my belief that Mr. Tenenbaum is, and has always been, a dedicated, loyal and professional civil servant in the service of our Nation.

Very Respectfully,

Claude M. Kicklighter

Attachment

ACKNOWLEDGMENTS

This book would not be complete unless I expressed my deep gratitude, thanks, and appreciation to those who have supported myself and my family throughout our "ordeal" and bringing this book to fruition.

This book would not have been possible if not for the support of Dr. Michael (Moishe) Engelberg, the executive director of the New York Center for Civil Justice, Tolerance & Values. Dr. Engelberg has been a trusted and close family friend for more than forty years. He not only provided the much-needed funding for this book, but was also always there to lend an ear for moral support for myself and my family.

My attorneys Mayer (Mike) Morganroth and Dan Harold have been working my case for almost twenty years. Mike took my case on as a cause because of his outrage over the injustice and the false accusations against me based solely on the anti-Semitism within the US government and how this anti-Semitism caused the death of American soldiers. The lack of accountability by the US Army has only spurned him on to continue the fight to obtain justice in my case.

My ghostwriter, Erica Orloff, who did an amazing job of translating my story onto paper and became connected to my family in the process.

My editor, Kris Spisak, who was able to take the manuscript and make it even stronger.

My publishing team at Post Hill Press.

My community, who never for a moment lost trust in me and the belief that I was falsely accused of being an Israeli spy.

And most of all, to my family for their love and constant support through almost twenty-three years of a story that is still ongoing.

"NEVER AGAIN"

ENDNOTES

A War Story

1   Madeleine Brand, "Coping with Heat in Iraq," NPR, June 18, 2008, http://www.npr. org/templates/story/story.php?storyId=91639449.
2   David Sessions, "How Hot Is Iraq?" *Slate*, September 12, 2007, http://www.slate. com/articles/news_and_politics/explainer/2007/09/how_hot_is_iraq.html.
3   "What is it like to get hit by an IED?" Quora, https://www.quora.com/What-is-it -like-to-get-hit-by-an-IED.

Chapter 1

1   Torie Rose Deghett, "The War Photo No One Would Publish," *The Atlantic*, August 18, 2014, https://www.theatlantic.com/international/archive/2014/08/the-war-photo -no-one-would-publish/375762/.

Chapter 2

1   Uniform Code of Military Justice and United States Code, according to AR 381-12, 4-2.
2   "Home," United States Army Intelligence and Security Command, last modified June 19, 2019, https://www.inscom.army.mil/MSC/902MIG.aspx.

Mogadishu

1   Gina Dimuro, "The Battle of Mogadishu: The Harrowing True Story Behind *Black Hawk Down*," https://allthatsinteresting.com/battle-of-mogadishu-black-hawk -down-true-story.
2   "Battle of Mogadishu (1993)—Black Hawk Down," Military Factory, last updated 2019, http://www.militaryfactory.com/battles/battle_of_mogadishu.asp.

Chapter 3

1   Doug Templeton, interview with FBI, as cited in *Tenenbaum v. Simonini* Civil No. 98-CV-74473-DT, 6.
2   Stephanie Samergedes, memorandum to various government agencies on December 9 and 23, 1996.
3   Dan Meyer, personal interview with the author, 2006.
4   Deposition of Steve Twynham, February 2, 2000, as cited in *Tenenbaum v. Simonini*, 44.

ENDNOTES

5 Deposition of Michael Shropshire, August 31, 2000, as cited in *Tenenbaum v. Simonini*, 61.

6 R. Jeffrey Smith, "Defense Memo Warned of Israeli Spies," *Washington Post*, January 30, 1996, https://www.washingtonpost.com/archive/politics/1996/01/30/defense-memo-warned-of-israeli-spying/6a9492ce-5f10-4362-8ae7-f22a041f3e72/?noredirect=on.

7 Ibid.

8 Jeff Stein, "Does the CIA Stereotype Jews as Security Risks?" *Salon*, June 10, 1998, http://www.salon.com/1998/06/10/news_58/.

9 Deposition of James Gugino, September 2, 1999, as cited in *Tenenbaum v. Simonini*, 131.

10 Discovery documents found via Juan Matteo, 1999–2000.

11 Deposition of John Simonini, May 25, 2000, *Tenenbaum v. Simonini*, 124–125.

12 Wikipedia, s.v. "Demographics of Israel," Wikipedia, last modified September 9, 2019, https://en.wikipedia.org/wiki/Demographics_of_Israel.

13 Deposition of Paul Barnard, September 30, 1999, *Tenenbaum v. Simonini*, 60.

14 Ibid.

15 Ronald Duquette, personal interview with the author, December 4, 2015.

16 Deposition of Barnard, September 30, 1999, 52.

17 Duquette, personal interview with the author, December 4, 2015.

18 Martin Terry, interview with the author, April 13, 2016.

Chapter 4

1 Deposition of Robert Riley, April 4–5, 2000, *Tenenbaum v. Simonini*.

2 Deposition of Jim Thompson, December 13, 1999, *Tenenbaum v. Simonini*, 57.

3 FBI District Office, correspondence to Louis Freeh (Director of the FBI), September 24, 1996.

4 Ibid.

5 Deposition of Gugino, August 1999, *Tenenbaum v. Simonini*, 111.

6 32 Gugino, FBI memorandum, December 12, 1996; Simonini, interview with the FBI, March 25, 1997; FBI memorandum, January 23, 1997; Simonini, sworn statement, January 22, 1997.

7 Simonini, "Subject: TACOM Request for Info," memorandum, October 11, 1996.

8 Simonini, briefing slides, October 11, 1996.

9 Deposition of Simonini, May 25, 2000, *Tenenbaum v. Simonini*, 85.

10 DIS Report of Investigation, February 19, 1997, 6.

11 DIS Report of Investigation, February 1997, 6–7.

The Olympic Park Bombing

1 Olivia B. Waxman, "When Terror Struck the Summer Olympics 20 Years Ago," *Time*, July 27, 2016, http://time.com/4417773/atlanta-olympic-bombing-1996/.

2 Scott Freeman, "Fallout: An Oral History of the Olympic Park Bombing," *Atlanta*, July 1, 2011, http://www.atlantamagazine.com/great-reads/olympic-park-bombing-oral-history/.

3   Gregg Zoroya, "How the IED Changed the U.S. Military," *USA Today*, originally published December 18, 2013. https://www.usatoday.com/story/news/nation/2013/12/18/ied-10-years-blast-wounds-amputations/3803017/, accessed May 21, 2018.

Chapter 5

1   Depositions of Barnard on September 30, 1999, 60, and on October 14, 1999, 39.
2   DIS Report of Investigation, February 19, 1997, 8.
3   Ibid.
4   George Maschke and Gino J. Scalabrini, *The Lie Behind the Lie Detector*, anti-polygraph.org, 17–18.
5   *Tenenbaum v. Simonini*, 18, paragraph 66.

Chapter 6

1   "The Truth About Lie Detectors," American Psychological Association, originally published August 5, 2004, http://www.apa.org/research/action/polygraph.aspx.
2   Deposition of Sean Nicol, November 10, 1999, 14-16.
3   Deposition of Albert Snyder, May 23, 2000, 7–8.

War Zone Training

1   Jen Judson, "Counter-IED Training Prepares Soldiers for Unexpected," *Defense News*, November 30, 2015, https://www.defensenews.com/training-sim/2015/11/30/counter-ied-training-prepares-soldiers-for-unexpected/.
2   David Sommerstein, "IEDs Now Form a Part of Army Base's Training," NPR, September 27, 2006, https://www.npr.org/templates/story/story.php?storyId=6154815.
3   Judson, "Counter-IED Training."
4   Vee Terrell, personal interview with the author, May 3, 2018.

Chapter 7

1   DIS Report of Investigation, February 1997, 9.
2   *Tenenbaum v. Simonini*, 18, paragraph 66.
3   DIS Memo for Record, February 18, 1997, 11, paragraph 48.
4   DIS Report of Investigation, February 19, 1997, 11.
5   DIS Report of Investigation, February 19, 1997, 10–11.
6   Deposition of Gugino, September 2, 1999, 129–130.

Chapter 8

1   DIS Report of Investigation, February 19, 1997, 13.
2   Marty Crandall, interview with Erica Orloff, April 12, 2016.

"Going Boom"

1   Zoroya, "How the IED Changed the Military."
2   Geoffrey Ingersoll, "Combat Medic Gives Stirring First-Hand Account of the Day He Stepped on a Bomb," Business Insider, May 16, 2013, http://www.businessinsider.com.au/medic-ied-amputee-army-2013-5.

Chapter 9

1   Deposition of Gugino, September 2, 1999.
2   Deposition of Gugino, September 2, 1999, 90–91.
3   Crandall, interview with Orloff, April 12, 2016.
4   Deposition of Roger Pendenza, February 7, 2000, 55.
5   Deposition of Nicol, November 10, 1999, 14–16.

Chapter 10

1   Deposition of Simonini, October 31, 2001, 127–128.
2   Duquette, interview with the author, December 4, 2015.
3   Duquette, email to website, September 29, 2015, https://www.justanswer.com/mili-tary-law/9by74-retired-army-i-ve-worked-army-civilian.html.

Improvised Armoring

1   Michael Moran, "Frantically, the Army Tries to Armor Humvees," NBC News, April 15, 2004, http://www.nbcnews.com/id/4731185/ns/world_news-brave_new_world/t/frantically-army-tries-armor-humvees/#.WyfVDadKjIU.
2   Ibid.

Chapter 11

1   David Josar, *Detroit News*, February 1997.
2   Deposition of Gugino on August 19, 1999, 113–114.
3   Dan Meyer, David A. Clarke School of Law presentation at the University of the District of Columbia, citing Guidelines B and C.
4   Duquette, interview with the author, December 4, 2015.

Chapter 12

1   Deposition of Gugino, August 19, 1999, 27.
2   "The Truth About Lie Detectors."
3   Deposition of Simonini, October 31, 2001, 222–224.
4   Deposition of Gugino, August 19, 1999, 37–38.
5   Deposition given of Gugino, August 19, 1999, 43–44.
6   "Memo for Record," March 17, 1994, SAEDA 1985 occurrence, 109–111.

The Anxiety of Travel

1   Terrell, personal interview with the author, May 3, 2018.

Chapter 13

1   Deposition of Dr. Richard McClelland, July 14, 1999, *David Aaron and Madeline Gail Tenenbaum v. Lt. Col. John Simonini et al.*
2   Jerry Abraham, interview with Orloff, April 13, 2016.
3   Ibid.

Stranded in the Desert

1   Terrell, personal interview with the author, May 3, 2018.

Chapter 15

1 "Polygraph Statement of Mark Mallah," AntiPolygraph, https://antipolygraph.org/statements/statement-002.shtml.
2 Ron Kampeas, "The Ups and Downs for Jews in the US Security Services," *The Times of Israel*, February 19, 2015. https://www.timesofisrael.com/the-ups-and-downs-for-jews-in-the-us-security-services/.
3 Yitzhak Benhorin, "New Details Uncovered in CIA Anti-Semitism Case," *Ynet News*, April 24, 2012, https://www.ynetnews.com/articles/0,7340,L-4220781,00.html.
4 Ibid.
5 "John F. Kennedy and Religion," JFK in History, John F. Kennedy Library, http://www.jfklibrary.org/JFK/JFK-in-History/JFK-and-Religion.aspx.
6 Seymour M. Hersh, *The Samson Option: Israel's Nuclear Arsenal and American Foreign Policy* (New York: Random House, 1991).

Chapter 16

1 Deposition of Simonini, October 31, 2001, *David Aaron and Madeline Gail Tenenbaum v. Lt. Col. John Simonini et al.*
2 Bill Meyer, "Bogus Spy Probe of Orthodox Jew Cost GIs Lives," *The Cleveland Plain Dealer*, August 5, 2008. http://www.cleveland.com/nation/index.ssf/2008/08/bogus_spy_probe_of_orthodox_je.html.
3 Testimony of Paul Bernard, deposition of September 30, 1999, *David Aaron and Madeline Gail Tenenbaum v. Lt. Col. John Simonini et al.*

Franz Gayl, Fellow Whistleblower

1 Government Accountability Project, "Interview with MRAP Whistleblower Franz Gayl," *Whistle Where You Work*, 2009, https://youtube/VxcV-bK1R24.
2 "Franz Gayl, Troop Safety Whistleblower," Whistleblower, https://www.whistleblower.org/franz-gayl-troop-safety-whistleblower.
3 Heather R. Smith, "Army Researchers Help Reduce MRAP Maintenance," U.S. Army, August 15, 2013, https://www.army.mil/article/109310/army_researchers_help_reduce_mrap_maintenance.
4 "Interview with MRAP Whistleblower Franz Gayl."
5 Ibid.
6 "Franz Gayl, Troop Safety Whistleblower."

Chapter 17

1 Gugino, deposition of August 19, 1999, *David Aaron and Madeline Gail Tenenbaum v. Lt. Col. John Simonini et al.*
2 Gugino, personal conversation with the author, 1998.
3 Duquette, personal interview with the author, December 4, 2015.

Chapter 18

1 Deposition of Gugino, August 19, 1999, *David Aaron and Madeline Gail Tenenbaum v. Lt. Col. John Simonini et al.*

2 Duquette, personal interview with the author, December 4, 2015.
3 Ibid.
4 Richard McClelland, personal conversation with the author, April 1998.
5 Deposition of Gugino, September 2, 1999, 185–188.
6 Emily Bacon, email to Jerry Chapin, March 1998.

The Marble ER

1 Erik Storm, personal interview with the author, April 20, 2018.

Chapter 19

1 McClelland, personal conversation with the author, April 1998.
2 Duquette, personal interview with the author, December 4, 2015.

Chapter 20

1 Deposition of McClelland, July 14, 1999, *David Aaron and Madeline Gail Tenen-baum v. Lt. Col. John Simonini et al.*, 31–34.
2 Deposition of Gugino. August 19, 1999, 23.

Mike Helms, Insult to Injury

1 Dana Liebelson, "The Whistleblower Who Fell Through the Cracks," http://www.pogo.org/our-work/articles/2011/wi-wp-20111207.html.
2 Ann Scott Tyson, "Service Civilians and the Wounds of War: Many Fill Vital Roles in Iraq, but Medical Care Can Be Spotty," *Washington Post*, July 25, 2007, http://www.washingtonpost.com/wp-dyn/content/article/2007/07/24/AR2007072402459_pf.html.
3 Dana Liebelson,"The Whistleblower Who Fell Through the Cracks," POGO, December 7, 2011, http://www.pogo.org/our-work/articles/2011/wi-wp-20111207.html.
4 Marisa Taylor, "Pentagon, CIA Instructed to Re-Investigate Whistleblower Cases," McClatchy, June 23, 2015, http://www.mcclatchydc.com/news/nation-world/national/article28348576.html.
5 Dana Liebelson, "The Whistleblower Who Fell Through the Cracks."
6 Ibid.
7 Tyson, "Service Civilians and the Wounds of War."
8 Ibid.

Chapter 21

1 John W. Dean, "ACLU vs. National Security Agency: Why the 'States Secret Privilege' Shouldn't Stop the Lawsuit Challenging Warrantless Television Surveillance of Americans," FindLaw, June 16, 2006, https://supreme.findlaw.com/legal-commentary/aclu-v-national-security-agency-why-the-state-secrets-privilege-shouldnt-stop-the-lawsuit-challenging-warrantless-telephone-surveillance-of-americans.html.
2 "Pentagon, DOJ Used State Secrets Privilege | As Cover for Anti-Semitism, Engineer Says," Courthouse News Service, February 20, 2009, https://www.courthousenews.com/pentagon-doj-used-state-secrets-privilegeas-cover-for-anti-semitism-engineer-says/.

Chapter 22

1 Dan Harold, personal interview with the author, April 12, 2006.
2 Ibid.
3 Mike Morganroth, personal interview with the author, April 12, 2006.
4 Harold, personal interview with the author, April 12, 2006.

New Convoy Operations Training

1 Seth Robson, "IED Survivor Talks About Humvee Safety," *Stars and Stripes*, June 15, 2006, https://www.stripes.com/news/ied-survivor-talks-about-humvee -safety-1.50379.
2 Ibid.
3 Jerry Wilson, "JMRC Soldiers Train NATO Forces to Combat IED Hazards," U.S. Army, April 23, 2007, https://www.army.mil/article/2808/jmrc_soldiers_train_nato _forces_to_combat_ied_hazards.

Chapter 23

1 Letter from Senator Carl Levin to Mike Morganroth, March 14, 2006.
2 Personal discussions with anonymous source.
3 Interview with anonymous source, July 6, 2015.
4 Ibid.
5 Ibid.
6 Affidavit of John Crane, dated February 2016.
7 Jeff Stein, "Joseph Schmitz, Donald Trump's Foreign Policy Adviser, Left the Pentagon Amid Controversy," *Newsweek*, March 21, 2016, http://www.newsweek.com/ donald-trump-joseph-e-schmitz-foreign-policy-pentagon-dod-germany-wrong- doing-439239.
8 Marisa Taylor and William Douglas, "Trump Adviser Accused of Making Anti-Semitic Remarks," McClatchy, August 18, 2016, http://www.mcclatchydc.com/news/ politics-government/election/article96421087.html.
9 Meyer, personal interview with the author, 2016.
10 Deposition of John Simonini, May 25, 2000, 50.
11 Dana Milbank, "The Price Gina Gray Paid for Whistleblowing," *Washington Post*, August 20, 2013, https://www.washingtonpost.com/opinions/dana-milbank -the-price-gina-gray-paid-for-whistleblowing/2013/08/20/9fe80c98-09cb-11e3- 8974-f97ab3b3c677_story.html.
12 William H. McMichael, "Dover Mortuary Works to Redeem Itself after 2011 Scandal," *USA Today*, June 24, 2013, http://www.usatoday.com/story/news/nation /2013/06/24/dover-mortuary-works-to-redeem-itself-after-scandal/2451315/.

Chapter 24

1 Affidavit of John Crane, August 16, 2016.
2 Interview with Dan Myer by the author, January 2018.
3 Ibid.

ENDNOTES

Photography of the Army Dead

1   Elisabeth Bumiller, "Pentagon to Allow Photos of Soldiers' Coffins," *New York Times*, February 26, 2009, http://www.nytimes.com/2009/02/26/us/26web-coffins.html.

Chapter 25

1   POGO Staff, "POGO Letter to Members of Congress Regarding the DOD Inspector General," POGO, May 1, 2008, http://www.pogo.org/our-work/letters/2008/go-igi-20080501.html.
2   Ibid.
3   Ibid.
4   Letter from Mike Morganroth to IG-DOD, April 24, 2008.
5   Meyer, 2016.

Chapter 26

1   Email from David Tenenbaum to his supervisors, July 2008.

The Restriction and Replacement of Humvees

1   Carly Everson, "Army Humvee May Soon Be a Relic," *CBS News*, February 12, 2010, https://www.cbsnews.com/news/army-humvee-may-soon-be-a-relic/.
2   "Senior U.S. Commander Restricts Humvee Use in Afghanistan," *CNN*, July 1, 2010, http://www.cnn.com/2010/US/07/01/afghanistan.humvees/index.html.
3   Grant Turnbull, "End of an Icon: The Rise and Fall of the Humvee," Army Technology, September 29, 2014, https://www.army-technology.com/features/feature end-of-an-icon-the-rise-and-fall-of-the-humvee-4381884/.
4   Ibid.

Chapter 27

1   Michael Engelberg, interview with Orloff, April 2016.
2   Affidavit of Crane, August 16, 2016.
3   Ibid.
4   Anonymous letter to Morgonroth & Morganroth, PLC, May 30, 2008.

Chapter 28

1   Senator McCaskill's staffers, personal conversation with the author, February 2018.

Author's Note

1   "Faces of the Fallen," *Washington Post*, http://apps.washingtonpost.com/national/fallen/causes-of-death/ied/.
2   David Wood, "Beyond the Battlefield: Afghanistan's Wounded Struggle with Genital Injuries," *Huffington Post*, originally published March 21, 2012, http://www.huffingtonpost.com/2012/03/21/beyond-the-battlefield-afghanistan-genital-injuries_n_1335356.html.

Appendices

1 Frank Felsenstein, *Anti-Semitic Stereotypes: A Paradigm of Otherness in English Popular Culture, 1660–1830* (Baltimore: Johns Hopkins University, 1995), 2.
2 Army Regulation 381-12, 4-2.
3 Deposition of Simonini, October 21, 2000, 27–28.
4 Deposition of Gugino, September 2, 1999, 129–131.
5 Deposition of Gugino, August 19, 1999, 127–128.
6 Deposition of Gugino, August 19, 1999, 128–130.
7 Deposition of Gugino, August 19, 1999, 64–67, 128, and 133–134.
8 Seymour M. Hersh, *The Samson Option: Israel's Nuclear Arsenal and American Foreign Policy* (New York: Random House, 1991), 145–146.
9 Meyer, interview with the author, September 22, 2018.
10 IG-DOD Report, July 2008.